1-800-AM-I-NUTS?

To the Bishop's School
Scholarship Fund—
Best wishes,
Margo Kaufman

1-800-AM-I-NUTS?

MARGO KAUFMAN

random house new york

The essays that appear in this work were originally
published in *Cosmopolitan,* the *Los Angeles Times
Magazine, LA Weekly, The New York Times, Working
Woman, USA Today, The Los Angeles Reader, The Village Voice,* and *Pug Talk.*

Library of Congress Cataloging-in-Publication Data
Kaufman, Margo.
1-800-AM-I-NUTS? / Margo Kaufman.
p.   cm.
ISBN 0-679-42004-5
1. American wit and humor.   I. Title.
PN6162.K38 1993
814'.54—dc20   92-50509

Manufactured in the United States of America
24689753
First Edition

Book design by Debbie Glasserman

For my husband, my beloved muse,
who shall remain pseudonymous

ACKNOWLEDGMENTS

It took me so long to get a book published that I began to suspect that I burned libraries in a former life. Luckily, I had the following people around to help me overcome my bad karma. A million thanks to:

Eric Mankin, for taking the time to read and edit every essay in its most larval stage, and for his wise counsel, deftness with a delete key, and unflagging sense of humor.

Loretta Fidel, for believing in me, selling me, and having such great taste in restaurants.

David Rosenthal, for saying yes.

And Jon Winokur, for his terrific advice and pep talks.

I also owe a huge debt of gratitude to: Nancy Newhouse, at The New York Times, for giving me more credibility than I ever had in my life; Emily Young, at the *Los Angeles Times Magazine,* for making sure I was grammatically correct; Russ Smith, former editor of the *Baltimore City Paper,* for letting a woman who walked in off the street write a column; James Vowell, editor and publisher of *The Los Angeles Reader,* for giving me my first job in L.A. and my health insurance; Ann

Marie Wilson, editor of *Pug Talk* magazine, for keeping me in touch with the pure joy of writing; and Rob Asghar of the University of Southern California News Service, for keeping me well supplied with experts.

In addition, I'm deeply beholdened to my sister, Laurie Goldberg, whose hilarious commentary helped me make a deadline more times than I'd care to admit. And I'd never hear the end of it if I didn't acknowledge the rest of my family and friends who were willing to go on the record whenever I called, most notably: Grandma Flora; my brother, Bobby; my sister-in-law Robbie; Annette Appleby; Léon Bing (for teaching me not to be a good sport); Marjorie David; Marc Glassgold; Nancy Hathaway; Marilyn Hulquist; Richard Kaufman; Robin Moorad; Wendy Raebeck; Cherri Senders; Margot Slade; and Suzy Slutzky. Special thanks from the bottom of my heart to my dear friend Marian Bach, and to my mother, Gloria Asnes, for being there.

Finally, I'd like to thank Bess, Stella, and Sophie, who snoozed through every page.

Margo Kaufman
Venice, California

CONTENTS

INTRODUCTION

I owe my career in journalism to a cardboard box. Years ago, after a divorce, I left Los Angeles (a city I like because it's easy to tell who the strange people are) and returned to my hometown of Baltimore (a town that has always made me nervous because even the ax murderers wear suits). My plan was to become an interior decorator, so I enrolled in the Maryland Institute of Art. I thought I was going to study something fun and creative, like Introduction to Sofa Buying or Fabric Swatches 101, but instead I was forced to enroll in Basic Drawing (a talent I've never possessed).

I knew I was in trouble the first day of class, when the teacher put a cardboard box in front of me and instructed me to draw it. I quickly sketched two intersecting squares and connected the edges, a trick I learned in third grade to make a box drawing look three dimensional. The teacher was unimpressed. "I can't *feel* your box," she complained.

I don't believe that it's necessary to *feel* a cardboard box. It's only necessary to know how to pack one. But my teacher made me draw that carton three hours a night, three times a week. She even sent it home with me, so I could get to know it better. I suppose she was just trying to teach me to draw on the right side of my brain, but before I learned how, my left brain snapped and I started writing about the absurdity of this experience. This led to a humor column in the *Baltimore City Paper* and the end of art school. Within six months I was back on my beloved Côte Gauche, roller skating along the bike path overlooking the Pacific Ocean, and the rest is, well, my résumé.

Although my work has appeared in *The New York Times,* unless you live in Los Angeles or subscribe to *Cosmopolitan* or *Pug Talk* (yes, there really is such a publication), you may not know who I am. You've never seen me on the *Young Comedians* on HBO. My picture hasn't flashed across the screen on *America's Most Wanted.* And I'm not a recovering fill-in-the-addiction former child star.

I'm just a married lady, complete with a husband and pugs, who is trying to make sense out of life in a society where the 911 number at my local police station is answered by voice mail ("Press one, if you are being mugged") and where I can buy area rugs and silver platters at the car wash. The line between ordinary and bizarre is very hazy.

Granted, my line is hazier than most. I live in what has got to be Lunatic Central—Venice Beach, California, the seedy but artsy, always on the brink of gentrification beachfront community whose boardwalk is the second biggest attraction in L.A. after Disneyland. In my neighborhood, chain-saw jugglers, limbless dancers, and bodybuilders the size of the Bob's Big Boy icon are a common sight. If I have a career dilemma or a dispute with my husband, I can run down to the corner and seek guidance from one of a dozen sidewalk tarot readers, palmists, and clairvoyants.

The essays that follow are a deluxe assortment of sanity checks. I've always wished there was a hot line that I could call when I was confronted by a bizarre situation. For example, if my husband accuses me of being too demanding because I expect a birthday present (this from a man who clipped out and handed me an ad for a shortwave radio before his birthday), or I turn on the television and see a model demonstrating a Flowbee (a revolutionary new precision hair-cutting system that attaches to a vacuum cleaner), instead of standing there dumfounded, wondering is it me, I could pick up the phone, dial 1-800-AM-I-NUTS?, and check.

Lacking access to such a hot line, I did the next best thing. Whenever I stumbled upon something peculiar, I called friends, experts (one of the few perks of free-lance writing is the access to free advice), my sister, even my grandmother. And then I sat down and wrote a column to try to make sense of it all.

I hope it helps.

ON
VENICE
BEACH

BLIGHTED BEACH MEMOIRS

It's amazing what you find on the beach these days. I was strolling along Venice Beach, trying to have a spiritual encounter with the ocean, when I tripped on a broccoli. Not a random floret, mind you. An entire head of broccoli.

What's a broccoli doing on the beach, I wondered? It didn't strike me as the sort of thing that gets mislaid, or accidentally falls out of the combination folding chair/tote. True, it wasn't a mass of used syringes like you find on New York beaches. But it wasn't a seashell either.

"Broccoli? What's unusual about that?" scoffed senior lifeguard Conrad Liberty when I called lifeguard headquarters to ask if there had been a salad-bar spill. "There are storm drains and that kind of stuff gets up on the beach. Dead animals—mice, dogs, cats—come out of the storm drains too. Of course," he added hastily, "we don't have them wall to wall."

There isn't any room. On any sunny Sunday most Southern California beaches look like a gigantic garage sale. I have actually seen video cameras, pillows, playpens, guitars, and plastic wading pools strewn across the sand.

People didn't used to require so much equipment to enjoy the beach. I can understand bringing a small folding chair and a beach towel, even a giant beach towel with a near life-size likeness of Kareem Abdul-Jabbar arching for a skyhook. Or sun block, a sweatshirt, a book, a cold drink, and some fruit.

But patio furniture? A different strength sunscreen for each and every body part? A Playmate cooler the size of a compact car? A boom box the size of a station wagon? A portable TV?

"I've seen TVs everywhere," Liberty said. "That is not a good thing to bring, because it's so bright that you really can't use it."

"Why would anyone watch TV when they could watch the ocean?" I asked my ex-husband, a television addict and the only person I know who actively detests the beach.

"It's just water," Richard said. "Why would you want to watch that? Usually it's just dirty water. Would you tell people, 'Don't bring a Walkman' so you can listen to the children screaming?"

I know better than to argue with Richard. For years, he has tried to convince me that the beach is a large ashtray. "How can you relax when you're lying in cigarette butts?" he asks.

But even less cynical friends are beginning to complain. "The beach used to be a place to go because it was serene," Doug said. "But now there's too much action. If you're not killed in the time it takes to duck the Frisbee, you're hit by a softball. It's like going to the Olympics."

It's also like going to the zoo. There are dogs. There are police on horseback ticketing people for bringing the dogs. There are monkeys. There are parrots. "And now they're bringing reptiles," Marissa said with a sigh. "When someone sits down next to you with this giant thing coiled around their neck and they say, 'Touch him, he's not slimy,' what can you do besides move your blanket?"

You can pray that the boa gets run over by the *Santa Monica Art Tool,* an enormous sculpted concrete roller that stamps a miniature impression of Los Angeles when it is towed across the sand. I don't understand why it was necessary to spend sixty thousand dollars on a contraption to create a *faux* sand city when there were already three hundred thousand people lying there, so I called the Santa Monica Arts Commission.

"You didn't see people pretending that they were Godzilla and walking over Los Angeles [in the sand]?" asked Henry Korn, executive director.

"Most of the people I saw were just trying to get out of its way," I said.

"People love the *Art Tool,*" he assured me. "Have you seen the *Singing Beach Chairs?*"

Yes, I have. And in my opinion, the boundary between the ocean and land is not improved by seventeen-thousand-dollar fourteen-foot-high musical chairs. Why not commission art for places that need improvement? The corner of Sepulveda Boulevard and Saticoy Street in Van Nuys springs to mind.

That would be a greater test of the artist's skill. After all, as advertisers well know, anything looks good next to an ocean: cigarettes, trucks, soda, wine coolers, beer, Dennis Weaver on a horse. There's even a commercial featuring an air conditioner on the beach, surrounded by sea gulls and test pilot/Right Stuff expert Chuck Yeager.

The air conditioner probably enjoyed the beach more than the new white Chevrolet Beretta I saw being photographed in the surf. It was surrounded by klieg lights, reflective panels, generators, cameras, and even a backup black Beretta. ("We've got to see which looks better against the ocean," the assistant director explained.)

A police officer yawned as the crew raced to position the cars in time to catch the last fleeting rays of sunset. "The cars got stuck four times on the way down," he reported. "They finally sent for someone to build a track."

"It would have been easier to build a beach," I suggested.

The sports car was supposed to emerge from the ocean like Venus being born from the wave foam and race merrily along the water's edge like a frisky pony. The director barked,

"Action!" Three seconds later the pony was embedded in the sand up to its axles. "Help!" barked the director. Crew members frantically pushed the car out of the path of the incoming tide.

Suddenly, I realized that my puzzle was backward. The mystery was not "Why is there broccoli on the beach?" The only mystery was "Where is the Hollandaise?"

LOATHE THY NEIGHBOR

Not having access to a thermonuclear weapon, my friend Jon recently put pen to paper. He reads me what he wrote.

"Dear Neighbor," he begins. "I can't decide what it is about you that I hate the most. Is it the display of bric-a-brac on your patio wall? Is it the huge American flag that hangs seven days a week, twenty-four hours a day, from your balcony? Is it your filthy garage, where who knows what vermin is breeding this very minute? Or is it your enormous head?"

I picture a Macy's Thanksgiving Day Parade balloon with an imbecilic grin hovering above Jon's property line. And I wonder. Jon lives in a Pacific Palisades neighborhood that is as peaceful and orderly as Switzerland. What is it about neighbors that turns an otherwise reasonable person into a tight-lipped, beady-eyed turf defender bent on revenge?

It's not just Jon. Everyone has a flash point. It could be a sprinkler that overwaters, or a dog that barks or bites, or a stereo that puts the bass right through the floor. But it's always something.

Jon's letter continues: "Is it the fact that you don't have the intelligence to remember that you have a car alarm—so every time you get into the car, I'm treated to the sound of it going off?"

Jon acknowledges that he would go nuts in my neighborhood. I live in Venice. It's kind of like living in the strainer in the kitchen sink—you never know what you're going to find. The day after I moved here, I went for a walk and saw a man wearing nothing but seaweed dancing down my street. I rushed back to tell my husband.

Duke, a longtime Venetian, was completely unfazed. "It's just one of the neighbors," he said.

Over the years, his response has become like the punch line of a bad running joke. It's covered such strange sights and sounds as gunfire, a ferret on a leash, and the large black DIE YUPPIE SCUM sticker plastered on the back of a new Jaguar. Just the other night we were sitting down to dinner when we were jolted by a crash of breaking glass.

"It's just one of the neighbors," Duke said automatically. Sure enough, one of the Battling Bickersons next door had hurled a five-gallon Sparkletts water bottle through a second-story window. And my friends think *they* have neighbor problems.

"No matter what time I go to bed, at that exact moment my neighbor starts having sex," says Annette, who has a condo in Encino. "I'm trying to sleep, and it's boom, boom, boom upstairs. She must sneak down and see when I'm home." Either that or she never leaves her bed.

"My neighbor was having a birthday party for his girl-friend, and he strung colored banners around my trees," says Doug, who lives in the Hollywood Hills. "He didn't even ask permission. I wanted to kill. You move into a house for a sense of space, and then people invade it."

Nobody likes being reminded that their control over their environment is limited. Even my husband, the world's most tolerant human, ran out of patience when a neighbor acquired a novelty record from hell, *The Best of Sitcom Theme*

Songs, and played it—loud! Once was amusing, but daily . . . "No jury would convict me," Duke said. (Frankly, I didn't know which was scarier—the fact that such a record existed or that I knew all the words to "Car 54, Where Are You?")

It used to be that people dreamed of having neighbors like Ward and June Cleaver; "next door" was a friendly place to borrow sugar and swap gossip. But in these days of overcrowding, people dream of neighbors who travel all the time, whose only sign of life is the security guard who stops by three times a day to check the locks. Neighbors who aren't remodeling.

As are the people who live behind me. At seven this morning, I was awakened by the sounds of a nail gun. At eleven, my driveway was blocked by a large catering truck. And at three, I was asking the foreman to please get his building debris out of my trash cans.

Still, most of the time I'm really glad that my neighbors are there. A lot of them are friendly and fun to talk to. And I know that if I ever screamed, someone would hear me and call the police.

Suddenly, there is a furious banging on my front door. Oh, no, I think nervously. But it's Jane from up the street, inviting us to dinner. I accept happily.

"What was that?" Duke asks.

"Just one of the neighbors," I reply.

GUMHEAD CONFIDENTIAL

After two days of suffering, I thought of a solution: Kill Moe. It wasn't that I disliked him—quite the contrary, but he was the only barrier between me and a supply of my beloved Nicorette, the prescription chewing gum with nicotine that helped me quit smoking.

Frankly, I liked Miss Nicky (the Nicorette gum character in "Doonesbury") much better than I ever liked Mr. Butts. When I smoked, I had to brush my teeth every twenty minutes. And every time I inhaled a cigarette, I felt guilty about endangering my health.

But I never felt guilty chewing (actually, you don't chew, you park it on your gums); instead I enjoyed a mild nicotine rush and the keen sense of moral superiority and relief that goes with becoming a nonsmoker. I was very grateful the gum was there for me.

And it would *still* be there for me if Moe, my pharmacist, hadn't opened his big mouth. "You've got to stop chewing this," he exclaimed when I went to pick up my weekly supply. "It's pretty obvious when someone's hooked," he chided, adding that *most* people manage to give up the gum in a few months. I stammered something about not really being a gum junkie. But Moe wouldn't let it drop. "You don't go around shaking and dribbling at the mouth," he said. "And you're not selling your body on the street. Still, it's not that difficult to spot a problem." How? "Forty-eight refills is a clue," he said with a superior smile.

"I can stop whenever I want," I said defensively. But why would I want to stop? I loved my wonderful gum. With cigarettes I faced public humiliation and social ostracism. But not with Miss Nicky. There were no "Chewing" and "No Chewing" sections in restaurants and airplanes. Strangers didn't lecture me on the dangers of secondhand gum fumes. I wasn't ordered outside in the middle of a dinner party if I wanted a chew.

Hardly anyone knew I was chewing. And who cared? There were no ashes, no overflowing ashtrays, no foul odor clinging to my breath, clothes, and hair. There was no danger of starting a fire with gum. I wasn't going to accidentally burn down a forest or a bed, or even singe a sofa. Once in a while, a piece might get stuck to a sofa cushion, but a little ice would take it off.

It was no big deal, except to Moe. If it hadn't been for him, I wouldn't have casually suggested to my husband, "Hey, honey. Let's drive to Tijuana." Duke looked at me with alarm. I loathe Tijuana, but it's the only place on the planet I know where they have flyers for the *farmacia* ("We have Retin-A!") in the government tourist office. And in Mexico they sell Nicorette over the counter.

"Have the doctor call the prescription in to another pharmacy," Duke said. I considered it, but I knew I'd still imagine Moe's accusing voice saying, "Gumhead, gumhead!"

So there I was, crazed, frantically rummaging through the wastebasket, hunting for scraps of Nicorette; gnawing four packs of Chiclets a day. Chiclets wouldn't do. Finally, I hit on the solution: Kill Moe.

It would be really easy.

He and my husband are longtime acquaintances, and we often run into each other at social gatherings. In fact, we expected to see him that night at a benefit on the Santa Monica Pier. I'd lure him over to the end of the wharf, on the premise of discussing my addiction. And then a quick shove would do the rest.

But Moe didn't come. I didn't see him for three weeks. And by then, I was already over the worst withdrawal symptoms. It wasn't just physical, oh, no—that discomfort lasted only a few days. What really rankled was the utter lack of social cachet involved in my noble sacrifice. When I told my friends that I was quitting smoking, I got compassion, I got admiration, I got useful tips. But when I said that I was giving up Nicorette, eyes glazed, subjects changed, people remembered urgent previous engagements.

Later, I called an expert to find out what diseases I'd managed to avoid. "There's no disease caused by Nicorette gum," said Nina Schneider, associate research psychologist at UCLA and the first American to study Nicorette. "There's no evidence that it's unsafe. Even if you're on gum for five years, you're not going to get emphysema, lung cancer, or even heart disease."

Still, I guess I'm glad I quit. Duke's proud of me. And so is Moe. Recently, I confessed I'd planned his murder. "Nobody's ever told me that," he said. "It's a pharmaceutical first." I was about to tell him I appreciated his concern. But Moe said, "You know, I would have given you another box. I'm not stupid. You may have been addicted to the nicotine, but at least you weren't smoking."

I think I'm going to kill Moe.

SHADES OF STATUS

"**N**ice sunglasses," sneers my ex-husband, Richard. "All you need is a cupful of pencils." This is what you get for buying three-dollar shades on the Venice boardwalk, chides an inner voice. "Get a decent pair," orders Richard, who is wearing one-hundred-dollar Serengeti ("like the African plain") Drivers. "You look ridiculous."

I generally hate to admit that my ex-husband is right. Besides, I'm not one of these people who thinks that sunglasses are a fashion statement. I don't like glasses. The happiest day of my life was the day I got contact lenses. Of course, *I* only wear sunglasses for utilitarian reasons: My contacts get scratchy when I'm in the sun. But everyone else seems to have gone sunglass-crazy.

"I love my Ray-Bans," exclaims the woman sitting next to me at the beauty salon. What's to love? I wonder. Ms. Blond Highlights caresses her Dark Metal IIIs. "They're my alter ego," she reveals. "I put them on and I'm tough."

Some people think a pair of dark glasses can define you, like your blood type. I don't understand it, though in a way

I'm not surprised. First it was real estate. Then real estate got too expensive. Next it was cars. Then cars got too expensive. So now it's sunglasses.

"I've got two pairs," my hairdresser, Carole, says fondly, as if she's talking about her children. "One's collegiate, my Anne Kleins. And then I've got my 'killer' sunglasses, my L.A. Eyeworks. The ones I spent two hundred dollars on."

For two hundred dollars, I could fly to Hawaii. But Carole maintains that her sunglasses also provide an escape from reality. "They have aluminum frames and mirrored lenses," she explains. "I wear them when I want to create an attitude without having to get into it. My sunglasses make me unapproachable. People leave me alone."

Sure they leave her alone. There's nothing more annoying than trying to have a conversation with a person hiding behind mirrored sunglasses (which they rarely, if ever, remove). Not only can you not make eye contact, which means flirting is out of the question, but you also keep noticing that your hair looks funny and your makeup is smudged.

And, Carole warns me, "Cheap sunglasses won't protect your eyes from damaging invisible rays."

Mr. Cheap on the Venice boardwalk has this angle covered. He's put enormous ULTRAVIOLET PROTECTED stickers on his entire line of Nok-Offs. "Those lenses are terrible," argues Judit Putter, the owner of Snooty Fox Eyewear. What else would she say when she's selling nine-hundred-dollar Cartier sunglasses made of twenty-two-karat gold?

"The first thing people notice about you is your face," says Putter, a licensed optician in Santa Monica who has just fit a one-year-old client with $290 Miklis. "You can wear the greatest clothes in the world, but you'll make a rotten impression if your glasses are wrong." I begin to panic.

Even my own sister is sunglass-obsessed. "I wouldn't wear cheap sunglasses," says Laurie, who regards her hundred-dollar Vuarnets as an alternative form of jewelry. "They always hurt your nose more. And you can never lose them."

This is true. You can throw a pair of cheap sunglasses out of the car window in Tijuana and they'll walk home to L.A.—like Lassie. Cheap sunglasses will even dig themselves out from under the sofa cushions.

But expensive sunglasses disappear before your check clears. "I had these great white Emmanuelle Khanhs with brownish tinted lenses," my friend Lynne recalls, hastily explaining that this was back when Khanhs were in. "I adored them," she says. "Then I went horseback riding and the instructor decided to teach us to trot. My glasses went flying off my face and bounced down a canyon. I seriously gave thought to going after them. I lost my company ID card, too, but I didn't care at all about that."

Lynne is a self-described sunglasses addict. "I believe in total coordination," she says, adding that she once bought a pair of hand-painted frames to match her car. "I've got at least twenty pairs." She used to have twenty-one pairs, but recently she was robbed. "They stole my Miklis," Lynne complains. "They passed over all the others and went for my gray granite Miklis."

"You've got to keep them on a leash," says Putter, the optician. "I've heard every horror story in the world. Customers set their Carreras on the table and the busboy steals them. I've known people who had their car windows smashed to get a pair of Persols left on the dashboard. Everyone wants hot sunglasses."

Not everyone, I think smugly. But a few weeks later, the hinge of my inferior shades breaks. I'm in Mexico, on a glass-bottom boat surrounded by ten sunburned noses supporting two thousand dollars' worth of designer frames. To make matters worse, the ocean is murky, so there's nothing for anyone to stare at but the paper clip that is now holding together my glasses.

I can't stand the shame. As soon as I get back to Los Angeles, I hurry to the nearest eye-fashion salon. After trying on everything from buffalo horn to sterling silver, I sheepishly choose a pair of *faux* tortoise frames, which, the salesperson assures me, I can wear with "almost anything." I can't tell you how much they cost. I can't even tell my husband.

Still, he notices.

"Nice sunglasses," Duke says when I return home. "Do we need a rider for our insurance policy?"

THE FAMILY CIRCUS

I may have suffered a setback in my effort to get along with my in-laws. But it really wasn't my fault. One minute I was up on stilts. And now here I am, looking at my splint and crutches, wondering when I'll be able to drive again.

I was just trying to fit into my husband's family. Duke's brother Danny was in town with Make a Circus, an arty San Francisco troupe. Danny, a juggler, was performing with his wife, Maria, a puppeteer/acrobat/clown. Duke and I drove out to Ganesha Park in Pomona to see the show.

The circus was terrific. But by the middle of the first act, I began to feel stodgy and conventional—my usual response to being around Duke's kin. Danny was masterfully tossing clubs in the air. Maria was dancing on stilts and playing the concertina. And I was just sitting on the grass, sipping a Diet Coke from a fluorescent sports bottle.

I haven't felt so out of it since I watched Duke's sister Joan, the star clown of San Francisco's renowned Pickle Family Circus, wriggle around on her back and play the sax. It was the first time in my life that I regretted giving up the baton.

What a contrast. Last week my brother, Bobby, his wife, Robbie, and their daughter, Erica, came to visit. Bobby runs a family company back East, and Robbie runs the house. They regard me as daring and bohemian.

Duke found this hard to believe—at first. But then he heard my brother describe his ideal solution for coping with stress. "I'd be really, really mellow if I had twenty million dollars in CDs," Bobby said wistfully.

Duke turned a little pale and gently pointed out that a lot of people might be able to cope with that.

"OK," my brother said amiably. "Make it five million."

Still, I really enjoyed Bobby and Robbie's stay. All they wanted to do was eat in nice restaurants, take aerobics classes, and shop—things I do well. There was no pressure on me to try something strange or fantastic. There was no pain either, unlike my in-laws' most recent visit.

Danny hoisted Maria onto his shoulders and in tandem they began to jump rope. When do they practice this? I wondered. Before dinner? After sex? Gosh, I hope not while they're having a fight.

"What would you think if I decided to take up knife throwing?" Duke whispered. "We could do it together."

Actually, we *had* planned to go hiking together after the show. But then Danny announced that there would be workshops so that the children in the audience could hone their circus skills. Tumbling attracted the younger kids. Juggling drew slightly older kids. And then there were the stilts.

"Honey," Duke said, "would you mind if I gave it a try?" How could I object? Obviously, the circus was in his blood. He picked up some stilts and followed the kids into the ring. Not wanting to be a stick-in-the-mud, I tagged along.

Mark, Danny's longtime juggling partner, was teaching Stilt Walking 101. "Make chicken wings with your arms," he said, flapping his elbows. "And remember to lift the stilt with your hands at the same time you step with your feet."

Suddenly, it all came back to me. I was ten, I was at

summer camp, and a bunkmate let me try her birthday present—stilts! I was pretty good on them, too. It's probably like riding a bike, I thought.

So I grabbed some stilts. In a few minutes, I actually managed to walk a few steps. "You're being such a good sport," Duke said admiringly.

"Be sure to look up," Mark said. "You can get in trouble only if you look down."

Yeah, right. "Honey, the footholds on these stilts are a little narrow for me," Duke said. "Let's switch." He gave me the death stilts.

A minute later, I was writhing on the ground in agony. I didn't know what hurt more: realizing that my in-laws would consider me a geek because I couldn't master a basic circus skill or my rapidly swelling right foot.

Which, as it turned out, is broken. The doctor in the emergency room said I can't put any weight on it for the next six weeks. I think I'm going to lose my mind.

"We better call Uncle Henry," Duke says. What's he? I wonder. A sword swallower? A fire eater?

No, Duke's uncle is chief of orthopedics at a prestigious New England hospital and chairman of the orthopedics department at an even more prestigious university medical school. He assures me that although I'll feel some pain, I should be able to hobble around in a hard-sole shoe. He also refers me to a good orthopedist.

I thank Uncle Henry profusely. Then he says, "I'll be in town this fall. Maybe we'll have a family reunion."

I think I'll sit that one out.

A WEARING EXPERIENCE

The miracle has happened again. I was sad, the sun wasn't shining, the computer was making funny noises. Fortunately, I knew exactly what to do. And now, sitting in my closet, carefully wrapped in tissue paper, emanating healing radiance, is a pristine white cardigan. And I'm cheerful and optimistic.

Saved! By the miracle of new clothes.

I'm lucky. I can afford to ease my pains with a shot in the wardrobe. And I'm female. I know what joy a silk camisole or a paisley scarf can bring. Men don't seem to get the same kick out of clothing acquisitions. Not once have I heard my husband say, "Honey, look at the great socks I found today."

"Men don't use clothes as a mood-altering drug," Duke says. "We go for cars and boats."

Clothes take up less space. Besides, the only thing you can control in life is your wardrobe. Cars break down when you least expect it. Boats eat money and gas. Your house, your mate, your friends, your family, even your career, are beyond your control. However, you're in total command of what you put on your back each morning.

"But sometimes what I have to wear takes over," argues my sister, Laurie. "Like if I have a business meeting, I have to put on the power suit. I can't wear the funky dress with the fringe."

That's only because that dress is olive and Laurie lives in Manhattan, where the women are in official mourning. "Everyone wears black all the time," she concedes.

A few months ago, I went to New York on business. At the time, the only black thing I owned was my car. I stood in the baggage-claim area at Kennedy Airport, wearing a teal-blue coat and red pumps, surrounded by women in funeral garb who stared at me as if I were Bozo the Clown. It was a little disconcerting.

"Put this on," Laurie said tactfully the next day when I appeared in a tropical print. She reached into her closet, rummaged through racks of black skirts, black blouses, black sweaters, black shoes, and even black sneakers—and handed me a black jacket. It made me look and feel surprisingly sophisticated. "You should get one," my sister said.

I was bound to succumb. The beauty of new clothes is that you can magically change your image with the wave of a charge card. Besides, fashion is a universal female bonding experience. My friends and I used to dress Barbie. Now we dress ourselves.

"Male bonding is about sports," Duke says. "When a man visits another man, the last thing in the world they would do is try on each other's clothes. Or shop. I can't imagine saying to another man, 'Hey, that sweater would look really great on you.'"

He doesn't know what he's missing. My sister took me to Nicole Miller, a sleek boutique on Madison Avenue. The ultrachic, ultrathin saleswoman in widow's weeds was aghast when I pounced on a red miniskirt. "No, no, it comes in black," she cried. But red always makes me happy.

"I don't know how you found that," my sister marveled. "I've been shopping here for three years and never noticed any color." Laurie did get me to buy slinky black slacks and an elegant black coat dress with jet buttons. But I returned the favor. I talked her into a purple suit.

"Maybe *I* need a new look," Duke said when I modeled my purchases. Unfortunately, he was joking. As far as he's concerned, the old shoe is the best shoe.

For years, I've been trying to purge his closet of a pair of virulent green velvet pants—the color of an old wine bottle or Astroturf, depending on the light. Recently, I took them to the cleaners. "What do you want me to do?" the cleaner asked.

"Lose them," I replied. (Alas, they're still here.)

For the record, I'm not one of those slaves to fashion who refuse to wear the same outfit twice. And I'm not a compulsive buyer. I just like to wear pretty things. I wander through boutiques the way I wander through gardens, checking out the flowers in bloom. But I can say no.

"Try this little dress," my friend Wendy said recently, holding up a dainty floral frock. We were in Suji, the cozy shop in Santa Monica where she works.

"I don't need the little dress," I said.

"It's only forty-eight dollars," Wendy said. "It would look cute with lace leggings." True, but when I tried it on, I didn't get the feeling that something wonderful could happen at any moment. And what's the point of new clothes if you don't get that feeling?

"Duke would really love it," Wendy said. I couldn't argue with that, but . . .

Fortunately, at that moment, a dejected-looking woman trudged into the shop. Her face lit up when she saw the little dress. "Oh, what a beautiful dress," she said wistfully.

Saved! By the miracle of new clothes.

THE GODS MUST
WEAR REEBOKS

God help me, I've found religion. And it's all Marissa's fault. We were lunching at Zucky's one fateful Saturday. A truly lousy spot to launch a quest for enlightenment, even if eating their chef's salad, or even believing there *is* a chef at Zucky's, is a true test of faith. Anyway, Marissa gave a sorrowful sigh over her glass of iced dishwater.

"Look, I can't figure out what to do about painting my kitchen. You mind driving over to Main Street and doing the psychic?"

"She picks paint chips?"

"No, my building's up for sale. And I shouldn't paint if I have to move. Besides, there's a bunch of things I've gotta know. Like when I'm going to meet my twin flame."

"Sure, why not? She can tell me if I was crazy to buy that red fringed sweater."

"Why? You love the sweater. It's gorgeous." Marissa, a fashion writer, is a much more secure shopper than I am.

"Well, my electric car antenna died as I was leaving the French Connection. I'm worried God's punishing me for spending so much money."

Ten years of Hebrew school left more of a mark than I like to admit.

"No, you saved money because now you have something to wear with your linen skirt."

Thus reassured, I climbed in Marissa's car and we drove to Aleph Books, one of the myriad of metaphysical bookstores in Los Angeles that play aural Valium music and sell three ancient *I Ching* coins for a dollar. It's a real mystery to me just where archaeologists unearthed the scores of ancient Chinese coins for sale in this city. I have a horrible suspicion they're stamped out in Monrovia and chemically aged.

Resident weekend mystic Reverend Annalee Weatherly was doing readings behind the rebirthing blankets. Twelve dollars per fifteen minutes. Enter and sign in, please. Pick out your healing crystal while you wait.

She was having a slow day, so we both secured appointments. I wasn't worried about the future, but I've never been able to resist a bizarre experience. Especially a cheap bizarre experience.

So I placidly sat in front of the sweating, overweight, polyester-clad psychic. She dipped her hands in water, mumbled some mumbo jumbo, and reached for my hands. Which she carefully weighed, explaining the left hand signified the past; the right, the future. I was fairly balanced.

Then why was I there?

"Margo, you have to remember that you chose your family to fulfill karmic requirements. If your father goes to jail, it's not your problem. You just have to be happy and not blame yourself."

My father was in serious legal trouble. A disconcerting fact the psychic couldn't possibly know. It wasn't written up in *Metaphysical Digest*.

"And you shouldn't kill yourself working. Even if they do want you to play with toys . . ."

I'd been working marathon hours in an advertising agency. My workload had just been expanded to include a toy account.

"Look, your aura's fine but you're missing a spiritual core. Find something you believe in. For inner peace."

Fran Lebowitz once said, "There's no such thing as inner peace. There's just nervousness and death."

The psychic lit up a Camel while I was writing a check. This was a bit disconcerting. Such earthly behavior confused me. Indicated disregard for the body. Still, if I wanted to undermine her credibility, her parting words deterred me.

"Take care of yourself. But get your car antenna fixed."

Marissa and I drove home entranced.

"So, what's the story on the paint. Or the twin flame. Whatever that is."

"It's a soul mate. Won't find him for months. But in the meantime, I can paint. How 'bout you?"

"I'm supposed to find God."

"That's got to be easier than finding a soul mate in Los Angeles. Check the Bodhi Tree," Marissa said as she kissed me good-bye.

Admittedly, there's something spiritually offensive about searching for God in a bookstore. But I have total faith in the power of the written word. My ex-husband swears if he'd taken all the things he screamed at me, published them in a pamphlet, and slipped them under the locked bathroom door, we could have avoided divorce.

Thus, I heeded Marissa's advice and drove over to the Bodhi Tree. I was in sad need of faith. My car mechanic had informed me it would cost $150 to fix my antenna. And he wouldn't accept my sweater as payment.

The Bodhi Tree was selling *I Ching* coins for three dollars. Prices on Melrose are inflated.

"Need any help?" asked the clerk. "Or some herbal tea?"

"I'm looking for religion."

"Anything in particular?"

"Something sort of eclectic. That supports the notion God lives in every new pair of sneakers."

"I don't think we've gotten that in yet. If you have the author, I can look it up."

I opted to wander. There are certain basic principles of the universe I swear by. Hair always looks perfect the day before it's due to be cut. You meet the man of your erotic dreams as soon as you go off the Pill. And the right book finds you when you're ready.

What found me was *Eight Thousand Years of Wisdom* by Tao master Ni Hua Ching, and *Creative Visualization* by Shakti Gawain. I threw them on my MasterCard with a quick, longing glance at Robert Schuller. Yes, I was tempted, but I'm too snobby to find God in a book they sell at the 7-Eleven.

At any rate, I returned home and speed-read my way through the millennia. Thrilled at this concept of God as a master energy force behind the universe. Actively fantasizing about moving to China to contemplate clouds from a mountaintop, I even called Pan Am to price tickets.

Then I got to the 180 Observances.

Do not tattoo your body or anybody else's. Do not dig for hibernating creatures in winter. Only heal a person if they request it. Do not cause a flood. Easy sacrifices in the name of inner peace.

Do not keep pets.

Beulah the Buzzer screamed in my head. Good-bye, inner peace. Bess and Stella, my pet pugs, are the loves of my life. Half my Chinese fantasy involved taking them back to their homeland. Where thousands of years ago they were gourmet fodder.

Crestfallen, I reached for *Creative Visualization*. Tao for Walter Mitty. The first exercise involved imagining a place in which you felt comfortable. I knew I was disillusioned when I pictured Neiman Marcus. The second exercise involved writing an affirmation, or positive thought, over and over until it sunk into the subconscious and wafted out into the universe to manifest destiny.

Everything works if I want it to, I typed with a basic lack of conviction. Fifteen times. Obediently, I recorded my negative responses: This sucks; I'd rather be a heathen; why am I listening to a psychic?

Frustrated beyond belief, I stomped out to the car in search of a more palatable panacea. Frozen yogurt. Vast quantities of French vanilla melted through my imagination. I wrenched on the ignition. Slammed into reverse. Hit the radio knob by mistake.

And lo and behold, my electric car antenna rose from the dead.

Everything works if I want it to?

Unbelievable.

Only in Los Angeles can faith move Mazdas.

THE BIG FIX-UP

I think I'm going to lose my mind. I'm sitting in my office, which used to be a sanctuary, listening to Pedro and Martin sing "La Cucaracha" as they chip paint off the windowsill with a scraper. Are they ever going to finish working on our house? I wonder.

Actually, I've been wondering that for quite some time now, and the end still isn't in sight. Though when it comes to home improvements, the end is never in sight. To own a house is to be its slave. No matter what you put in, no matter what you rip out, there is always another imperfection that demands your attention. And that imperfection (be it large or small) invariably leads you into the Land of Chaos.

Still, I feel guilty for complaining. I'm lucky to own my own home. For years I dreamed of living in this little white house by the sea. I imagined a cozy cottage with a picket fence, peg-and-groove floors, a flower garden, and plenty of storage space. But I never imagined how much time, energy, and aggravation this fantasy would actually take.

Who does? "You're fed this bill of goods that it's smart to buy a house," says my friend Marjorie, who bought a house last October. "You get equity. You get a tax break. You're not wasting money paying rent. But rent isn't a waste of money. It's what you pay to not have to deal with a house."

Of course, Marjorie's deal with her house sounds more like a deal with the devil. She's taking off the roof and building a second story—just as soon as she finds a contractor. Meanwhile, she and her mate are shelling out mortgage payments, interest on their construction loan, and rent on the house they're currently living in. "And we don't know anything of misery yet," says Marjorie, "because construction hasn't even begun."

Why not? "It takes months to make the design. And even longer to get the permits," Marjorie tells me, thus strengthening my resolve to never build anything bigger than bookshelves. "And if you're asking for a variance, you've got to get approvals, which take forever. And then you find a contractor, and he gives you a bid, and the bid is fifty thousand dollars more than you ever thought you'd spend."

In my experience, any home improvement costs more than you ever thought you'd spend. Then again, I used to believe that God gave you kitchen cabinets, asphalt driveways, and hardwood floors. Other people are more realistic.

"Whatever the problem, it's always a thousand dollars," says my friend Nina. "It's this magical figure. It can be a pane of glass. Or a little plumbing. You name it." (While this seems impossible, homeowners quickly discover that there's no such thing as a minor repair. You go out to replace a five-dollar bolt, and before you know it, a man in a giant payloader is pouring concrete in your window.)

But Nina has never hired anyone, so she has no idea of what the actual cost could be. "When someone gives my husband a price, he flips out and says, 'I can do it myself for much less,' " she explains. "And I can't justify spending the money when he's so handy. Though I'd like to say, 'Honey, I don't doubt that you can do it, but I was kind of thinking that it would be nice to have it done this year.' "

The problem is, like many do-it-yourselfers, her husband

finds it easier to start a home-improvement project than to
finish it. The demolition always goes quickly, even for semi-
skilled laborers. But as for putting it back together . . . Nina
has been doing without a kitchen floor for eight months now.
And the wife of another Handy Andy I know has gone two
years without ceilings. I would find living in a house with an
open wound to be more than a little bit stressful. Of course,
I get nervous watching my husband drill holes to install mini-
blinds.

Ironically, "many people become slaves to their homes to
reduce anxiety," says Los Angeles psychologist Gary Emery.
"They've got something else in their life that they can't
manage, so their house becomes the distraction, the one thing
they can control."

As far as I'm concerned, the only person who has his house
under control is Pop Larsen, the fictional sage of Builders
Emporium. As for the rest of us . . . "The more you try to
control something, the more out of control it becomes,"
Emery explains. "Nothing stays perfect. Even if you get it
fixed for fifteen minutes, something else goes wrong. You
start by changing the doorknob and wind up having to redo
the whole house."

Case in point: Three weeks ago, my husband arrived home
from the office with Pedro and Martin. "They're looking for
work," Duke said. "I thought they could clean up the yard."

It seemed like a good idea at the time. The yard was
overgrown with withered rye grass and weeds. It had to be
cleared out before we could plant whatever mystery shrub
happens to thrive in total shade and sand. So Pedro and
Martin started digging.

"The yard looks a million times better," Duke marveled
that evening, his heart swelling with the pride of home ownership. For a moment I, too, basked in the satisfaction that
comes with putting your house in order. Then he suggested
that the back of the house could use a coat of paint.

We really hadn't planned on painting the back of the

house. But making home improvements is an addiction that can be cured only by bankruptcy. "As long as they're here," said Duke, who eagerly rushed to Standard Brands and wrote a large check for brushes, rollers, masking tape, a fourteen-foot ladder, and a five-gallon tub of paint.

"You bought the wrong color!" I wailed with dismay two hours later when I discovered that the back of our house was now French vanilla and the rest of the house was snow white.

"No hay problema, Señora," Pedro said cheerfully. *"Podemos pinar toda la casa."*

"The whole house really does need to be painted," Duke said. That was easy for him to say. He doesn't work at home. While he's safely insulated in his office, I'm home juggling deadlines and Pedro and Martin. The minute I receive a long-awaited long-distance call from an interview subject or editor whom I've been chasing for weeks, I hear another urgent cry of *"Señora!"* Which is my cue to drop what I'm doing and fetch *"más pintura,"* *"más Hefty bolsas,"* or *"más dinero."*

Still, I must admit that Pedro and Martin are doing a wonderful job. And I would be thrilled except that a freshly painted house just points out how shabby the fence is, how dilapidated the roofing tiles look, and how badly the driveway needs to be paved. And my editors are beginning to wonder why all my stories are late.

"You know what we should do to our house—" Duke says when he returns home.

"Live in it," I reply.

AGENT DEAREST

If you asked me, I could write a book about agents. It wouldn't be a Jackie Collins saga about some shrewd hustler willing to kill for his ten percent. It would be the truth, which is stranger than fiction (which is why I've changed all the names except my own).

Chapter One. I send a sample chapter of my novel to Vince, a literary agent who had read an article I'd written and asked to represent me. I wait a month for Vince to return my call and inform me I am the next Franklin Allen Lieb—the man who got a six-hundred-thousand-dollar advance from Fawcett for his first novel. Instead, I get a call from my agent's assistant. "Vince is having a major life crisis. If you want him to represent you, you'll have to be patient." If I am patient, I will have a life crisis, too, I complain to my friend Todd.

Chapter Two. Todd suggests I call Annette. He bills her as the rising star of Talent Unlimited, a multimillion-dollar New York agency. "She can make things happen," Todd assures me. "She's the next Swifty Lazar."

"Sure, I'll read your proposal," the next Swifty says. "Todd's so cute. Does he have a girlfriend?"

"Not that I know of."

"The reason I ask is that he took me out to dinner last week and he didn't make a pass at me. He stared at me, and I felt like there was chemistry, but I'm not sure . . ."

"He wants to get to know you," I explain. "Todd's very old-fashioned."

"Oh, I feel much better," Annette says with a sigh. "Thank you."

"Thank you," I say gratefully. "I'll send the chapter Express Mail."

She calls three days later. "You know, I went out for drinks with Todd last night. And I asked what he was looking for in a relationship. He seemed really uncomfortable."

"Todd doesn't like to be pushed," I say. "Did you get the manuscript?"

"I'm very busy," she says. "I can't waste time with a man unless we have a future."

"About my novel—"

"It's a good idea, but I would have written it in the first person. If I were you, I'd do it over."

Chapter Three. I do it over. I not only rewrite the chapter, I also go to New York in the hope that a personal meeting with Annette will speed my ascent on the best-seller list.

"Cute outfit," Annette says when I walk into her office. "You mind going shopping? I have a big date Saturday night—with a doctor." I didn't fly three thousand miles to improve her wardrobe, but I look on the bright side. An agent with a serious shopping habit has motivation to sell my book.

She leads me to a boutique on Fifth Avenue that seems to specialize in slutwear. Who am I to judge a woman with good publishing connections, I think as she tries on leopard-print leggings, jumpsuits with industrial zippers, and leather halters. "Won't this drive him wild?" she asks, modeling a white fishnet toga.

"I think it will drive him away," I confess, then suggest she put it on hold until after lunch. "Did you like the chapter better in the first person?" I ask after she finishes complaining about how it is impossible to have a perfect job, apartment, and relationship at the same time.

"Yes, but it's not there yet," she says. I go home discouraged. But Annette keeps me in mind.

Chapter Four. "Chick at Silver Lining Press is looking for someone to write a relationship book for dogs," she calls to inform me. "I gave them your name."

"A relationship book for dogs," I stammer. Annette explains it is easier to sell a first novel if I have a nonfiction book in print. It sounds like good advice. When Chick calls the next day, I am elated. I send him pages two weeks later. Two weeks later, Chick calls back.

"Chick likes my proposal," I report exultantly when Annette calls late Saturday night from the doctor/boyfriend's apartment to ask if I think she should sleep with him even though he isn't officially divorced.

I advise her to postpone sex. She advises me the pages don't work for her. She enumerates fifty words she would change, thirty phrases she would add or subtract, twenty jokes she thinks are funnier than mine.

"But the publisher likes it."

"I'll tell you what. Tomorrow, I'll call Chick and tell him exactly what's wrong with the book."

An image flashes before my eyes. A salesman knocks on an apartment door. "Oh, good," says the occupant. "I can use an encyclopedia." "Wait," says the salesman. "Let me tell you what's wrong with these books."

I try to stay calm. "Please don't," I beg Annette.

But Annette is as good as her word. Chick calls the next day. "I've talked to Annette and we both agree that you're talented but the book isn't there yet. Why don't you take another shot at it?" I am weak. I know who I should take a shot at, but I hold fire.

Chapter Five. I incorporate Annette's changes into a second draft and send it back to her.

"I can't sell this book," she says after reporting that her doctor/boyfriend had sexual problems on their last date even though she had bought a leather miniskirt. "But don't be depressed. We can still be friends."

A TRUDGE
DOWN THE AISLE

"**S**hall we shop?" Duke asks invitingly, as if he's procured two front-row tickets to *The Phantom of the Opera* instead of a grocery cart with a wobbly wheel. I roll my eyes and trudge through the automatic doors.

Unlike my husband, who actually enjoys supermarket shopping, I consider it to be a loathsome chore, only one notch above doing laundry in a Laundromat. When I lived alone, I avoided the market at any price—even if it meant a daily run to the 7-Eleven. But Duke, not unreasonably, refuses to live on a diet of apples, bagels, and Diet Coke.

"It's comforting to make sure that the old larder is provisioned," he says cheerfully, as he ambles toward the dairy section. He believes that laying in a sufficient supply of produce, pasta, dried fruit, coffee, and Japanese soup offers subconscious reassurance that you can survive the upcoming week's apocalypse.

Well, if you can survive a trip to the supermarket with your mate, you can survive anything. Not only must you cope with the usual supermarket unpleasantries—the pungent aroma of a Clorox spill in the meat aisle, shopping carts that maneuver as if the shortest distance between two points is a figure eight, talking cash registers, screaming babies, and the citizen sneaking eighteen cans of cat food and a bottle of vodka through the express checkout line—you also must cope with your loved one's convictions on everything from cottage cheese to garbage bags.

It isn't easy. "I always think that this is where the relationship is going to end," says my friend Leslie. "In the market. Over the toilet paper." A one-ply versus two-ply clash? "I want plain, white toilet paper," she says firmly. "No scent. No little daisies. The cheapest you can find. After all, where is it going? But John wants the most expensive toilet paper. He believes that you should buy only the best stuff."

But everyone has his own definition of what the best stuff is. "Not that yogurt," Duke chides, when I casually toss a container of Dannon into our cart. Don't take it personally, warns an inner voice as my husband puts the container back on the shelf and reaches for a brand with a thousand-year-old Bulgarian on the label. "This is five cents cheaper," he says.

As far as I'm concerned, life is too short to worry about saving five cents on a tub of yogurt. But Duke is of the "those-crooks-will-never-gyp-me-out-of-an-extra-nickel" school of grocery shoppers. Still, over the years we have learned to compromise. He no longer drags me from market to market in search of the cheapest peach. And I do without the designer paper towels that match the kitchen.

Even so, "people have such personal styles about how they handle grocery stores," says my friend Claire, who has at least one supermarket spat a week. "I make a general list and systematically start at one end of the store. But Fred wants to explore. He's up and down the aisles, reading the backs of boxes. He picks food with no regard for what we really eat or have time to cook. It drives me nuts."

Not for long. "Fred seems to have a limited attention span," Claire explains. "Once he reaches a certain point, no matter what aisle we're on, it's time to go. We might have done only two aisles. It doesn't matter. He says, 'Let's grab a few things and split.' It takes all the fun out of shopping."

I don't think there is much fun in grocery shopping. My friend Roger agrees. "It's hell," he says. "I like to do it like a commando raid: hit and run. I don't want to wait around while Fran tries to decide whether to buy Kellogg's Corn Flakes or All-Bran. Who cares? It's all grain," he says. "And she gets so upset if I buy the frozen food first. What's the big deal? We don't live 180 miles away. It's not going to defrost."

Roger is convinced that the only solution is to shop alone. "It isn't a good event to share," he says. "It's one thing to say, 'Let's go pick out the new carpet.' Or 'Let's go buy the baby's furniture.' But 'Let's go to the supermarket and bicker about whether we want Granny Smith or Red Delicious'? There's no thrill involved."

My friend Sabina would argue with that. "I think marketing is a very loving, warm, intimate thing to do together," she says. "With my ex-boyfriends, I played soccer with the cantaloupes and threw around the grapes. Obviously, those relationships weren't going anywhere. But Anthony and I seriously read the labels together. We don't want to buy something that has cottonseed oil in it, God forbid!"

Chocolate is a different story. "The other reason I like to shop with Anthony is, I try to be so stoical about what I eat," Sabina confesses. "I buy the lettuce, the broccoli, the healthy food. But Anthony goes straight to the cookies and ice cream. I love having the cookies. And since he put them in the cart, I don't have to take responsibility for buying them."

In exchange for sharing his cookies, Anthony gets to share her coupons. "I cut them out," says Sabina, "but he really loves it when we get to the point where you turn them in. So we both get to enjoy the elation of building a financial future together by saving money. We leave the market as a team. What more could a couple want?"

"Detergent," Duke remembers, just as we're about to

reach the front of the checkout line. He leaves me with the groceries and bolts down the aisle. My blood pressure slowly rises as I empty our cart onto the conveyor belt and realize that my husband has disappeared with our checkbook. The shoppers behind me are glaring as I politely ask the surly checkout girl with the five-inch fingernails and the pierced nose not to total the bill yet. Just as a brute in a sweat suit begins slamming his cart into my ankles, Duke returns.

"Look, honey, I saved fifteen cents," he says proudly.

"Get me out of here," I reply.

FAREWELL, MEDIUM RARE

This never would have happened if Annalee hadn't disappeared.

I've always had a weakness for the supernatural. I don't transchannel Cleopatra, mind you, but I do enjoy getting a teeny glimpse into the future. Annalee was my psychic. For years I relied on her "channel of prognostication."

She was some seer. "A car crash," she once warned me. "I don't see you getting hurt, but I see you parked somewhere when you're hit hard on the driver's side." Twelve hours later, the door of my Mazda had a rendezvous with destiny—a.k.a. the Big Blue Bus.

"Ask her when the next earthquake will be," scoffed my disbelieving husband, whose romantic tendencies she had been correctly tracking, unbeknown to him, for two years.

"October," said Annalee. October 1986 came and went, reinforcing Duke's skepticism. But on October 1, 1987, Whittier's windows fell into the streets. "She did say October, didn't she? And she didn't say what year," he said with begrudging respect. But by October 17, 1989, when the Bay

Bridge collapsed, Annalee had disappeared, her clairvoyant powers unable to foresee a visit by spiritually benighted Santa Monica gendarmes who demanded to see her business license. "Isn't that just like a magus to vanish into thin air?" Duke jested. But I felt like I'd been abandoned by Mary Poppins.

I suppose that I could have left the rest of my life to chance. But as Nancy Reagan wrote: "Why take chances? It may be nonsense, but does anybody really know? And people have certainly been fascinated by astrology for thousands of years."

I usually don't listen to Nancy Reagan, but I always listen to my friend Léon. Usually the voice of reason, she badgered me to see her astrologer. "Erin's as accurate as anyone can be," said Léon, a writer who wouldn't submit her book proposal until the moon was in the right place. I thought she was nuts. "If the moon can control the ocean, it doesn't take a genius to figure out it might have some effect on your life, too." Léon said. And a major publisher gave her a six-figure advance, on "the very day when Jupiter trined the ninth house."

So, here I am in Hollywood, sitting in a charming, beautifully appointed old garden apartment (the kind you'd need extraterrestrial guidance to find) with sixteen-foot ceilings, a fireplace, and a lovely view. The former First Lady would feel right at home. Me? I'm staring blankly at a computer printout that looks like a blueprint for a merry-go-round, struggling to stay awake while Erin, a gracious, conservatively dressed ex-model with a Marilyn Quayle flip, methodically reveals the secrets of my natal chart.

"As you well know, you have a Leo sun sign," she begins, speaking into a studio microphone hooked up to the surprisingly sophisticated stereo system that's recording this reading (or should I say, celestial consultation?). This is so mainstream, I marvel.

"In addition to the sun in Leo, you have the planet Pluto there, and Mars there," Erin continues, hastily assuring me:

"Don't worry if you don't know what I'm talking about; you hopefully will in a few minutes."

But it's been ninety minutes and I'm completely bewildered—overwhelmed by quasigeometric lingo and hopelessly lost in space. Erin believes that "anything in our solar system and beyond can be used as an interpretive factor." But life's too short to worry about the influence of asteroids and planetoids, or whether sun spots cause fluctuations in the stock market.

Frankly, if I wanted to know this much about the cosmos, I'd have stayed up late and watched the *Voyager* transmissions. All I want to know is if I'm going to receive a large chunk of cash. But she keeps talking about the transiting nodes.

I really wish she would go into a trance. When I pay good money for an otherworldly experience, I want mumbo jumbo; I want drama, smoke, lightning, and crystal balls. Perhaps a bearded man in a peaked wizard's hat and a cloak covered with silver stars. But this earnest, intelligent stargazer in the black patent pumps is so aggressively normal. Annalee spoke in a mysterious voice of indeterminate gender. Annalee did readings in a metaphysical bookstore, behind the rebirthing blankets. But here, the only mystery is whether or not Erin takes MasterCard.

Still, she's been amazingly accurate about my personality. She even seems to understand what makes Duke tick. I wouldn't get on an airplane if she said it was a bad day to fly. But I want magic.

"Your Mercury is in the sign of Cancer," says Erin. "I think you're capable of being rational."

Then why am I tempted to ask her when I'll find Annalee?

LET'S GET SMALL

I fell off the wagon—all because of my sister. I'd been clean for years. But the other day, before I could stop myself, I bought a four-poster bed, a table, a Tiffany lamp, and a door. I put them in my purse and carried them home. How can I explain my behavior?

I, Margo, am a dollhouse junkie, a compulsive builder of miniature rooms. For weeks I've been cheerfully sawing tiny cornices, painting bantam bay windows, and running to the copy shop to reduce books to a Lilliputian scale. I know there are more important things I could be doing. But a hobby, like a habit, makes you forget about important things in life.

"I wouldn't know," my sister, Laurie, said when I pointed this out. "I've never found a hobby I liked. I hated needle-point. I was bad at clay. I grew plants, they died. Fish died. I don't have any patience or time." But she does have a passion for intricately detailed model rooms. "You build one for me," she exclaimed right before her birthday.

"It's been ages," Michael Lyttle said when I walked into his cavernous store, Miniature Estates (without so much as a backward glance at the twelve-thousand-dollar Victorian mansion in the window). I explained that I had kicked the habit. I just needed to do one more project. Lyttle rolled his eyes. He knows the early signs of hobby abuse.

"One middle-aged man, in one of his many dollhouses, had a tiny glass fishbowl," Lyttle said. "And he actually bred fish in a big tank, so he had a tiny baby fish swimming in the tiny glass bowl at all times." I began to hyperventilate. "And then there was the woman who wouldn't buy a particular chair because, when she pressed down on the seat with her finger, it wasn't soft enough."

For the record, even at the height of my minimania, I was never out of touch with reality. I didn't expect the itsy-bitsy clay avocado pit sprouting in the teeny-weeny glass on my diminutive kitchen windowsill to grow. I quit because I became obsessed. Once I actually told my ex-husband: "Not tonight, dear. I'm shingling the roof."

This doesn't surprise my friend Bob, a model-train fanatic. He's built three very complex—"they even have graffiti and things like that"—layouts in his garage. "I'd be in a lot better shape if I didn't stay up late building these things," Bob says. "But it's so peaceful. Just you and yourself tinkering away, squinting real hard. It's tough to get it out of your system."

Hobbies are one of the few arenas in life in which a person can always feel in control. Whatever the pastime—collecting baseball cards, growing orchids, flying fighter kites, or putting ships in bottles—you set your own pace; you do what you want, and nobody criticizes you.

"It's your one chance to show how you'd reshape the world if you were given the chance, which you never are," Bob says. "I can build a whole city and not worry if it's going to fall down in an earthquake. Though I did have a building fall over in the last one." (All he had to do was pick it up, dust it off, maybe glue the roof back on.)

Of course, this sense of power doesn't come cheap. Whether you're hooked on photography, stamps, skiing, or if-you-have-to-ask-how-much-you-can't-afford-it follies like sailing, there's always some new prize or piece of equipment that you see and desperately crave.

"It makes it hard for me to tell my kids I can't afford to send them to private school," Bob says. "I know I could. But it's all disappearing into the garage."

I tell myself that I quit making miniatures once and I can quit again. But my sister's gift is almost finished, and suddenly I'm not so sure. My editor called, and I said I'd have to call her back because I was varnishing the pygmy parquet floor. Then I bought a cordless phone so that I could do business while I was outside gluing dwarf spider plants onto a midget *étagère*.

But what really scared me was that I found a new supplier right near my house, and I keep finding excuses for stopping by. "My regular customers drop in all the time for a fix," says Sue Garfield, owner of Petite Designs, an elegant dollhouse boutique. She confides that she can always spot an addict because "anything they see in the real world they're trying to figure out how to create in miniature."

I shuffle my feet guiltily. Ever since I visited Organizer's Paradise, I've been dreaming about building a small shrine to organization. I'd need built-in bookcases and high-tech furniture and maybe track lighting and . . . Sue laughs and leads me to the back room where her resident craftsman, Dale Kendall, is showing a customer how to electrify a pint-sized kitchen.

"Dale can help you do anything," Sue promises.

"See you tomorrow," I reply.

VANITY OF VANITIES

I didn't want much. Just a small, simple vanity for the bathroom. I pictured it quite clearly: a plain, unobtrusive white cabinet with flat doors and a couple of drawers. I was willing to spend a reasonable amount of money to get something attractive. It didn't seem like the impossible dream.

But there I was, standing in a warehouse the size of an airplane hangar, feeling like a shrunken-down Alice in Home-ownerland. Buffeted by frantic shoppers pushing colossal carts, I surveyed a line of vanities that stretched out to the crack of doom. I could get an Early American piece of junk, a French Provincial piece of *rebut,* or a Spanish Colonial piece of *basura.*

"Vanity, thy name is ugly," said Duke.

Suddenly, I spied what looked like a sleek white vanity a quarter-mile down the aisle. Sure enough, it was the only non-wood-veneered unit in the place. It was streamlined and practical; there were plenty of drawers, a gray Formica top, a white enamel sink, and snappy chrome faucets that said HOT and COLD.

It turned out this vanity was sold á la carte. I flagged down a bored salesman, who was cruising the aisle on a giant fork-lift. "How much?" I asked.

"I don't know," he said, yawning. "I missed that class." He probably missed arithmetic, too, or he could have added up the various parts and arrived at a sum large enough to buy a round-trip ticket to the Milan furniture mart for me and a one-way ticket back for the vanity that I'd buy there.

Actually, I would have gladly gone to Italy, but I didn't have time. The contractor was coming in a week to fix a rotted hole in our bathroom floor. He had to rip out our old vanity, which was why we were frantically searching for a new one.

I realize that this may not sound like a major problem, especially if you compare it to serious life challenges such as finding a parking space in Westwood on a Saturday night. But I'm the kind of person who is politely called "sensitive about her environment" and impolitely called "picky." I've bought everything in the house—from my computer to the garbage can—because I thought it was cute. And frankly, something called a vanity should be cute.

Usually when I go shopping, I can find one or two cute models amid the chaff—a microwave oven without wood grain (why must appliances look rustic?) or fireplace utensils that aren't cheapened with shiny, embossed brass. But I couldn't find a single vanity that didn't look like it came out of the Sleepy Time Motel. And I looked in a lot of places, enough to speculate that vanities are a black hole in American mass marketing.

Finally, I found myself meandering around a Designer Quality Bath Furnishings Showroom, gaping at flushable, drainable works of art such as a majestic pedestal sink in "Pompeii Lava," which looked like an altar font and sold for an ungodly figure.

Not that I wanted it, or the porcelain washbasin with the hand-painted flowers and the matching hand-painted (why?) toilet bowl. I was just killing time, waiting for the show-

room's twenty-seven-year-old power-bobbed bath investment counselor to call my number and reveal how much the
plain white vanity in the corner cost. (For some strange reason, there were no price tags on any item less than one
thousand dollars).

"You're probably looking at about three or four hundred dollars," she said, adding that this didn't include a sink
(one hundred plus), a top (three hundred plus), faucets
(one-fifty plus), or even drawer pulls (ten plus). Still, I was
desperate. The contractor was now coming in three days.
"You're probably looking at about a four-to-six-week
wait," she warned me.

She was probably looking at an emotional breakdown.

"Vanity of vanities, saith the Preacher; all is vanity," Duke
said when I returned home despondent.

But, happily, all is *not* vanities. The next day we found a
chic little bath and tile shop that had an acceptably adorable,
acceptably affordable, red and white pedestal sink in stock. Of
course that means we won't have any storage space . . .

I don't want much. Just a small simple medicine chest for
the bathroom.

WHAT PRICE LUXURY?

Lately, three money pits are ruling my life. Two of them wag their tails, and one leaves a suspicious puddle in my driveway. I don't know which one gives me the most grief. My twelve-year-old pugs? Or my nine-year-old car?

One thing is certain. Whenever I'm feeling complacent, along comes a new crisis that invariably requires a hefty infusion of cash. I realize that people with kids have it worse. But with a child, your obligations and priorities are fairly straightforward. The child comes first.

With pets and cars, you're constantly practicing triage. There are so many decisions to make, and each one comes with the caveat that if you choose wrong, your beloved (fill in the species) will suffer. Or your car will blow up during rush hour on the 405. Or you'll be facing a Visa bill like the one you get after a long vacation.

For the record, I'm not complaining about the high cost of automotive or doggy luxuries. My car doesn't have a phone, a compact disc player, or an alarm with electronic digital motion sensors. My pugs don't have jeweled ID tags or marble feeding bowls. They don't even see a psychiatrist as does my sister's dog, Elvis.

"I spend an outrageous amount on Elvis," says Laurie, whose basset-hound budget includes Medipet insurance, a prescription pet-food delivery service, gourmet dog biscuits, and the Pet Pickup, which taxis Elvis to and from doggy camp. Of course, Laurie can afford these indulgences. She doesn't have a car.

I, however, write every third check to the mechanic or the vet. And these expenses never end; there is no bottom line.

Yesterday I drove to the Mazda dealer to buy a seventy-dollar pair of switches so that the automatic windows in my car would go down. On the way, I noticed my steering was loose. Roy, the mechanic I met in the parts department, offered to check it out. He scowled as he peered under the hood: "This baby hasn't led a tender life."

Roy told me the steering box needed adjustment, and then he reeled off what else was wrong: radiator, air-conditioning, transmission, belts, thermostat, ignition—you name it, my car needed it.

"It's still probably cheaper than the dog," said my husband, Duke, when I got home.

A few weeks ago, Bess, my black pug, collapsed on the Venice boardwalk with what I hoped was only heat prostration. When her tail suddenly became uncurled the next day, I rushed her to Bel-Air Animal Hospital. Norman Weiner, my vet of twelve years, suggested a geriatric physical, an in-depth examination that costs as much as a major tuneup. He explained that it could prolong Bess's life.

Now what was a little thing like my bank balance compared to that?

Alas, vets, like mechanics, tend to find other things to do once they're under the hood. Dr. Weiner recommended a teeth cleaning, which costs as much as an alignment and steering adjustment. "Why does Bess need this now?" I asked.

"The plaque bacteria could get into her bloodstream and affect her heart," Dr. Weiner replied.

As long as he was knocking Bess out for her teeth cleaning, I suggested, he should implant an ATM slot so that I wouldn't have to see the bill. "They do make implants now that send off a signal in case you lose your dog," said Dr. Weiner. But even he feels that's a little much.

"It's probably manufactured by the same people who do the Lojack tracking system for cars," Duke said later.

Despite Bess's medical treatment, I remained concerned. A week later her tail was still flopping lifelessly. But on the day my check cleared, Bess's tail miraculously recurled. So I guess my money was well spent.

And it could be worse. "My son's nanny is living in a little guest house that I could easily use as my office," says a friend, who is too embarrassed to let me use her name. "Only my son doesn't need a nanny anymore. And I need an office." So why doesn't my friend ask Nanny to move?

"Well, because our old, rickety dog loves her," she says sheepishly, "and it would be hard for him to adjust to a new pet-sitter. So my husband and I are spending a great deal in construction so our grouchy pet can have a live-in nanny."

Makes sense to me. I've just noticed that Stella, my fawn pug, has another eye infection. Mind you, this is in spite of the prophylactic prescription drops (at eleven dollars a bottle) that I've been putting in her eyes three times a day for the past six months. I love Stella, but the last thing I want to do right now is drive her to the vet.

So here I am in a modern quandary. On the one hand, I have Roy's warning that my car radiator could blow at any minute (naturally, he couldn't get around to fixing it for the next two weeks). And on the other hand, I have the image of a blind pug with a cane and a cupful of pencils.

Excuse me, I've got to find Stella's leash.

STAR-CROSSED

Why don't celebrities stay where they belong? On TV. In the movies. Or in the rack at the checkout counter.

To see them in real life only makes for awkward moments. You think you know them, but you don't. You feel compelled to say something, but there's nothing to say. They take the best tables. They draw fire. What good is having them around?

"Isn't that . . . ?" I recently wondered as a pert blonde with a body to die for walked into my aerobics class. I stared in rapt fascination. She looked a little old to be that daffy, giggly comedienne who danced in a bikini. Then again, I'd followed her career for at least twenty years.

Still, I was careful not to get excited. I live in Los Angeles. I know the unwritten commandment: Thou Shalt Not Acknowledge the Rich and Famous. (That's for gushing tongue-tied tourists from Iowa who buy maps to the stars' homes.) Besides, I tend not to recognize people out of context. I wasn't sure this was the face that launched a thousand fanzines.

Then she began to sing. Class had just ended; there was no music playing to sing along with. Yet she blithely pranced across the dance floor warbling a merry tune. Even the most studiously blasé among us took notice, if only to furtively check for plastic-surgery scars.

"You know who you look like?" said a brazen classmate. The star giggled—so coyly that my fillings almost fell out. "Are you related to her?" my classmate continued obtusely. Frankly, I was so embarrassed for both of them that I skipped the denouement.

If celebrities would simply stay in the tube or on the screen, then everyone would know how to act. But when they wander out on the streets, it gets confusing. It's uncomfortable for the celebrity. And it's uncomfortable for me.

Recently, my husband and I went to the opening of the Moscow Circus. There was a panoply of famous people, few of whom I recognized until Duke pointed them out. (I have no memory for faces. My husband says that he could introduce a hot-water heater to me as George Lucas.) There was the younger, beef-jawed son of the longtime sea hunter. And the martial-arts monarch fresh from defeating a million pre-glasnost communists.

"Have you met Walter Mondale?" a man asked. I stared blankly at the bell-captainly gentleman sitting next to him. There was a resemblance.

"I think I voted for you," I said stupidly.

"That man never ran for anything except a tip," Duke said later.

I did recognize the short, genial, teddy-bearish everymensch—L.A.'s dream tax attorney—with his tall, brittle blond wife. And the perennial boy of the video West (co-winner with George Hamilton of the Dorian Gray award). He stood next to me, grinning expectantly. But what was I supposed to say—"Miss the prairie?"

"Why spoil a perfect relationship?" Duke said.

Secretly, I was a little disappointed that none of the stars said hello to me. After all, it's impossible to turn on the TV or the radio without hearing whom they've married, whom they've divorced, whom they've impregnated, and/or what drugs they've just kicked. It seemed inconceivable that they didn't know *my* name.

On the other hand, what could they possibly say that I'd find interesting—besides "Hey, how would you like a job?"

I felt silly taking covert looks at the household names, but I wasn't half as silly as the paparazzi who preyed on them like carp coming up for a feeding. The more polite ones yelled, "Mr. So-and-So," before firing off a barrage of flashbulbs. But most of them just hollered, "Hey, Kevin, over here. One more," as they dogged him to the men's room.

The most awkward moment came when the teddy-bearish every-mensch's young son asked for a hot dog. I could imagine the beleaguered star standing in the concession line, surrounded by hordes of fans shouting his character's name. I was actually tempted to get the hot dog for him.

But who was I to spoil the fun? After all, a long time ago I was a celebrity—once removed. I was sixteen years old and visiting Los Angeles for the first time on a cross-country tour. I was walking around Beverly Hills when I noticed the persnickety and fastidious half of a sitcom duo. "Aren't you . . . ?" I stammered. He smiled and asked my name, and we chatted for several minutes. Afterward, nobody believed me.

But the next day, while members of my tour and I were strolling around Huntington Library and Botanical Gardens, we heard a familiar voice. "Aren't you Margo?" the persnickety and fastidious star exclaimed. You'd be surprised how popular I became that summer.

It never would have happened if he'd stayed where he belonged.

A CLOSED-DOOR POLICY

"**Y**ou can't be as bad as I am," says Jon about house guests. Jon is wrong, I think. "I had a friend," he continues, "a good friend, probably my best friend, stay with me, and he got on my nerves."

In how many days? "What do you mean days?" asks Jon. "On the way to the airport to pick him up, I began to feel put out. Then I thought: Why does he have to let his feet touch the carpet when he walks?"

Maybe Jon *does* understand how I feel about house guests. My friend Marcella, on the other hand, doesn't have a clue. Recently, she told me that we couldn't have lunch for the next two months because she's having company.

"Here I sit, juggling my schedule for the onslaught of the House Guest Season," said Marcella, who entertains at least twenty-five visitors a year, mostly between May and September. "I even keep a guest book. There are probably five hundred names in there."

Despite Benjamin Franklin's astute (if conservative) observation that fish and visitors smell in three days, Marcella's guests stay an average of *five* days. "Though we did have one who stayed for three months," she recalled, "and that really was too long. There cannot be a nicer guy, but I wound up hating him."

I would have wound up killing him. I work at home. House guests (I don't care who they are, how much I like them, or how long it's been since I last saw them) are pests, much like roaches and mice. But there are differences. You can trap roaches and mice. And they don't want you to drive them to Disneyland.

Don't get me wrong. I'm glad to see out-of-town visitors. They're welcome at my house for breakfast, lunch, or dinner—as long as they call first. It's when they want to *stay* in my house, disrupting my life, fogging up my bathroom, tying up my phone, that I act like a mama bear defending her lair.

My husband found this out the hard way. When we moved in together, he blithely suggested that we turn the room that was earmarked for my office into a guest room. "You can always work on the sun porch," Duke said, noting that the porch wasn't big enough or private enough for overnight visitors.

I immediately went off like a car alarm.

"I guess it's the couch in the living room if they stay," Duke hastily conceded. Or a bigger house. Or a motel.

I'm all in favor of motels. Sure, they cost forty dollars a night, but they save a lot of aggravation all around. Frankly, the only thing as draining as having a house guest is being one. In your effort not to be any trouble, you do twice as much housework as you ever do at home, and still your hosts' faces grow longer and longer as they knock themselves out trying to be cheerful.

And this is assuming that they don't have a convertible sofa designed by a chiropractor who wants to increase business, or an unhousebroken but amorous dog. Being a house guest might be fun if you had a good experience in the army, or if you come from a large family. But otherwise . . .

"In the South, it's just something you do," says Marcella, who's from Arkansas. "If you don't stay with people, it's an insult." I've yet to meet anyone (and this includes friends and relatives) who was offended not to have me as a guest.

"If I travel the world, I can collect my debt," Marcella says. "I could stay anywhere." That would be an advantage, I suppose. "Of course, my husband wouldn't dream of it," she says. "Here I spent all these years working out a wonderful trade agreement, and he wants his own place with a private bath. He doesn't like the people. Probably because they've been house guests."

Probably. "The real problem with house guests is you can't have sex whenever you want," my friend Sabina says. "That they wake up earlier or later is unimportant. What gets me is when you're in the kitchen doing the dishes, your husband comes in, starts nibbling on your ear, and your house guest wants a glass of milk."

What gets me is when you're in the kitchen doing the dishes while two ardent house guests are rolling around on your living room floor.

"You're just not a hostess," says my sister, who once threatened to buy me a welcome mat that said GO AWAY. "You would never buy a sofa bed." I shuffle my feet guiltily. "The first piece of furniture I got was a sofa bed," she says.

Actually, it's pretty comfortable. I slept on it for five days last fall when I was in New York. And I must confess I had a wonderful time. Laurie didn't feel the slightest need to entertain me, and I didn't feel obliged to be compulsively neat. We just basked in the intimacy of being sisters. Of course, Laurie, a workaholic, was hardly ever home.

Which brings me to the reason she's calling me now. "Guess what?" she says. "I'm coming to L.A. on business."

"Want to stay with me?" I automatically reply.

SHALL WE TRANCE?

Whenever I think that my job is tough, I get this little reminder from the Universe that it could be worse.

As I confessed in a previous column, I have a weakness for the supernatural. Perhaps it's just part of being a free-lance writer, but I'm continually drawn to metaphysically fit folks who have mysterious ways of knowing where my next assignment is coming from. And they keep telling me that being a swami is no bed of roses.

Take Thomas Jacobson of Beverlywood, a genial ex-marine-turned-successful-trance-medium. He and "Dr. Peebles," his spirit compadre, have appeared on national television and radio and are the subject of a new book, *To Dance with Angels*.

Still, "people are constantly accusing me of fraud," Jacobson says. "Or, at best, of being a well-intentioned, deluded person."

I can sympathize. It's bad enough going to parties and telling people I'm a free-lance writer, which everyone's job-status converter instantly translates into "failed real estate agent." But at least I can drop the names of publications, for validation.

"At the beginning, I told people I was in alternative communications," Jacobson says. "Finally, I got up the courage to tell people I'm a spiritual medium." That must be some icebreaker at a party. "The reaction is never boring," he acknowledges. "Either they have to go to the bathroom all of a sudden or they want to talk all evening."

Mystics are also besieged by curiosity-seekers. "You have to let people know that you're out having a good time, just like everybody else," says Louise Woods, a Santa Monica seer who identifies herself as a metaphysical counselor. "People say, 'Oh, you're psychic. Tell me about this and this.'" She handles it the way a doctor or a lawyer would. "I give them my business card and tell them to make an appointment," says Woods. "I don't do house calls."

Speaking of houses . . . "Imagine me trying to get a loan on a home," says Jacobson, who listed "voice medium" as his occupation on both his loan application and his tax forms. (Can he claim Dr. Peebles as a dependent? I wonder.) "It's tough," he says. "You're trying to be credible, but you're doing something that most people see as incredible."

Actually, I don't think what he does is any more incredible than the theory of continental drift. But you can't go by me. In my profession, I have to make numerous leaps of faith. For example, I work on spec.

"I've had a real quandary with business," Jacobson says. "On the one hand, there's this attitude: If you're so psychic, why don't you make money? But on the other hand, if you make a lot of money, you're not considered to be very spiritual."

No matter what you earn, authorities will view you with suspicion. "When I first started working, I called downtown and asked what statutes were on the books," says Erin, a Los Angeles astrologer. "They said, 'You have the wrong office. You need to talk to the vice squad.' So I called. They answered the phone with 'Bunco.' I inquired about getting a business license, and they sneered. 'What exactly do you do, lady?' "

Actually, Bunco could use someone like Erin. "I'd been reading for a very nice woman who worked at a bank," she recalls. "And I'd given her some dates for little things. Then one day she came in and said, 'Oh, Erin, these dates have worked out real well. Now I want you to do something important. I want you to pick out a good time for me to do some embezzling.' I said, 'Number one, your chart doesn't look good for that and, number two, I don't do that.' "

Gee, and I thought it was frustrating sitting alone in a room for hours, staring at a word processor. At least I don't have to divine where and when my editor will meet a tall, dark, handsome stranger or hold myself up to public ridicule when my predictions are printed in the *National Enquirer*. No one expects miracles from writers, only words.

But some days they don't come easy—to me anyway. Of course, I haven't taken any courses in mediumship like Molli Nickell. "I learned automatic writing," says Nickell, editor-publisher of *Spirit Speaks,* an all-ghost-written Brentwood-based magazine created to share guidance and wisdom from the spirit plane. "I shift into a meditative state and say a little prayer and ask my spirit teachers for guidance, and words come into my head and I just write."

Right. I'm sitting in front of my computer with my eyes closed. I've said a little prayer and begged my spirit guides to help me finish this column. That was an hour ago. And this piece is due by the end of the day. Suddenly, I get a message.

"We don't work on deadline," the spirits say.

part 2

LOVE
IN THE TIME OF
TELEPHONE
TAG

LES MISERABLES

Why are men such babies when they get sick? My husband has just announced for the third time in twelve minutes that he doesn't feel well. "You married him in sickness and in health," chides an inner voice, so I stop writing and hurry into the living room where he is lying in state on the sofa. "What's wrong, honey?" I ask, bracing for an up-to-the-minute bulletin on his Battle with Disease.

"I have the sniffles," Duke says in the sepulchral whisper used to broadcast golf tournaments and state funerals. He looks up at me with the plaintive stare of a grievously wounded mastiff.

"Oh, no!" I exclaim. This can't be the same man who carefully relocated a rattlesnake from a trail when we were hiking, the man who has his teeth drilled without novocaine. My maternal instincts are immediately inflamed by the absence of machismo. "Let me get you some aspirin," I say.

"Do you think that vitamin C would help?" he asks.

Actually, I suspect that nothing—and that includes vitamins, garlic, Contac, or Extra-Strength Excedrin—helps a sick man as much as the knowledge that a busy woman dropped whatever she was doing to go and get it for him. "Lie still," I say. Not that he has the slightest intention of moving. "I'll run to the drugstore."

"It's comforting to have you with your little Florence Nightingale cap on ministering to me," Duke says. With his last ounce of strength he reaches for the remote control and switches on his favorite channel—Channel 18—where he watches two giant Koreans clad in shorts and garter belts wrestle in a sandbox. I am tempted to remind him that Magic Johnson played in the NBA Championships when he had the flu.

But I know better than to spoil his fun. In my experience, I have discovered that unlike women, men basically enjoy ill health. Still, before I risked the wrath of half the population by putting this in writing, I got some expert opinions.

"When I get sick, I feel great," confesses Glen, thirty-eight, a lawyer. "My God, nobody can expect anything of me when I'm sick. I can just sit around and catch up on magazines and programs I've taped on the VCR, and of course sleep. And I also can take an Empirin and codeine to make myself feel better without feeling like a drug abuser."

Dr. Alfred Coodley, emeritus clinical professor of psychiatry and behavioral sciences at USC School of Medicine, suggests, "For a certain portion of men, who throughout life have needed to be tough, competent individuals who can deal with everything, illness provides a convenient escape from life. He no longer feels obligated to maintain that defensive, powerful, independent attitude. He has a legitimate opportunity to, in a sense, cop out: 'It's OK to be childlike because I'm sick. I'm entitled to be taken care of because I'm sick.' "

"I don't know how I got the sniffles," Duke moans.

"You swam in the ocean on a very cold day," I reply, composing my face into an attentive bedside manner. I know better than to suggest that he sat in a draft. Men like to believe their illness, like a war wound, was honorably gained.

"The water was unusually cold for this time of year," he agrees. Then he gives me a news update: "My sniffles are getting worse." He sneezes once or twice to make sure I get the message.

I get the message. I run into the bathroom and bring him a box of Kleenex. Then I run into the bedroom and bring him a quilt, then a pillow, the television listings, a trash can (used tissues are multiplying on the carpet faster than germs), and a cup of Red Zinger tea. "I'm very grateful," Duke says. "As you know, I have the sniffles."

Of course I know. I wouldn't be this obliging if he were well.

"Getting sick is one of the little tests men have for women," says Rob, thirty-two, a screenwriter. "If a woman doesn't perform well in your sickness, it will never happen." What's a good performance? "A full mother. My last girl-friend did the right thing. When I had a cold she immediately bought some chicken and made some soup. She even had her own concoction of hot water, lemon juice, and honey, which she called Sickee Tea. The important thing about Sickee Tea is that you don't make it yourself; someone has to make it for you."

Robert explains that "a woman who behaves badly is a woman who tells you that when she is sick, she never gives in, she goes out and does anything. You don't want to hear that a woman is more macho than you. I had a girlfriend who actually said, 'What are you doing in bed? Let's go to a concert.' She didn't understand that I was really kind of enjoying my cold. I thought it was something that we could share together. She didn't see it that way. She thought I was a wimp."

There is a limit to how long even the most understanding woman can cater to a man who lies in a pool of sweat (a man who is too sick to take a shower, but not sick enough to see a doctor) without contemplating euthanasia.

"The only thing you should ever do for a sick man is offer

to drive him to the hospital," sneers Claire, an interior designer. "Or drive yourself before he drives you crazy. Fred
actually expects me to sit by his side and do anything he
wants. There's no use leaving the room—as soon as you do,
you'll hear a weak moan that sounds like a request. And I'll
say, 'Did you just ask me for a heating pad?' and he'll whim-
per, 'What? What? Don't make me yell. I'm sick.' Or worse,
he'll say things like, 'I'm not hungry but don't you think I
should eat something?' which of course means he wants me
to make something but he won't tell me what—I'm supposed
to guess the magic potion. He's thirty-eight years old. Can
you believe it?"

"Maybe it's because men are used to be being spoiled by
their wives and mothers," speculates Dr. Harry Sperling, an
Encino ear, nose, and throat specialist.

"Men can act like babies when they're sick, and that is
reinforced by a woman's responses because women are
known behaviorally to be more nurturing than men," says
Dr. Thomas Lasswell, professor of sociology at the James A.
Peterson Human Relations Center at USC.

"My tummy hurts," Duke reports the next day. I am not
surprised. He has digested the entire Channel 18 lineup: Farsi
lounge acts, Indian music videos, *Armenian Teletime,* and the
weekly Yugoslav show (with its slogan, "From the Adriatic to
the Pacific"). "Have you seen my Merck Manual?" he asks.

"No," I lie. Reading a Merck Manual is guaranteed to
prolong even the most minor ailment. In case you don't
know, the Merck Manual is to bodies what the Chilton
Manuals are to cars. It is a hypochondriac's bible, 2,462 pages
of small print that details everything you never wanted to
know about common, rare, fatal, or merely life-threatening
diseases.

Here's what happens when a man gets his hands on a
Merck. One Sunday afternoon, Duke cut the grass with a
Weed Eater. Half an hour later, I found him poring over his
Merck.

"What's the matter?" I asked, alarmed when I noticed that he was reading about multiple sclerosis.

"My hand keeps trembling," Duke said.

"Was it trembling before you mowed the lawn?" I asked. Duke shook his head.

"Then why don't you assume it's vibrating from the Weed Eater?"

"I guess it could be," Duke said, sounding disappointed.

My friend Léon, who swears that "all men are hypochondriacs beyond belief," has never been with a man who didn't have a Merck. But she has learned how to use it to get revenge. She called her boyfriend, who was complaining about "intestinal heaviness," and said, "I'm looking through a medical book and I think I found what's wrong." Then, she says, "I read him about fourteen symptoms to which he eagerly answered, 'Yes, yes.' You would have thought the prize at the end was a Maserati. Then he asked, 'What have I got?' I really enjoyed telling him: 'A tipped uterus.' He hung up the phone. He later complained that I didn't 'take his symptoms seriously.' "

Here's another surefire way to heal a sick man in a hurry:

I trudge slowly into Duke's sickroom. "I don't feel well, honey," I moan. Duke bounds out of bed and throws on his clothes. "Excuse me," he says. "I've got to flush the cooling system in my car."

A MARCH
DOWN THE ISLE

"There's no such thing as a small wedding," I warn Monica when she tells me she's getting married in May. Weddings follow a law of geometric progression: If you invite A, then you have to invite B and C; if you have just A, B, and C, you'll offend D, E, F, G, H, and I.

"But all we want is an intimate ceremony with our family and friends," Monica argues.

That was what my fiancé and I had wanted, too. "We can get married in our front yard," said Duke. "Or better still, on the beach." It sounded like a good plan. How difficult could it be?

Let me tell you.

"When's the wedding?" asked my sister the minute I called New York to tell her that Duke and I would no longer be living together on spec.

"I don't know yet," I stammered as my pulse began racing for the escape hatch. (Remarriage is an excellent test of just how amicable your divorce was.)

"You must set a date," Laurie ordered. "I want to get a cheap fare."

Duke and I decided January would be a good time for a wedding, mostly because it was the first available month that didn't include holidays, birthdays, or former wedding anniversaries.

"You must get married by the end of the year to file a joint tax return," my father decreed.

We decided Thanksgiving would be a better time for a wedding, mostly because we could cook a traditional turkey dinner ourselves and save the expense of a catered reception. But a head count of our parents, stepparents, siblings, their spouses, and their children revealed we were looking at a minimum guest list of fifty people—if we excluded all our friends.

"You must invite Duke's aunt and uncle," insisted my future mother-in-law, who had already invited them for me. "They live in Boston. They won't come."

But you can't rely on anyone not to come to a wedding, especially a wedding in Southern California. Within weeks, everyone we had ever met—long-forgotten friends, ex-lovers, even college roommates—found out about our wedding, "wouldn't miss it for the world," and had, in fact, purchased nonrefundable plane tickets. I began to panic when I got a postcard from a friend in Tasmania.

"You must hire people to help you," exclaimed my future sister-in-law.

We decided to call a caterer. I discovered that we would have to pay fifteen hundred dollars for a turkey dinner and triple overtime for people to serve it because it was Thanksgiving. Duke sent me to check out a beachfront restaurant.

"You can sort of see the ocean from the dining room," I reported glumly. (My doubts were growing faster than the Homeless City of tents that blocked the view.) "And it's twenty dollars a person."

"I guess that's OK," Duke muttered morosely.

"Are you sure you want to go through with this?" I fretted as he ran out of the house to enjoy a few peaceful hours wandering the aisles of Pep Boys.

"I don't care," he snapped.

I didn't think it could get worse, but then it did get worse.

"You must ask Zara to be your flower girl," my future father-in-law informed me in front of his four-year-old granddaughter. (My brother's wife had already taken the liberty of buying her six-year-old daughter a dress.) Grandma called from Florida to threaten that my ailing grandfather would die if a rabbi didn't perform the ceremony.

"My wedding is turning into a pageant," I complained to my friend Lori. "And it's not as if the British government is picking up the tab and I get to ride in a glass coach."

"Albert and I started out with six people and wound up with one hundred twenty-seven," she consoled me. "One of my cousins was seriously into alcohol. She drank all the white liquor and went to work on the brown. She ripped off the bottom of my wedding gown as I walked into the reception." I began to reminisce about the good old days when I was dating.

Duke was on the phone making inquiries about the price of a one-way ticket to Mexico City when I got home. "I'm canceling our wedding," I announced before he could read off his Visa number.

I haven't seen Duke so relieved since Magic Johnson flattened the Celtics in the championships with a miracle junior sky hook. "That's great, honey," he said. "Will you marry me?"

Curiously enough, everyone was more understanding about the wedding being canceled than they were about the wedding being held.

"Whatever makes you happy," said our friends and relatives, who effortlessly located doctors to attest to urgent inner-ear infections forbidding air travel, allowing refunds on their nonrefundable tickets.

So, Duke, an enormous bridal bouquet, and I took a boat to Santa Catalina Island. We checked into the Call of the Canyon Room at the Zane Grey Pueblo. Fern Whelan, the justice of the peace of the city of Avalon, agreed to marry us at five o'clock.

At noon Duke suggested we take a little hike up the airport road. The only hike I felt like taking was to the hairdresser, but I didn't want him to think he was marrying a poor sport. At three o'clock I was sunburned, weary from walking uphill, and too desperate to find a bathroom to marvel at the wild buffalo cow and calf that kept me from going behind a tree.

"Let's turn around," I said. "Just a little farther," Duke coaxed.

At four o'clock we were past Black Jack Mountain, some seven miles away. Duke suggested a shortcut back through the restricted area where hunters were shooting wild pigs.

I jumped in front of a speeding truck. "Stop!" I shrieked. "I'm late for my wedding."

All's well that ends well. We were married against a beautiful sunset on our terrace overlooking the harbor. The hotel graciously supplied champagne and a witness.

There is such a thing as a small wedding.

IT'S IN THE MALE

Where can I get a male ego? Anyone who believes that men and women have the same mind-set hasn't lived on earth. A man thinks that everything he does is wonderful, that the sun rises and sets around him. But a woman has doubts.

Recently, my husband and I were in an elevator, waiting to ascend from the depths of Parking Level Five to Ground Zero. After a few moments, I had a revelation. "Honey," I said, "we're not moving."

"Sure we are," Duke said with more certainty than I ever feel about anything.

We waited a little longer. The lights on the control panel were dark and there wasn't the slightest sensation of motion. Yet he insisted that everything was under control because, he explained, "I pushed the button."

I hate to argue with a man who has pushed the button (men frequently take it personally when a machine disobeys their commands). But I was getting claustrophobic. So *I* pushed the button and immediately—noticeably!—the elevator began to rise. Duke was unabashed. "There must be something wrong with that button," he exclaimed.

I don't know one woman (though I'm sure some exist) who would have come to that conclusion. I, for one, would have assumed that I had made a mistake. That's why I want a male ego. Men rarely seem to assume that they've made a mistake.

"You're looking at the basic premise of the male ego," my friend Doug says. "Men are always right." But this implies that when I disagree with one, I am always wrong. "You've got the picture," he replies.

I detest the picture. But "it's the thing that let our ancestors go out and kill woolly mammoths," my friend Rob argues. "If you let any doubt creep in, you're history. You've got to go out like it's the only thing to do and you're just the guy to do it. It's the only way you've ever got a shot."

I don't want a shot. I just want to be treated fairly and paid well. Still, armed with a male ego, I could do battle over almost anything—the placement of my name on a memo, for example, or who gets served coffee first when I'm in a meeting. "Titles are really critical," says my sister, Laurie, who believes that there should be a theme park based on the male ego, only "there's not enough land."

"There's a guy in my office at the exact same level as me," she says. "Yet he fought for six months—screaming!—to be called a Senior Media Supervisor instead of Senior Media Executive. Finally, our boss asked if I minded that Harold had this title—did I want it as well? I said, no, the title I wanted was Senior Media Goddess. So he put that on my door. Now Harold is fighting for a bigger office."

My husband isn't surprised. "A man's ego is quite large," Duke says. "But it's very delicate."

He's telling me? In my experience, the male always seems to be discovering a cure for something, no matter what he's doing. And whatever it is, it's invariably more important than what the female wants to do. I'd be willing to bet that if one day a woman walked barefoot to the moon and back and a man cleaned out his desk, when the two of them sat down to dinner that night, he would groan, "Boy, was that desk a mess."

"It's protective," Rob says. "Would we ever do anything if we couldn't convince ourselves and our loved ones that it was the most critical thing on the planet?"

I don't know. Some guys seem to be without shame. Not too long ago, I was reading the Trump-versus-Trump coverage in the New York *Daily News*. Marla Maples was on the cover wearing something revealing (does she own a regular dress?). The headline read, BEST SEX I EVER HAD. None of my girlfriends (for the record, I don't know Cher, Roseanne, or Madonna) would be flattered to wake up and find that in giant letters on her doorstep. But . . .

"Reading that headline was the best sex Donald Trump ever had," Duke said admiringly. "The male ego can always use an amorous press release." (Actually, any stroke will do.)

I wonder if I could go to Sweden and have ego-change surgery or to Houston and get a male ego transplant. One useful side effect would be that I'd no longer feel the compulsion to straighten up the house. The next time I got lost, instead of asking for directions, I'd drive around in circles, clenching my teeth, trying to read the map while going forty miles an hour. And if I happened to run into an abusive, frothing maniac, I could get into a nose-to-nose shrieking confrontation with him instead of discreetly slipping away.

On second thought, maybe the house isn't big enough for two male egos.

NO TIME FOR PASSION

Forget money. Forget in-laws. Forget real estate. The biggest conflict between modern mates is time. After all, you can make more money. You can move to another state to escape his or her parents. You can fix up the house. But you can't put more hours in a day.

"I think everyone has discovered that time is at a real premium," says Marcia Lasswell, a Claremont family therapist. "Both husbands and wives have such busy schedules. It's tough to find time when they can be together."

She's telling me? "Isn't this romantic?" Duke asks as I morosely drag our shopping cart around the supermarket. Duke has just started a new job and has been working fourteen hours a day. And I'm in the throes of a writing frenzy, so my schedule is equally crazed. Today is Sunday, and we've cut work back to four hours so we can share a few precious moments. "What a great deal on cantaloupes!" my husband exclaims.

This isn't my idea of meaningful conversation. But I really can't complain. Our timetables are so hectic we've been living out of takeout cartons. The cupboard is bare, the refrigerator is empty, and even if one of us actually found a few spare seconds to tackle the last two weeks' worth of laundry, we'd have to do it without soap.

Still, on the Quality Time Scale of 1 to 10, a trip to the supermarket rates a 2. Our next stop, the dry cleaners, rates a 1. And our next stop, the hardware store, gets a minus 6. There's no romance to be found amid the plumbing supplies and the dead bolts, no matter how advantageously priced.

Yet I really should count my blessings. Many mates can't even get together to run errands. "I never get to see my husband," my friend Nina says blithely. I shake my head in dismay. When I called her to lament that Duke and I were fighting the clock, I expected sympathy.

"Ed always works a minimum of seventy hours a week," Nina informs me. "And he jogs every other night. And then there's softball league. And computer club." Doesn't she mind? "I'm just grateful he's not a surfer," she says with a laugh. "They have to get up at five every morning and check the waves."

Whatever happened to stopping and smelling the roses? Duke bounds out of bed at seven in the morning. "Gotta run," he says, hurriedly kissing me good-bye. "I've got a breakfast meeting."

"Remember the good old days, when we used to have romantic breakfast meetings in bed?" I ask wistfully.

"I'll call you," Duke promises. And he does call. But I'm at the gym. And when I call him back, he's in a meeting. And then I'm doing an interview. And then he's got an important call on the other line. And so it goes. Love in the Time of Telephone Tag.

Some duos don't connect for days. "I get bummed out when he gets home after I'm asleep and then he wants to talk," says my friend Sabina. "But then you wake up the next morning, and you realize that you don't know what he did yesterday and he doesn't know what you did. It's a little strange."

A little strange? Lately, it seems as if the unhurried life isn't worth living. Couples aren't simply juggling marriage, careers, and children anymore—they're juggling his friends, her friends, their friends, families, therapists, pets, charity functions, hobbies, and sports.

"My girlfriend's schedule is such that I can work as long as I want Monday through Friday without feeling guilty," my friend Andy says. "But golf takes up at least five hours a weekend. In order to schedule golf, I've got to encourage her to do more things. She'll say, 'I'm thinking of checking out this store.' Great, I'll play golf. 'Volunteer work?' Great, I'll play golf. Of course, I get really irritated if she's not there as soon as I'm done."

Even so, "a marriage isn't going to thrive on neglect," warns Lasswell, the family therapist, who adds that "any relationship needs energy and time put into it. And not poor-quality time when you're both too pooped to do anything but just crash." I shuffle my feet guiltily. "Busy couples have to schedule togetherness time or they won't get it," says Lasswell, who recommends that husbands and wives make appointments to see each other, "a month in advance if necessary."

I can't believe that the Day Runner has become a marital aid. But Nina informs me that she and her husband book time for everything—"including sex." Whatever happened to getting carried away by the moment? "Not having spontaneous sex isn't so terrible," Nina assures me. That may be true.

But this doesn't sound like my kind of foreplay. "Whenever we set up a sex date, we always have a fight," Nina confesses. "There's no intimacy, so we have to fight first to reconnect."

Of course, many couples spend their precious moments in heated combat. On the Quality Time Scale, an intense discussion over why she insists on dragging you to a shopping mall when she knows you hate to shop rates a 4. Giving him the cold shoulder because he's paying more attention to the Dodger game than to you rates a 3. And packing your suitcases and threatening to fly to Hawaii—alone—to see if your mate will even notice that you're gone rates a 5.

But if you really want to ruin the day or evening, there's nothing like trying to find a significant Quality Time activity. "It's not enough to read the Sunday papers and just hang out together," my friend Claire laments. "It's got to be hot stuff. Get the band. Get the majorettes. Get the pompons. You're really under the gun to have serious fun."

It's as bad as New Year's Eve—which, for the record, I've never enjoyed. In fact, most of the good times in my life haven't been planned—they just happened.

"Honey, I'm home," says Duke. But it's only five-thirty. In the afternoon. "Want to go for a walk on the beach?" Duke asks.

Excuse me. I've got to run.

FINDING LOVE
AMONG THE RUINS

"If he leaves one more dirty coffee cup lying under the bed, I think I'm going to lose my mind," says Monica. She and Jack have been married only a couple of months, but she tells me that the honeymoon is over. "I'm married to the slob," she laments.

Half the women in America are married to "the slob," I would think—and half the men. In my experience, Cupid's arrows rarely strike two people with the same definition of cleanliness. One partner usually feels like he or she is being asked to live in a furniture exhibit in the British Museum. The other partner remains convinced that he or she is forced to contend with the human version of Hurricane Gilbert.

"Jack just sits on the floor, and in a matter of moments there's a mess," says Monica. "A pair of sandals, three empty cans of Diet Coke, an ashtray, a drawing of a shelf he plans to build, a list of things to do, and fourteen magazines. And it stays there until I clean it up."

"Hire a maid," I suggest. It is a waste of time and energy to try and reform the slob. In my opinion, if a person has reached the age of thirty without developing an aversion to baseball-sized hairballs in the bathtub, it is unlikely that person is ever going to change.

"I believe that every individual should be responsible for his or her own mess," says Monica.

I used to feel that way, too. Then I met my husband, who makes Pigpen from "Peanuts" look like Felix Unger from *The Odd Couple*. The first time I walked into Duke's bachelor apartment, I wanted to run out and get a typhoid shot.

"Look out the window," said Duke, as I waded through stacks of yellowing newspapers, piles of sporting goods, and eighteen days' worth of dirty laundry. I wound up spending a lot of time looking out of the window at the glorious view of the Pacific Ocean, particularly since the alternative was to look at what was growing in the carpet.

I tried to remember that one person's mess is merely another person's filing system, but by our fifth date, I found myself cleaning in self-defense, afraid of what might come out of the kitchen sink in the middle of the night. And three years later, I am still cleaning.

"I would never clean up after my husband," says Lori. "We both make the same money and I'm not going to spend my weekend picking up after him. He has certain rooms to do around the house, and if he doesn't do them, I just step over the mess and start leaving my stuff around."

"I can't leave my stuff around," I say. "There isn't any room." Lori tells me that the disarray would disappear if I would only learn to outslob my husband. "Just get out the chocolate candies and read in the living room," says Lori. "It's really liberating to stretch out on the sofa in the middle of a messy living room and refuse to do anything."

In my opinion, life is too short and love too precious to spend time arguing about who took out the trash last. Of course, I am lucky. I am not married to a man who expects me to do all of the housework. Duke does his fair share of the domestic chores, albeit the high-profile glamour chores, like cooking, fire-building, going to the supermarket to make his coupon kills and dragging them back to the lair as Mr. Cro-Magnon did in the Ice Age.

Last month, for example, Duke whipped up a four-dish Asian dinner for six people, cooking three of the four dishes simultaneously in a ten-minute flurry of split-second stir-frying that set off every smoke alarm in the house. When he finished, there were splashes of Chinese condiments on the wall, the floor was splattered with tenaciously clinging clumps of mung bean thread, chopped scallions seemed to be growing between the tiles on the kitchen counter, and the wok was dripping grease on the stove.

Scorecard: Number of guests who praised Duke's cooking—six. Number of guests who praised my cleanup—zero. Still, my sister has the opposite problem. Every man she has ever gone out with is neater than she is. "I want to find a sloppy man," says Laurie. "Then I would have the upper hand: I could complain about him rather than vice versa." It is true that the central advantage of being neat is moral superiority—you are always right.

Laurie continues: "The man I'm dating now is meticulous. One night he unexpectedly slept over and I waited until he was asleep. At four in the morning I tiptoed into the bathroom and scrubbed the tub so he wouldn't find out how messy I really am. I looked into his closet once; it was actually organized. To me, a closet is where you hide things that you don't want people to see."

Still, I suspect that Laurie will eventually find happiness with a neat freak. I believe that deep down, most neat people have a basic need to be messed up, and that messy people have a similar need to be tidied. It seems to be a sensible balance of nature, the way plants need both sun and rain to grow. Two neat people would only find themselves arguing about whether to file the records alphabetically or chronologically; two slobs would find themselves buried under a stack of empty pizza cartons.

But of course I can afford to be philosophical about being married to the slob. I finally convinced him to split the cost of a cleaning service. So on a recent bright sunny Monday morning, our house was invaded by a cheerful crew of three white tornadoes who in the space of a few hours got the fingerprints off the light switches and the gray patina off the white Venetian blinds. Duke's eyes widened in wonderment as he surveyed the freshly waxed floor. He turned to me and smiled.

"It's like fairyland," he said.

Then he reached for a glass. "Don't touch a thing!" I told him.

MONEY, HONEY

"We need to talk about money," says my husband. I clench my fists and begin to hyperventilate. Duke and I have a modern attitude about finances: We don't trust each other. Does anyone?

"Are you free Monday night?" he asks.

"I can't fight Monday night," I reply. "I'm on deadline." The last thing I need to think about is how much we spent on Christmas and how much we're going to have to spend on taxes.

"We're just going to balance our checkbook and pay some bills," he assures me. "We're not going to fight."

I want to believe him. But when I think back on the arguments that we've had since we got married, it seems as if every one began as some petty monetary crisis. There was the brawl over whether our food budget was expected to cover Milk-Bones for my pugs. There was the skirmish over how I could pay 75 cents for a can of Diet Coke when Vons was selling six-packs for $1.29.

There was the battle over why two people who had already

made the commitment to share their lives could not commit
to sharing a checking account.

"Show me a couple who's been together for longer than
three months who doesn't have a conflict about money and
I'll show you a his-and-hers crypt at Forest Lawn," says
Duke.

Experts agree. "People are going to argue about money,"
says Constance Ahrons, associate director of the Marriage and
Family Therapy Program at USC. "It doesn't make much
difference whether money is tight or not. People are going to
fight about money anyway, especially if their values are different."

How different are our values? Let me put it like this. My
mother's motto was: "The best is none too good." Duke's
father taught him that he would go to hell if he paid retail.

"We've gotten much better about money in the last year,"
Duke reminds me.

This is true. We no longer go to war over sums under
twenty-five dollars. We opened a joint checking account for
household expenses. We saved for vacations. We even filed
a joint tax return. Still, none of these improvements were
made without raising our voices.

"Money is probably the major marital problem," says Ahrons. "It's harder to talk about than sex."

Actually, money, like sex, is only difficult to discuss with
one's partner. It's quite a popular topic of conversation
among friends. My friend Claire, for example, is annoyed
because her husband has a strange concept of what is and is
not economical. "Fred has no problem going to a restaurant
and spending thirty-five dollars apiece," she complains. "But
let one head of seventy-nine-cent lettuce go bad in the refrigerator, and it's a whole different thing. He goes insane.

"We split most general amounts of money. But I have to
go through the phone bill and highlight every call that I've
made. It's easier than hearing about it. I don't want him to
say, 'Don't call information,' so I write him a check."

Monica would like to be able to write her husband a check. Jack just announced that he doesn't know how she's going to afford to go on their nine-day ski trip to Sun Valley.

"I stood there dumbstruck," Monica reported when we met for lunch the other day. "And then Jack said in a very smug voice that *he* can afford to go."

"But you're married," I argued, even though I realize that "for richer and for poorer" is a purely academic part of the marriage vow for many double-income couples. "Why doesn't he just pay for you? Or lend you the money?"

"He feels that if he makes things easy for me he's setting a precedent that he really doesn't want to set," Monica said with a sigh. "And I agree that it's very important for me to be contributing half, so I'm my own worst enemy."

"In theory, keeping money separate keeps you from fighting about how you spend it," says Ahrons. "But what started out as a system to preserve equality and independence has sort of run away with itself. It's gotten to a point where couples have arguments like, 'You owe me seventeen cents for postage stamps.'"

And their accountants find themselves acting as referees. "More and more couples are telling me their woes," says Joel Lewinson, our long-suffering CPA. "They spill their guts out to me. Wine, women, whatever. I'm like their financial shrink."

But he doesn't object. "Any accountant can put numbers together," says Joel. "To plan ahead, you want to know what everyone's doing."

Often he is the first to know. "I'll be sitting down with a couple doing the sale of stocks," he says. "And the husband will turn to the wife and say, 'I didn't know you bought that.' Or there's interest from a savings account that the wife doesn't know exists. It's a very trying time when couples come in and get their taxes done."

What's especially trying? "When I have to go through mental gyrations and do the return as if they were single and

as if they were joint so they each contribute their own fair
share," he says. I shuffle my feet guiltily.

Sometimes I think that life is easier for one-income couples. But recently my brother and sister-in-law came to visit
from the East Coast. Bobby believes that it is his duty as a
husband and father to be the breadwinner, and Robbie is
happy to have bread won for her. As part of their official tour
of Los Angeles, I took my sister-in-law to visit my favorite
soothsayer. "How much does your fortune-teller charge?"
my brother asked nervously while she was having her reading.

"Fifteen dollars," I said.

"Would she take a bribe?" he asked. "I'd give her a grand
if she'd look into her crystal ball and tell Robbie: 'I see that
you spend too much money. You don't appreciate how hard
your husband works. You really don't need to move to a
bigger house.' "

Curiously, it turned out that Robbie had already received
divine financial guidance. She returned from the reading
clutching a malachite egg. "It's a prosperity crystal," she
explained. "The psychic promises that it will make us rich."

"Maybe we should buy a prosperity crystal," I tell Duke
while we're blaming each other for the three unrecorded
checks in our checkbook. "A really big prosperity crystal."

"That's a good idea," he says. "Maybe I can find one on
sale."

AND DOGGY MAKES THREE

Can this relationship be saved? My sister calls from New York in tears. Her boyfriend refuses to let her basset hound sleep on the bed. "I can understand him not wanting Elvis between the sheets," Laurie assures me. "But what's wrong with on top of the covers?"

"Many men do not like to be in bed with more than one species at the same time," I tell her.

"But Elvis is used to sleeping on the bed," my sister insists, adding that her boyfriend considers it objectionable to find nonhuman hairs on his jacket.

I search for a way to break it to her gently. This relationship cannot be saved. In my experience, a couple can disagree on many subjects—where to eat, whom to vote for, what movie to see, even how to spend money—and still get along fine. But couples with major disagreements about pets—and by that I mean how many, if any, what kind, and how to treat them—are virtually bound to wind up with irreconcilable differences.

My sister takes the bad news in stride. "Men who want

dogs to fetch are a good bet to avoid because they want you to fetch, too," sighs Laurie, who decides to take Elvis for a walk in the hope of attracting a pet-loving mate.

He shouldn't be hard to find. Recently, *The New York Times* reported that pet ownership is "at an all-time high, with 61% of American households, about 52.5 million, owning animals, in most cases more than one animal." These pet owners can accept almost anything: exorbitant vet bills, a year-round flea infestation, glossy copies of *Dogue* and *Catmopolitan,* even a surly half-housebroken destroyer of shoes. They just can't accept criticism about their pets.

"My dog is just as important to me as a child would be to a single mom," says Sabina, the "mother" of a one-hundred-pound German shepherd named Shane. "And if a man cannot choose to make my animal happy, that, in essence, is not making me happy, and the animal stays and the man goes."

Sabina admits that her "son" has caused some problems between her and her boyfriend, Anthony, even though Anthony "loves the D-word [dog] like a stepfather." What kind of problems? "We were spending a week on a houseboat," Sabina recalls. "Naturally, we were taking Shane along. We all went to the pet store to buy a harness so that if he fell in the water, we could pull him out. Anthony was working with the pet-store lady. She showed him a blue harness. I explained that 'Shane says that he would prefer red.' Anthony got so mad that he walked out of the store. He was really embarrassed. I didn't understand. Shane's the one who has to wear it. He might as well pick the color."

Curiously, I believe that this relationship *can* be saved. Sabina will never find another guy who is willing to take a German shepherd on a houseboat. And at least Shane accepts Anthony.

Dr. Richard Polsky, an animal behaviorist in West Los Angeles, has been called on to intervene in numerous instances where a pet refused to let a human come between it and its owner. "One woman couldn't embrace her boyfriend because her Rottweiler would attack and growl," Dr. Polsky recalls. "Every time a man would go near her the dog would get really aggressive, even to the point where she couldn't keep the dog out of the bedroom because it would bark and scratch and carry on."

Could this relationship be saved? "Yes," Polsky says. "We worked out the problem in terms of teaching the dog to be more independent, and we did some antijealousy training. This involved teaching the dog to accept someone he doesn't like by associating it with something positive, like Häagen-Dazs, Stilton cheese, Italian sausage. You've got to find out what turns the dog on."

Häagen-Dazs and Stilton for recalcitrant animals might get expensive in Judie and Michael's Old MacDonald–style relationship. These two animal lovers keep about fifty pets, including two horses, a pony, eight cats, a golden pheasant, and three French rabbits, with four California tortoises here and a goose there. Ee-ii-ee-ii-oh dear!

The downside? "They run our life," says Judie, who is awakened at five-thirty in the morning by the frantic quacking of Victoria, her black East Indies "house duck." She explains that "as soon as you get out of bed there are eight cats yelling, 'Feed me.' Then you open the door and the goats and the sheep yell, 'We're starving.' "

The upside? No danger of running out of things to say to each other. Judie reports that "Michael calls and says, 'What's new?' and I say, 'Bear the cat did this. The horse did that. We have a crisis in the aviary. Should I call the vet?' "

"I can tolerate small talk about the animals better than small talk about work, or a mutual friend's hysterectomy," Michael says.

I can't imagine what would happen if Judie and Michael found themselves in the position of Monica and Jack. They bought their cats, China and Tucker, when they first started living together. "When we broke up, it was horrible," Monica says, "like who gets the kids. It was finally determined that Jack would give them a better home because I had moved to a one-room apartment. I made him swear that he wouldn't turn the cats against me."

Fortunately, China and Tucker performed a stupid pet trick that is actually quite common but seldom seen on David Letterman's show: The cats played marriage counselor. Monica's visits to ascertain whether Jack was fulfilling his litter-box responsibilities resulted in a reconciliation that ended in a trip to the altar. That was one of the few trips that having a pet made easier.

Here is another. A couple of years ago, when my husband and I were still in the midst of the Commitment Wars, I had to make a one-week trip to the East Coast. At the time, I was living alone with Bess and Stella, my pug dogs. I happen to regard pugs as the crown of creation, though I realize that viewpoint is not universally shared.

In Baltimore I had dinner with Marc, who has been my friend for as long as I can remember. We discussed whether my relationship with Duke could be saved. "I'm afraid that he's never going to get over his ambivalence," I sighed.

"Wait a minute," said Marc, who has an uncanny instinct for grasping the crux of the matter. "Where are Bess and Stella?"

I explained that the girls were staying in Duke's apartment. "Duke loves all dogs, even pugs," I proudly reported. "And he hates to think of them locked up in a kennel."

"Duke took the pugs!" marveled Marc, who feels that pugs are a waste of good dog food and swears that he would eat a can of Alpo before he would be seen walking two small, wrinkled dogs with curly tails.

"Don't worry, Margo," he said. "Duke must really love you."

THE SILENT PARTNER

Can we talk? I'm rarely at a loss for words. As far as I'm concerned, talking is a natural biological function, like breathing—I do it all the time. Yet, my husband can hold his breath for hours, even days at a time.

The silence seems deafening. "Is something bothering you?" I ask, even though I realize that trying to pull words from the mouth of a man in the midst of a mute spell is as pointless as trying to make a telephone call when the line is dead.

Duke shakes his head. "Uh-uh," he mutters.

Unfortunately, talking is like tennis. You need two people to play. "It's a big problem in a lot of marriages," says family therapist Marcia Lasswell, who adds that the quiet one is usually the man.

Why? "Men have an easier time being silent than women," she explains. "Silence is almost a macho characteristic. Clint Eastwood, Gary Cooper—they don't say many words, they're all action. The strong, silent type is a masculine myth. But women get very frustrated."

Yup. My friend Léon was once married to a man of few words. "Not only didn't he speak, but when I did, he said, 'Shh!' " she recalls. "He wouldn't answer things like, 'Let's buy a house' or 'What did you think of that movie?' I tried notes, I tried signal flags; he wouldn't answer. Once, after a prolonged period of his not talking, I went outside the house and rang the bell. He opened the door and asked, 'Where have you been?'

"At first, I thought all that silence meant that he knew the secret of the universe and that in time he would impart it to me," Léon says. "But when it was not forthcoming, I began to think that if I killed him slowly, at least he'd say something like 'Ouch' or 'Stop it.' "

Nope. Threats won't make him talk. In such extreme cases, "it's like trying to force someone who isn't coordinated physically to dance," Lasswell says. "These really silent types are basically shy. Somewhere along the line, they learned that speaking up didn't get them anywhere."

Shutting up doesn't get them anywhere either. "I had a couple where the man was so nonverbal that he really had a terrible time," Lasswell recalls. "His wife yearned to hear the words 'I love you,' and he just couldn't get it out. So, we practiced and practiced. I told her to say it first so that he would feel safe. So she turned to him and said, 'I love you.' And he said, 'Ditto.' "

Recently, starved for conversation, I called my friend Claire. "I'm trapped in the Silent Zone," I said with a sigh.

"He must be angry," Claire concluded. "Fred always clams up when he's absolutely furious. I figure it's just as well, because if he said something, it would be something that I didn't want to hear."

"Duke's not mad," I assured her. (It's easy to tell when a quiet man is mad. He storms into the house, slams the door, and hits the wall, and when you ask what's wrong, he snaps, "Nothing.") "He's just not speaking."

"I'd go insane," Claire said. "I'd send myself into a busy

little circle wondering why he isn't talking. Pretty soon, I would start tossing plates around."

We don't have that many dishes. Besides, "you shouldn't take the silence personally," Lasswell insists. "You've got to remember that he didn't just start being silent when he married you."

Don't I know it. After a year of dating, I still didn't know where Duke went to high school. It's not that he conceals anything. He just doesn't go out of his way to reveal it.

Some day, I expect to find a ticket to Stockholm lying on the dresser. "What's this?" I'll ask. After ten minutes of cross-examination, he'll reluctantly inform me that he's won the Nobel Prize.

Now, if I ever won, I'd tell everyone in the city in a matter of seconds. So would my friend Jane, another life of the party, who's been married to a taciturn man for thirty-seven years. She's still trying to adjust. "You can't out-silence them," Jane marvels. "Things come up in this world like 'Hello' or 'The house is on fire.' You've just got to teach them that it's important to say, 'I'm home' when they walk through the door so you don't have to worry it's a robber."

I suspect that it's easier to teach a dog to "speak." So does Monica. "Jack can go through an entire family outing without saying a thing," she laments. "But it makes me very nervous. So the last time we went to my parents' for dinner, I asked him to please try to act interested. He said, 'I can't. I don't relate.' I said, 'Just try to say something to do with something they're talking about,' and he replied, 'I've got to be me.' Finally, I asked, 'Could you at least lean forward when they're talking?' "

Sometimes I feel guilty for talking more than my mate. But someone has to shoulder the conversational burden. "I suppose the worst thing for a man who doesn't talk would be a woman who doesn't either," Jane says. "He'd go crazy."

Experts agree. "I enjoy someone who's pretty much of a brass band more than someone who's just a flute," declares

Glen Esterly, coauthor of *The Talk Book: The Intimate Science of Communicating in Close Relationships*. Esterly, a self-described "silent man in a state of flux," admits: "An extrovert takes away the pressure to avoid what's referred to as awkward silence. If I'm going through quiet periods and I'm with a quiet woman, there's a lot of dead air time. I'm not uncomfortable with the silence, but most people are."

Yup. Duke is lying in bed, reading about irregular Spanish verbs. "Soon, he'll be able to be silent as fluently in Spanish as he is in English," I think. *"Buenas noches,"* I say, giving him a kiss.

"Mi charladorita," Duke says fondly. "My little chatterbox."

TRAINING YOUR MATE

"**T**his year, give her a valentine she'll never forget," reads an ad for a diamond- and ruby-studded bracelet. I shake my head sadly. So far, my three-year campaign to convince my husband that Valentine's Day is not just a merchandising ploy dreamed up by florists has been totally unrewarding.

My friend Sabina says that I can easily train my mate to give me a gift. "All mates have to be trained," she insists. I wince as she reports that last year, her prize student/boyfriend, Anthony, drove to the ends of the Valley and picked a bouquet of wildflowers to show that his love for her was boundless. "You can train a man to do anything," Sabina assures me.

Like a dog? "Essentially, yes," says Thomas Lasswell, a professor of sociology at USC. Lasswell calls it "operative conditioning." "You reward people for doing what you want them to do," he explains, adding that there can be difficulties. "For example, efforts to train a man to make a bed are going to be marginally successful if he doesn't value having the bed made."

Don't I know it. So far, I've had training difficulties not

only with bed making but also with the preferred storage area for dirty dishes (the dishwasher versus under the sofa) and soiled laundry (the hamper versus the chair/floor/doorknob). And numerous female acquaintances say that they are considering installing beepers similar to the seat-belt reminder in a car as a last-ditch effort to train their mates to leave toilet seats in the down, or closed, position.

Still, these are just routine housekeeping—or should I say, housebreaking—problems. Sabina, ever the optimist, is actually attempting to train Anthony to communicate—specifically, to pop the question. Not the big question, the ordinary question.

"I wait for hours for Anthony to ask me how my day was," Sabina explains. "We've completely discussed his entire day in elaborate detail. And I'll sit there thinking, 'It's got to happen. He's got to ask.' But he doesn't ask.

"So I say, 'Honey, it is now nine o'clock. You've been home for five hours. You still haven't asked me how my day was.' And then I throw in a little guilt like, 'How can you simply forget that I had a day?' "

Sabina maintains that the Guilt Method works, although you can't expect it to work the first time or even the first few dozen times. "There are going to be months and months of his never asking how my day was, and I will have to repeat the same lesson over and over," she admits. "But eventually, he'll get it."

I wonder. Once, when I complained to Duke that he wasn't giving me sufficient positive feedback, he marveled, "You mean, even if I think something really loud, you can't hear it?" For a while, I adopted the Pop Beads Method. I gave him a large bag of those plastic, colored beads that snap together, along with instructions to give me a bead every time he found something positive to say. The resulting necklace reminded him and reassured me that communication was actually taking place. This worked out so well that he offered to buy the second batch of beads. "I'm so lucky," he said. "Some women would prefer diamonds."

So would I. And my friend Léon has a way for me to get them. "Whip, chair, and pistol," she advises. "I've never been willing to say, 'Oh, sweetheart, whatever makes you comfortable.' Sure, I start off adorable. But the first time he breaks my Wedgwood, I find myself screaming, 'What do you think you're doing? You're not home, eating out of a carry-out carton over the kitchen sink!' "

A real animal trainer, Matthew Margolis, president of the National Institute of Dog Training and coauthor of *When Good Dogs Do Bad Things,* has another philosophy. "You've got to show or tell the animal what you want in a way that's firm but not harsh," he says. "If you want to train a dog, you have to use love, praise, and affection. That's what it responds to. It's the same with people."

Margolis contends that any mate can be trained if the trainer looks at the problem from the trainee's point of view. "You have to figure out what will make the dog feel really good and reward it." For example? "If you want a dog to kiss you, you put butter on your face," he explains. "So scent your face with whatever brings a gleam to your mate's eye. He'll respond."

An image flashes before my eyes. I'm lying in bed next to my husband with Laker tickets clenched in my teeth. Duke grabs the tickets, gives me a quick kiss, and races out of the house to drive to the Forum, like a mouse stealing cheese from a trap.

But affection really isn't the problem. Which is fortunate because, contrary to what Dr. Ruth says, you cannot sexually train your mate. Either he's got it right from the start, or you're doomed.

Still, the dog-training tips may help me avoid disappointment on February 14. Though Duke insists that he finally realizes that Valentine's Day is one of the Big Three gift days in a wife's year (along with her anniversary and her birthday), I am leaving nothing to chance. I marshal my pugs, Bess and Stella, into the living room with an ample supply of their favorite reward, onion bagels. "You're going to learn how to fetch long-stemmed roses from the florist," I say firmly.

COLLAPSE OF THE
MEET MARKET

Is it my imagination, or has the singles scene gotten a lot worse? I've been married for a few years, so I don't speak from firsthand experience. But I've been getting some pretty grim reports.

It's not simply a matter of deadly diseases putting a damper on flings. The age-old skirmish between the sexes seems to have degenerated into trench warfare. Maybe it's because my single friends are getting older and the field is getting smaller. But I listen to them and think: It *can't* be that bad. And then I wonder. *Can* it be that bad?

Last week, I met a friend—let's call her Barbie—for lunch at Angeli Mare. Barbie is a woman with everything going for her—looks, brains, personality, successful career. Still, she tells me it's getting harder and harder to find a date.

"Barbie's having trouble?" my husband, Duke, marveled later, his ears perking up.

"Not that much trouble," I assured him. But actually, I lied.

Recently, Barbie met an attractive attorney—let's call him

Ken—on a plane. "We hit it off and he wasn't married, so I agreed to go out with him," she said. "We went for a bike ride, and then to dinner. We're in the restaurant, we've been together a total of maybe three hours, and he says, 'I have a favor to ask of you.' I said, 'What? Already?'

"He asked if I'd ever heard of bachelor auctions," Barbie said. Blessedly, I wasn't familiar with the concept, but she explained that it was a cattle call of "fairly good-looking men, in tuxedos with name tags and numbers," who are auctioned off for a worthy cause. In Ken's case, it was the March of Dimes. He asked Barbie to bid on his "package," a five-day ski trip with him to Park City, Utah.

This request struck me as the nadir of modern courtship, even before Barbie told me that the prize included five nights in a *one-bedroom* condominium. Call me old-fashioned, but I prefer the good old days when Rhett Butler paid $150 in gold for one waltz with Scarlett O'Hara. Or even the so-so old days when you went to the movies together, Dutch treat.

Still, I don't know why I was shocked. Recently, I saw *Love Connection,* a television program that epitomizes the current dating scene. I'm probably the last person in America to have discovered this show, but I was riveted by its sheer awfulness. In comparison, its predecessor, *The Dating Game,* with its sophomoric but all-in-good-fun questions ("If I was a block of wood and you were a power tool, would you buff me, sand me, or saw me?"), seemed as tame as a romance novel.

On *The Dating Game,* the lucky couple (and a chaperon) won a free trip to someplace memorable—a beautiful holiday south of the border, in downtown Tijuana. But the big prize on *Love Connection* is the chance to go back on the show and find fault with each other, in embarrassingly explicit detail.

I guess it's not that much different from going out with someone you met at a party and then calling every friend in your Rolodex for a neurosis-by-neurosis, postdate postmortem—group analysis being an intrinsic part of every modern romance.

"It's a jungle out there," Duke said, dragging me from the TV.

Barbie agreed. "Today, you have to be aggressive," she declared. So she bid on Ken. "He offered to put up half. Of course, it was left up to me to decide how much I wanted to spend on him." To my amazement, Barbie set a one-thousand-dollar—"Hey, he's a tax write-off"—limit. She couldn't attend the auction, but ever-gallant Ken provided a proxy.

In a moment, the results. But first, a word from an eligible bachelor. "I guess I'm a romantic," says my friend Jon. "But I think you should meet Ms. Right cute, the way they do in the movies. Back into her car, stare at each other's bumpers, and fall in love at the body shop, instead of putting yourself up for sale at the meat market."

Jon may be sentimental, but like many single men, he's very set in his ways. "Dating requires doing things I don't ordinarily do," he says. "I won't go to a restaurant after five o'clock. Could I get a date to meet me at four-thirty with the early-bird coupon?"

Suddenly I understand the difficulties of Barbie's search for Mr. Right. Speaking of which: "Ken called the day after the auction," she revealed over dessert. "He said, 'You lost. I went for two thousand, seven hundred fifty dollars to a legal secretary named Taffy. And it didn't cost her a penny because she got donations from the people she does business with.' " Barbie wondered if Ken will call after he and Taffy get back from their trip.

Then her eyes twinkled. "Oh, look!" she exclaimed. "The cute guy in the corner just went to the bathroom. Maybe I can bump into him." Barbie freshened her lipstick and prepared to reconnoiter the ladies' room. "I have to time it just right. Men are so quick."

Is it my imagination, or has the singles scene gotten a lot worse?

LOVE BYTES

"Will you turn that damn computer off and come to bed?" I beg my husband. It's midnight, and he's been fooling around with his new modem for the past five hours. I'm beginning to wish that I was a pocket-size twelve-hundred-baud transmitter.

"In a minute, honey," says Duke, who said the same thing a couple of hours ago. "I just want to figure out this glitch in the automatic hang-up."

I know better than to suggest that he wait until morning and call the computer help line. While I tend to view my computer as a somewhat faithful servant (who has the disconcerting habit of calling in sick at the worst possible moment), Duke views his computer as a wild animal that he alone can tame.

I'm not the first woman to fall asleep to a lullaby of computer beeps. Recently, *The New York Times* reported that "women and girls use computers; men and boys love them." According to *The Times*: "While legions of women work with computers in their jobs and many excel as computer scientists and programmers, they are almost without exception bystanders in the passionate romance that men conduct with these machines."

Many of these romances seem more like fatal attractions. (If women were so entranced, there would be a self-help book out: *Women Who Compute Too Much*.) My friend Rob, for example, is having a torrid affair in a walk-in closet. "I can go in there and sit in front of the computer and look up and discover that it's four hours later," says Rob, who sometimes plays the game "Leisure Suit Larry in the Land of the Lounge Lizards" with his computer until two or three in the morning.

And he doesn't just spend time on his Compaq Deskpro; he spends money. "I covet things that I have absolutely no use for," Rob admits. "I realize that the fact that another CPU down the street can do thirty-two megahertz at the flash of a keystroke is irrelevant. But I still want to have the hottest computer on the block." Why? "For a man, a computer is a car equivalent."

No kidding. My friend Monica's husband actually turned their garage—"where you used to be able to park cars," she laments—into an enclosed, insulated, carpeted computer shrine. "You know what he gets into?" marvels Monica, a computer widow. "The table that his computer stuff sits on. It can't just be a table from a store. It has to be a nuclear-age, computer-material table."

"I'm a computer stud," her husband, Jack, proudly proclaims. Jack, a systems programmer who modifies software, feels that his technological wizardry gives him an edge over ordinary computer hackers. "I'm a lot more manly than most men who deal with computers," he says. "To me, everyone who isn't a stud is like a housewife—and that includes men and women."

Luckily, Monica is resigned to sharing her stud with a silicon rival. "I think that when Jack gave the computer a phone line that used to be mine, I got my first clue," she says with a laugh.

Some women aren't laughing. "Many women get very

jealous when their husband brings home a new computer," says Chaytor D. Mason, a USC associate professor who studies the psychological aspects of the work environment. "It's almost as if he has a girlfriend. He's totally enthralled. His wife gets no attention. She goes to bed alone and cold." (All the while wondering, what does he see in it?)

"I think part of the computer's allure to a man is mastery," Mason says. "Here's this thing staring him in the face. Can he get control over it? He's looking for self-proof, and after that, the feelings of excitement and victory will begin to fade. If a wife can stand the period of isolation and see it as a passing phase, she may be a little more understanding."

She'll be more understanding if she has her own computer. A computer can turn a self-sufficient woman into a damsel in distress faster than it can delete a critical file.

"I think women have been taught to be fearful of machines," says Constance Ahrons, associate director of the Marriage and Family Therapy Program at USC. "We use machines cautiously, just wanting them to service us. But men like to tinker with them; they're very interested in how the whole computer works. I don't know how my computer works," Ahrons confesses. "I know my program. I just pray that it works all the time. If something goes wrong, I have to find a man."

Me, too. "Help!" I cry. My husband rushes into the office to see what's wrong. I hand him a computer printout of what's supposed to be the final draft of this story. There are four crisply typed pages of gibberish. "My computer is speaking in tongues," I wail frantically.

"Did you check the connection?" Duke asks calmly. Yes, five times. I also triple-checked the software and every button on the printer, but I watch expectantly as my husband checks it all again. Computers often recover miraculously the minute a man starts whispering sweet binary nothings.

Not this time. "It's not printing the right characters," Duke informs me, as if I didn't already know. My anxiety mounts as he hooks up *his* computer to the printer, prints out a file, and sighs with relief as the text comes out in English. "It's not the printer," he says happily. "It must be *your* computer."

This is why I don't love computers. I call the computer store. "Nobody else has this problem," says the salesman, who has never understood anything I've ever said except my Visa number. It turns out that the only person who can fix my laptop is in Buena Park. I can spend three hours driving it there and then another three hours picking it up, or I can spend eighty dollars on a messenger. I opt for the messenger.

Later, the computer doctor calls and tells me that I can have the computer back in a week for one hundred dollars or he can fix it overnight for one-fifty. I feel as if I'm a contestant on *Let's Make a Bad Deal*.

But this is the price you pay for computer dependency. The following evening I'm frantically pounding the keyboard on my newly repaired laptop, trying to finish this story so I can pay for its upkeep. At midnight Duke knocks on my office door. "Will you turn that damn computer off and come to bed?" he begs.

IN LOVE WITH ROMANCE

In my next life, I want to inspire grand romantic gestures the way my girlfriend Léon does. Léon, a model-turned-author, is like a character out of Colette's *Gigi,* a time traveler from the Paris of a century ago, when the biggest news on the boulevards was the amorous adventures of the femme fatales. "It's just the usual," says Léon, "being flown places, being sailed to supper, getting the gifts every day. You know. . . ."

No, I don't. For weeks I've been trying to persuade my husband to take me to dinner at some dreamy little restaurant with tablecloths and candlelight instead of a two-for-one special. "What's more romantic than loading the dishwasher together?" Duke asks. "What could be more intimate?"

Maybe cleaning out the garage.

Don't get me wrong. I love my husband. But a woman needs a romantic pick-me-up now and then. I don't expect anything dramatic, like when Charles MacArthur introduced himself to Helen Hayes by giving her a handful of peanuts and saying, "I wish they were emeralds." I just want some small indication that Duke doesn't think of me as an old shoe.

"Honey," Duke asks, "do you think there's a woman on this planet who doesn't think she deserves more romantic attention from the man she's involved with?"

Yes, I do. "Here's my secret for getting the romantic gestures," Léon says. "I tell guys that I'm not a great romantic. Then they break their necks trying to turn me into one."

Take the World Famous Artist (W.F.A.) with whom Léon enjoyed a long relationship. Once, before she went away on business, W.F.A. took her out for a farewell lunch. "There was a highly personal drawing—framed, of course—wrapped up on my plate," says Léon, adding that this was the first of many such museum-quality offerings.

"I was thrilled," she says, "and then he exclaimed, 'No, it's not romantic enough. I've got to give you something that I really need.' And he handed me his driver's license. It made me curl up in ecstasy."

I confess that my response would have been a little more practical. "Are you out of your mind?" I would have stammered. "What if you get stopped by the police?"

"You can't be practical and complain about the dearth of romance," Léon says. "If a guy goes out and blows his paycheck on one hundred gardenias, say, 'Thanks.' Don't ask how he's going to make his car payments."

I wouldn't dream of it. Last night, when Duke brought me a loaf of rye bread, his car payments never crossed my mind. "I guess this doesn't rank with hiring mariachis to play 'Malagueña' under your window," he conceded. Actually, I really don't like "Malagueña," which only goes to show that romance is all relative.

"You know what romance is for men?" my friend Rob asks. "Romance is money. The more you spend, the more romantic you are. Sending a dozen roses is romantic. But three dozen roses is really romantic, and it's really expensive."

I hate to think that romance is just the reduction of a man to a desperately twitching checkbook. It's more the art of making your sweetheart feel special. Many men would be amazed by the results of an unexpected card or a seductive telephone call.

Of course, the fastest way to find romance is to leave town. "Want to drive down to Mexico?" I ask my husband after another stressful, unromantic week. A couple of hours later, we're cruising down I-5. Suddenly, around El Toro, the lights on the dashboard flash, and my car dies in the fast lane.

While I sit in shock, cursing the mechanic who just two days before handed me a large bill and assured me that the car was reliable, Duke takes command. My heart melts as he coolly pushes the car off the road and gamely pokes around under the hood, oblivious to the half-pitying, half-belittling stares of passing motorists. "Don't worry, honey," he says later as we climb into the tow truck. "I'm sure it's nothing major."

But the diagnosis at the nearest auto shop is that I need a new carburetor, which won't be available for five days and will cost a small fortune. Undaunted, Duke gets on the phone and miraculously finds a tiny garage in San Clemente with a mechanic who can rebuild my carburetor right away for a thousand dollars less. I haven't seen anything so romantic since *Gone With the Wind*.

I can't wait to tell Léon.

CHRISTMAS AT TIFFANY'S

Men! Are you wondering what to get that special lady for Christmas or Hanukkah? I can cut your agony in half. Buy gems. In my experience, almost all women want jewelry.

"You really believe that a man's natural function is to be a jewel buyer?" asks my husband, Duke.

Let me put it like this. If you're absolutely certain that your beloved has her heart set on a specific item—a red Mazda Miata, for example, or a suede jacket, a crystal ball, a *flacon* of Poison, a cashmere sweater, or even one of those limited-edition collector plates—then buy it with my blessing. But if you're just going to wander aimlessly around the shopping mall, eyes glazed, neurons malfunctioning, trying to decide among a basket of cheese balls, a hair-removal machine, and a copy of *The Curmudgeon's Garden of Love*, then run—do not walk—to her favorite jeweler.

"There's a certain amount of resistance to spending large sums of money on little tiny things," says Duke. "A man can buy something that fits into a matchbox, or he can buy a truck."

He'll get a lot more mileage out of the matchbox. Very few women want a truck—or many of the other popular gift items foisted upon us at this time of year. Recently, I went to a department store. I was riding down the escalator when I noticed an enormous display of artificial daisies arranged around a large-screen television set. That's strange, I thought.

Actually, it was *stranger* than I thought. A close inspection revealed that the daisies, some of which were wearing sunglasses and/or bow ties, were swaying in time to a Janet Jackson music video. A festive banner proclaimed that these were "Rockin' Flowers" and that they cost "only" $29.95. "Everybody's buying them for Christmas," said the salesman. "They're perfect gifts for children, for men, and especially for women."

Not this woman. (Or any other woman I know.) Frankly, the last thing I want for Christmas is a hyperactive fake bloom (especially when for the same price I could have a few dozen real blooms). I realize that I sound like an ingrate. But I don't like joke gifts. I don't understand what you're supposed to do with joke gifts, except titter politely when you open the prewrapped package, and then (later) shove it in the back of your closet.

"If you yell at Rockin' Flower, it wiggles," the salesman said. Who cares? I've never wanted to holler at a flower. And neither have any of my girlfriends. On the other hand, many of us have always wanted to own some breathtaking bijou—a marquise sapphire ring, perhaps, or a turquoise Zuni fetish necklace, a pair of silver earrings, or an Art Deco Cartier brooch. Or a fourteen-karat-gold charm bracelet, like the one I tried on in Beverly Hills the other day.

"Don't you feel guilty wanting jewelry when we're about to kill the last rhinoceros on the planet?" asks my friend Monica, who secretly wants an emerald necklace. Of course I feel guilty. Every woman with a semblance of a social conscience (and/or children to put through college) feels guilty for desiring some precious or semiprecious bagatelle. Still, it was a really pretty charm bracelet. . . .

"It was a really pretty necklace," Monica says with a sigh. "And it was on sale."

Even so . . . "There's a certain tendency among men to buy something useful," says Duke. "Something that might have a ricochet effect back to the giver—like a really good torque wrench or a set of weights." Or a Swiss army knife, like the one he gave me for Christmas the first year we were married. (I almost used it to slit his throat.)

"It's the feminine model," Duke said as he proudly showed me the nail file, the scissors, the orange zester, and the teeny tweezers. It's the thought that counts, I sullenly reminded myself. And, in all fairness, I must admit that the knife was (and still is) extremely practical. But . . .

"Women don't want things that are so useful," my friend Léon shrieks. "Like a plumber's snake, or 'Here, honey, all gift-wrapped, a thing for your steering wheel that locks it so nobody can steal your car,' or 'Just for you, my darling, an attachment for the Electrolux.' " (And, in general, few women are truly dazzled by anything that plugs in.)

"I want something that comes in a small but suspiciously heavy box," says Léon, who has no shame. "A little something for the toe of the stocking. Like a Fabergé Imperial Easter egg. Or an eight-karat emerald-cut flawless diamond. 'Oh, thanks, honey. Look how it sparkles on the little paw.' "

For the record, not all women like, or even want, a gigantic sparkler, though I don't know too many who would return one (they might have it reset). In baubles, as in cars, taste varies. Some women prefer ethnic jewelry or antique jewelry or costume jewelry or wearable artsy jewelry—so make sure that you pick up the subtle hints ("I want that"). But whatever kind of jewelry you buy:

"It's irrevocably the woman's, not yours," says Duke. "She takes it. She hides it. She has it. And she never gives it back. At least, if you give a woman a car, you can use the car. But you can never use the jewels."

That's what makes them so special. "It's a nice feeling to know that a man went into a jewelry store, which to him is like alien territory," says my sister, Laurie. "It's one thing for him to go into a lingerie store. That's pretty self-serving. But for him to go into a jewelry store when he doesn't get anything out of it except the fact that you're wearing jewelry—that's wonderful."

You bet. "I suppose that a man can rationalize it as being an investment if he's dumb," says Duke, who not too long ago rationalized an exquisite Edwardian choker that I'd been dreaming about for two years. I was very, very grateful. "I like it that it gives you so much pleasure," my husband admits. "So I controlled my hyperventilation and wrote the check."

Still, I don't see him writing a check for my charm bracelet in the very near future. Not unless I really step up the hints. "A charm bracelet?" Duke says, when I casually remark that I'd seen one. "Aren't they mostly for high school students?"

Oh, well, maybe next Christmas.

part 3

MORE
THAN I EVER
WANTED
TO KNOW

IRRATIONAL PASTIMES

I can't believe what passes for sports these days. "It's the Battle of the Monster Trucks and Mud Racing Spectacular," says the television announcer. My jaw drops as a giant truck with immense tractor tires drives over ten cars and squashes them like soda cans. "How can you watch this?" I ask my husband.

"It's riveting in its awfulness," Duke says as a foolhardy trucker tries to plow through a mud bog, even though his engine is in flames. "It amazes me that anyone would spend so much time and energy doing something this weird."

It's not just anyone. Pick a Sunday, any Sunday. Pick a town, any town. The beaches, mountains, stadiums, gymnasiums, playgrounds, and parks are mobbed with aficionados playing or watching some incredibly dubious sport. I can understand baseball, basketball, golf, track and field, tennis, or even football. But rattlesnake rodeos? Motorcycle racing on ice? Foot tennis? Executive war games, where weekend warriors dress up in combat fatigues and pay to shoot each other with paint pellets?

"Trash sports," exclaims John Cherwa, associate sports editor at the *Los Angeles Times*. "That's our official name for them. Because they're not traditional and, in many cases, they're not real. Supposedly, in Atlanta they have a thing called cat chasing." *What?* "They throw a cat out of an airplane and then different parachutists try to chase and catch the cat. I don't know if it's true, but I've heard it."

For the life of me, I can't figure out why anyone in his right mind would do such a thing. Of course, I also can't fathom what draws a person to competitive cheerleading, curling, hang gliding, or the granddaddy of dubious sports—synchronized swimming. Some sports are glamorous. Some sports are exciting. Some sports are good for your heart. Some sports are good for making money. But some sports are good for nothing.

"And there certainly are a lot of them," says my brother, Bobby, who lists target diving (training to be an arrow?), powerboat racing (go out on the water, burn gas and wreck your hearing), and air shows (die!) among the world's dumbest sports. "But kick boxing is as bad as it gets," he insists. "It's not enough that you've got a guy beating his opponent's face in with his hands. He's got to use his feet. And not only can he kick his opponent when he's down, if he kicks him in the head, he gets a point."

I think you should get ten points if you turn off the television. "Historically, a lot of these trash sports started in the seventies when major networks had sports anthology shows," Cherwa explains. "The networks were starving for programming, and all this bizarre stuff began showing up. There was one guy I'll never forget. He was called the Human Fly. They actually strapped him to an airplane, and they flew him around."

Technically, the Human Fly is more in the spirit of a publicity stunt, unless there's an American Federation of Human Flies out there, sponsoring tournaments somewhere in Arkansas.

"Have you heard about hoe-de-o?" asks my friend Sabina. This sport, which sounds like the world's worst date, is played by backhoe operators who don't get enough ditch digging during the regular week so they get together on weekends to turn on the old Caterpillar and watch the dirt fly. "In one event, they see if they can pick up an egg and race across the track without breaking it," Sabina says. "It gives all new meaning to the term *party game*."

I realize that America is a nation of sports nuts, led by a horseshoe-tossing, powerboat-piloting fly fisherman. But lately it seems as though the sports keep getting nuttier and nuttier. Forget about obvious death-wish sports such as parapenting (where you run down a hill with a wing on your back until you gain enough speed to fly) or acrobatic skateboarding in the gutters adjoining high-speed boulevards. (Duke believes that skateboarders have had the fear centers of their brains surgically removed.) I am struck by what is a popular and relatively mainstream activity—mountain biking.

According to the Bicycle Institute of America, 7.5 million people rode mountain bikes in 1988. Yet I can't figure out what's fun about this sport. I see these bicyclists painfully struggling in very low (rat-treadmill) gear to get up steep inclines on bumpy trails. I hear their anxious voices yelling "Get out of the way" as they hurtle past on the lips of precipices. And it's not as if those spandex shorts are really flattering.

Recently, when Duke and I were hiking up the Temescal fire road, I asked a mountain biker just what he saw in the sport. "How far did you get? Six miles?" sneered the biker, who looked as if he'd been freeze-dried on his bicycle. "I've come forty miles."

But if we were going for distance, we'd take the car. "Everyone wants to do something better than everyone else," Cherwa reminds me. "You go through the conventional sports. None of us can be the best basketball, baseball, tennis, golf, or football player around." So maybe we can be the best mountain biker or the best cat chaser. "At least we can be in the top ten," he says. "Just think, if you invent something that nobody else can do, you can suddenly declare yourself to be the world champion."

I wouldn't mind getting my picture on a box of Wheaties. But I can't think of a sport that someone else hasn't already thought of. There's bodysurfing, land sailing, snow boarding, jet skiing, wind skating, even Frisbee golf.

Still, if you want positive proof that the bottom of the sports barrel has been thoroughly scraped, check out the game of Hackey Sack. For the record, a Hackey Sack is a little square beanbag that groups of seemingly brain-dead youths stand in a circle and kick—sometimes for hours at a time. This is an unbelievably moronic activity, something that would appeal to people who spent all their time in college playing Frisbee. "It's a politically correct sport," argues Derek, a twenty-four-year-old beanbag kicker. "It doesn't hurt the environment and it fosters cooperation." I'll bet. "Everyone in the group has to take turns kicking it," he explains, "so there's no competition."

Derek boots the beanbag to me. I have my usual instinctive reaction to any flying object that comes my way—I duck. But the Hackey Sack bounces off my chest, which is legal. In fact, you can use any part of your body except your hands. Derek taps it back with his head. This is really dumb, I think, as I punt it back with my knee. Though I've got to admit that it's sort of fun, too.

"It takes a year to get really good," says Derek, who carries his Hackey Sack everywhere so that he can stay in shape. Imagine devoting a year to this cretinous thing, I think, as I tap the beanbag with my toe. Imagine standing in the hot sun for hours, I think, as I lunge to place a shot with my heel.

"Excuse me," I say. "Where can I buy one of these things?"

THOUGHT FOR FOOD

So what will it be? Dim sum? Greek? Mexican? Thai? Ethiopian? Punjabi? Decisions, decisions. New York pizza? Chicago pizza? California pizza? A person could starve to death in the time it takes to decide where to go to dinner.

It's not just a matter of having a lot of choices. Food has become everyone's three-dimensional Rorschach test, an edible tool for self-definition and social judgment.

Take my friend Katie's latest warning bell. "I never thought a man's eating habits would affect the way I perceived him as a potential partner," says Katie, a vegetarian. Recently, she accepted an invitation to the Hollywood Bowl. "I was doing the picnic," she says. "But when I asked what he liked, he said, 'There's something you better know. I don't eat vegetables or fruit.' I asked about pasta salad. He said no. Coleslaw, no. Potato salad, no. Finally, I asked, 'Well what *do* you eat?' And he said, 'Meat. Just meat.' "

What is he, a crocodile?

There's *always* something objectionable about another person's diet. If it's not animal fat, it's Milano cookies or too

much garlic. Or worse, it's some politically incorrect foodstuff that anybody with half a social conscience is boycotting.
(Why do they always boycott tasty products such as tuna and
grapes instead of things I'd never miss—such as turnips?)

Personally, I'm hoping for ecological sanctions against the
fryer, my sworn food enemy, which follows me wherever I
go. On a recent trip to the Southwest, it seemed that kitchens
had thrown away the broiler and the conventional oven and
replaced them with giant vats of bubbling lard. "All I want is
a baked potato," I feebly insisted as the waitress recited the
specials: deep-fried chicken, chicken-fried steak, french fries,
hush puppies, fritters, doughnuts. "Have you tried the Indian
fry bread?" she asked.

I'd also like to ban places that flaunt live originals of what
you're about to eat. I've learned to avert my eyes when I walk
into Chinese seafood restaurants and see the doomed fish
swimming around the tank. But does the management have
to put a guy in a chicken suit beckoning outside California
Chicken Burger?

Of course, it's better than in Spain, where animal legs with
hair are an essential part of the decor. I don't eat meat, but I
still have nightmares about the place in Asturias where my
husband scarfed a huge plate of cold cuts under a ceiling full
of dangling carcasses.

"Do you have a baked potato?" I asked meekly.

Actually, I'm not a finicky eater compared to a lot of folks.
I wouldn't dream of issuing verbal or written instructions to
prospective hosts before I go out to lunch or dinner. I'm not
kosher, hypoglycemic, or ovo-lacto vegetarian; I'm not doing
Pritikin or Optifast. And I'm not a food snob, either, unlike
my husband.

He views eating as a grand adventure, whereas I just see it
as a way to stay alive. We could land in a foreign country late
at night, famished, and still Duke would troll the streets
scrutinizing restaurant menus, seeking out the peak gastro-
nomic experience. I wouldn't dare suggest a coffee shop.

"For the same price, you can have something awful or you can have something really good," Duke says. Of course, his idea of really good is more evolved than mine.

I learned this early in our relationship. One morning, I found him in my kitchen, scowling at the contents of my refrigerator. There were apples, a pitcher of Good Earth iced tea, a tub of yogurt—my usual food staples—plus bagels and cream cheese that I'd bought because I knew he was coming over. "Don't you have a red onion?" Duke asked accusingly.

In an effort to score gourmet points, I later went to a designer produce store and asked for the best onion God ever made. Five dollars bought a Maui onion the size of a grapefruit, packaged in a net sheath with everything but a biography. Duke was mollified—briefly. Then he started looking for the capers.

These days, you can't be too much of a culinary sophisticate. "It's gotten into regions now," my sister, Laurie, complains. "People who can't find Florida on a map know the difference between Sichuan, Hunan, and Mandarin."

Frankly, I've never awakened in the middle of the night with a hankering for Middle-Altitude Andean food. If I have to pick a restaurant, a modern-day act of courage, I automatically head for my favorite sushi or salad bar. Needless to say, I'm not asked to pick very often.

"You're lucky," Laurie says. "There's nothing worse than being responsible for a bad meal. You sit there all evening muttering lame excuses like 'I swear there were more specials the last time.'"

Doesn't bother me. Just give me a baked potato.

WOMEN WHO
READ TOO MUCH

My name is Margo, and I am an addict. You'd never guess by looking in my eyes, or my medicine chest, or my liquor cabinet. But a cold, sober look at my bookshelves reveals the awful truth.

I am a self-help junkie.

Just last month I consumed *Creative Visualization, How to Negotiate Anything, Goodbye to Guilt, Anger: How to Live with It and Without It,* and *Women Who Love Too Much.* Every time I picked up one of these books, I swore it would be my last. I just wanted to ease the pain of living by learning how to do things right.

All I learned was how I do things wrong.

But I couldn't seem to control my thirst for advice. Whenever I thought my life was running smoothly, another book got published to prove it was not. The authors found things wrong with me even faster than my parents did. And I suffered from the delusion they truly understood me and really wanted to help.

I tried to resist. I wanted to read fiction. But whenever I

walked into Hunter's or Crown or Dalton I was possessed by a demonic urge to buy out the psychology section. I couldn't go on like this.

The road to perfection was eating up my MasterCard.

My friends were scared to confront me. They were afraid I knew something they didn't. They tried to lure me to the movies, or to parties, but I lied and said I had to work. I was ashamed to admit work consisted of one thousand affirmations, an hour of meditation, and a lesson from *A Course in Miracles*. I lived in fear they'd find out I couldn't run my life without my books.

Then Randy came over, and I tried to get her addicted, too. She came in very upset. "John just told me he is into spanking, and I don't know what to do," she sighed.

I rummaged under my bed and pulled out *The Joy of Sex, Nice Girls Do, Sexual Energy Ecstasy, How to Make Love to a Man,* and *Sex Tips for Girls.* In a moment of weakness, Randy reached for them.

"I guess I should try it. I don't want to seem repressed. What would you do if you were me?"

"I'm not you," I said (*Notes on How to Live in the World and Still Be Happy* had insisted I give up judgmental behavior). "But if I didn't want to, I'd say no."

"But he really loves me," she argued.

I walked over to my closet and got out the copy of *When I Say No I Feel Guilty* that I kept in my jacket. Then I retrieved my copy of *Men Who Hate Women and the Women Who Love Them.* (I'd hidden it in the bathroom.) Randy practically swallowed them whole.

"Mind if I borrow these?" she asked, unable to pull herself away.

I started to panic. I was terrified I might need them again. The minute she left, I ran to the Phoenix Bookstore to replenish my supply. I was out of control, but I couldn't fight it.

I had to get help before I destroyed my relationship with

my boyfriend Duke. Since we'd met, I'd been downing three
books a day. Any time we had a problem, I'd turn to my
library for reassurance that I wasn't making the same mistakes
that had led to my divorce. And you know what? I couldn't
win, no matter how hard I tried. Every single book said every
single relationship problem is every single woman's fault.

I felt helpless.

How come nobody writes self-help books for men? Like
Why Do I Think I'm Nothing Without a Porsche?; *Smart Man,
Foolish Penis*; *Everything You Always Wanted to Know About
C•MM•TM•NT But Were Afraid to Ask*? How come *I* was
staying up nights reading Erich Fromm and Leo Buscaglia
while *he* was reading computer menus and the *Sports Illustrated*
swimsuit issue?

"Why aren't there self-help books for men?" I asked Duke
casually, not wanting him to know the extent of my addiction.

"There is one, honey. *How to Pick Up Girls*."

I thought for a moment I was losing my mind.

I knew I was losing my reflexes. One night I arrived at
Duke's apartment. He was cheerful and glowing. "Jo Jo just
called and begged me to be her boyfriend. She's real lonely,
and she really wants to see me, but I said I had you."

In the good old days before self-help, I would have picked
up the phone and hit him over the head with it. Now,
numbed by self-awareness, charged with understanding, I just
laughed and praised his sacrifice. I actually considered sneaking out to the bookstore to pick up Nancy Friday's new book,
Jealousy.

That's when I vowed to kick the habit.

I've been clean for a week now. It hasn't been easy. I had
to cancel my subscriptions to *Glamour, Mademoiselle, Self,
Shape, Vogue,* and *Psychology Today*. I had to reset the buttons
on my car radio so I couldn't pick up Toni Grant or Dr.
Ruth.

I have to stay strong when people try to sabotage my
efforts.

Randy was all excited at lunch. "I just bought the greatest book. You have to read it. *Why Men Are the Way They Are.*"

My pulse raced. I wanted a fix. Just a quick look at the book jacket. I took a deep breath and shook my head.

"I don't want to know," I said firmly.

"I'm worried about you," said Randy. "I think you need help."

SMALL IS BIG

"**M**argo! What are you doing here?" exclaims George Schlosser, a painter from Connecticut whose Lilliputian versions of museum masterpieces hang in some of the finest dollhouses in the country. I begin to sweat. Once I was so hopelessly in love with George's miniatures that I was willing to spend hundreds of dollars on a few square centimeters of fine art, but that's all over now. At least I hope it is, because I am here at the Masters of the Miniature Arts Show and Sale at the Quality Hotel in Anaheim as a reporter, not as a collector.

"I haven't seen you since the show in D.C.," George says.

That was five years ago, I recall, slightly embarrassed by the memory. I spent one hundred dollars (that I had sensibly put aside to pay for dental work) on an elfin reproduction of Winslow Homer's *Croquet Scene*. Of course, it is comforting to note that while the value of my teeth has not appreciated, a similar minuscule painting is now selling for $250.

Miniatures are a lot bigger than they used to be. Sure, the standard scale is still an inch to the foot, but according to Bob

Bell, a member of the board of directors of the Miniature Industry Association of America, there are now between two and three million dollhouse and miniature collectors in the country who spend between eighty and one hundred million dollars a year on their hobby. He asks, "Does that surprise you?"

Me? Who once invested $350 in a limited-edition mini-Steinway concert grand made by a missionary in Kenya? All that surprises me is that collectors don't spend more. There are dollhouse boutiques everywhere. There are glossy dollhouse magazines such as *Nutshell News,* which is crammed with ads for any little thing (including the kitchen sink) that you might possibly need for your dream dollhouse. There are even travel agents selling deluxe packaged tours to historic European dollhouses.

And "the shows are going gang-busters," adds Tom Bishop, who produced this event. Bishop stages fourteen shows a year in major cities across America. He expects that this show, which features the handiwork of more than three hundred artisan craftsmen, will gross around seventy-five thousand dollars.

"The bigger shows do a hundred thousand dollars," he says. "I've seen people spend fifteen thousand dollars at a single dealer." Phil Nelson, a carpenter from Oroville, is waiting for just such a person. He is trying to sell a fifteen-thousand-dollar "board-by-board exact copy of the Morey Mansion in Redlands that took two years to build."

"You sure you don't want it?" he asks.

"No, thank you." I recently sold an ornate Victorian dollhouse and have no desire to acquire another. I have enough trouble finding space for the two dollhouses I still own: a turn-of-the-century Tudor mansion and a New York City tenement complete with fire escape, wee prostitutes, and bums.

But Elizabeth Garrow, a dealer from San Diego, has nine dollhouses, "everything from modern to a hacienda to Victorian." Garrow has been collecting since she was five and "fell in love with a miniature porcelain bathroom set, which I thought was the most exquisite thing that I had ever seen. From then on, miniatures were a part of my life," she says.

"Miniatures are like family," says Phyllis Cohen of Miami. She points to a display case crammed with midget brand-name products. It looks like a pixie supermarket. There are itty-bitty boxes of Raisin Chex, Tide, Rinso, Ritz crackers. There are itty-bitty spray bottles of Windex and Formula 409. "You have to get the copyrights from the companies," she tells me. "But who would object?"

Not these collectors, dressed in T-shirts that proclaim DOLLHOUSE LOVERS DO IT IN A LITTLE WAY, THINK SMALL, and MINIATURE MANIAC.

The room reverberates with oohs and ahs as aficionados discover treasures: wee track lights (five lights for sixty-one dollars) that throw microspots when you hook them to a twelve-volt transformer; a matchbox-sized puppet theater with a pencil-point Punch and a staple-sized Judy; an infinitesimal hummingbird feeder ($7.95), and brine-size anatomically correct sleeping infants.

"Aren't they darling?" coos Connie Hart, a Denver dealer. She explains that an artist named Lynn Fuller made these "teeny-weeny babies" out of Fimo clay and that I can adopt one for thirty dollars.

I am not ready to have a tiny clay child. Undaunted, she shows me a $40 white bronze breastplate the size of a half-dollar with two cocktail-toothpick-sized swords through it and a battle-ax suitable for swinging by a six-inch Saxon for $22.50, done by Fresno artist David Sciaca. "He also does a suit of armor, for two hundred seventy-five dollars," she assures me. "You could put it in your antique shop." I am ashamed to admit that I sold my desktop antique shop a few years ago to pay my full-scale rent. In fact, I stopped collecting when I realized that my dolls were living better than I was. They were sleeping in a $250 hand-carved sleigh bed, and I was sleeping on a $30 secondhand futon.

But Jayne Merchant sees it another way. She works as a bill collector, "so this is a nice break from it," she says. "When you're trying to collect money from people who are terminally ill, or the relatives of someone who has passed away, it's nice to come home and play dolls."

George makes one last pitch as I leave the show. "You have quite a few of my things," he says. "But you don't have this." He shows me a four-hundred-dollar copy of Edward Hicks's *Peaceable Kingdom,* which is painted on antique linen "rather than the usual canvas board."

"Don't tempt me," I beg. My mind works rapidly. If I buy one more painting, I can construct a dwarf art gallery complete with a smugly superior pink-haired picoreceptionist filing her nanonails. But where can I buy microscopic quichettes and bitsy bottles of bad wine to serve at the opening?

"I think I better go now," I tell George.

NAME BRANDED

It's amazing how certain names really bother people. Broad-minded, sensible, otherwise-tolerant individuals make snap judgments on the basis of a one- or two-name introduction. And it doesn't matter what you're called; you can't escape discrimination. Everybody is a name bigot.

Take me, for example. Recently, I got a call from my sister, Laurie. "I met a man," she began. "His name is Merlin." I didn't need to hear that he owned a crystal shop, that he had a sword hanging on the wall—Excalibur?—before I advised her to pass. Merlin is hardly a name that inspires confidence. As my friend Marjorie later put it more bluntly, "It means *bum*."

"You have to watch out for names from King Arthur's court," Laurie agreed. "You don't want to go out with any-one named Gareth or Percival. And Lancelot—or worse, Lance—is also a bad bet." In general, anyone named after a fictional character seems worth avoiding, if only because you'd feel pretty silly moaning, "Ivanhoe, Ivanhoe," in the throes of passion.

"How about a guy over the age of thirty who calls himself Scooter?" Duke asks later. How about a guy who calls himself Duke?

Name bias isn't rational. Then again, prejudice never is. Sometimes, a name just conjures up unfortunate images. "I went out with a man named Ray," Laurie said. "I couldn't even say his name out loud. I kept expecting him to spin a pizza dough."

Other names you just can't trust. Once, when Duke and I were dating, I was at his apartment when a statuesque blonde knocked on the door. When she learned he wasn't home, she sighed and said, "Be sure to tell him Bunny stopped by."

"Believe me," I muttered, "I will."

"Bunny was probably just lonely and wanted to talk," Duke said when he returned. But Bunnys (like Bambis, Brandys, Chrissys, and Tiffanys) aren't generally known for their snappy repartee.

"There's usually a problem when nicknames have a *y* on the end," says a friend who goes by the name of Preacher. "Take Freddy. That's a good litmus test. If you're not prejudiced against that name, then there's something wrong with you. Actually, any name with a *y*—Johnny, Tommy, Timmy— didn't these people ever grow up? And it's even worse for women—Sherry, Taffy, Candy, Kitty—it takes the dignity right out of a person."

Speaking of dignity, Preacher admits, "I'd be prejudiced toward someone with a name like mine. But part of the fun of having it is watching people's reactions and seeing if they're sensible." What's sensible? "The raised eyebrow, a smirk, a step back. The nonwise reaction: 'That's an interesting name. How did you get that?' "

Actually, in a way I prefer almost any moniker to some of the names that imaginative couples are currently giving their kids. My sister-in-law Robbie just named her third child Samara Leigh, a name she dug out of a baby-name book about the size of the *Oxford English Dictionary*. A roster of my other nieces and nephews sounds like cottages at a swanky resort in the Mediterranean: Zara, Erica, Alina, Adam, Elon, Imogene, Emma, Ariel.

My friend Wendy is aunt to Ruby, Tripoli, Matisse, and Jake. "Cathy and Barbara are beginning to sound nice to me," Wendy says. "I'm so sick of some of these yuppie names I can hardly get them out of my mouth. Like Zoe, Chelsea, and Dakota.

"Imagine your name is Dakota and you go to play school, and there are five others," says Wendy, who met two Dakotas last week. "Couples are actually going through the states. Carolina, Indiana, Florida." What'll be next? New York? "There's already a kid named Jersey on my block."

And to think that my friend Jane was contemptuous when her sister named her daughter Elizabeth. "I realized that if she could pick that name, I didn't know who my sister was," Jane says. "The only Elizabeth we had known was a person we both really despised."

Many name bigots feel that once you have a negative experience with someone, then anyone with that person's name is cursed, which leads me to believe that there aren't going to be a lot of little Saddams pitter-pattering around the United States anytime soon. And other chauvinists are suspicious of men with women's names and vice versa. And then there are names that seem like bad omens.

"I was looking for a new eye doctor," Laurie said, "and I called a friend. He said, 'I know a great ophthalmologist. His name is Dr. Tingle.' I immediately refused to see him. I don't care how good a doctor he is. Though I suppose it could have been worse. Dr. Tingle could have been a gynecologist."

Of course, some names do evoke a positive response. The last time I was in New York, for example, I met with a new editor. "Hello," she said, "My name is Margot."

I liked her immediately.

WHO'S THE BOSS?

Is it my imagination, or is this the Age of the Control Freak? I'm standing in front of the triceps machine at my gym. I've just set the weights, and I'm about to begin my exercise when a lightly muscled bully in turquoise spandex interrupts her chest presses to bark at me. "I'm using that," she growls as she leaps up from her slant board, darts over to the triceps machine and resets the weights.

I'm tempted to point out that, while she may have been planning to use the machine, she was, in fact, on the opposite side of the room. And that her muscles won't atrophy if she waits for me to finish. Instead, I go work on my biceps. Life's too short to fight over a Nautilus machine. Of course, *I'm* not a control freak.

Control freaks will fight over anything: a parking space, the room temperature, the last pair of marked-down Maude Frizon pumps, even whether you should barbecue with the top on or off the Weber kettle. Nothing is too insignificant. Everything has to be just so.

Just so *they* like it. "These people compulsively have to

have their own way," says Los Angeles psychologist Gary Emery. (And it isn't enough for the control freak to win. You have to lose.) "Their egos are based on being right," Emery says, "on proving they're the boss."

But how many bosses can one world take? It's gotten to the point where you can't make a simple telephone call without winding up in a heated game of one-upmanship.

"What gets me is when some person with absolutely no power has his secretary call and say, 'Please hold for Mr. Drek,' " my sister complains. But Laurie, a publicist who is on the phone all day, knows how to put spin on the ball, too. "I hang up," she says smugly. "And when the secretary calls and says, 'We seem to have gotten disconnected,' I tell her that I hung up. And then I say, 'Have Mr. Drek call me himself. I don't have time to hold.' Then he sends me a fax message because he's too scared to talk to me, and I know I've scored a victory."

Perhaps a Pyrrhic victory. "Control freaks are overconcerned with the means, rather than the end," Emery says. "So it's more important that the string beans are the right kind than it is to just enjoy the meal."

"What do you mean just enjoy the meal?" scoffs my friend Marc. "There's a right way to do things and then there's everything else." It goes without saying that he, and only he, has access to that Big Right Way in the Sky. And that Marc lives alone.

"I really hate to be in any situation where my control over what I'm doing is compromised," he admits. "Like if somebody says, 'I'll handle the cooking and you can shuck the corn or slice the zucchini,' I tell them to do it without me."

A control freak's kitchen can be his or her castle. "Let me show you the right way to make rice," said my husband the first time I made the mistake of fixing dinner. By the time Duke had sharpened the knives, rechopped the vegetables into two-inch squares, and chided me for using the wrong size pan, I had decided to surrender all control of the stove.

(For the record, this wasn't a big sacrifice. I don't like to cook.)

"It's easier in a marriage when you both don't care about the same things," says Milton Wolpin, a psychology professor at USC. "Otherwise, everything would be a battle."

And every automobile would be a battleground. There's nothing worse than having two control freaks in the same car. "I prefer to drive," my friend Claire says. "But no sooner do I pull out of the driveway than Fred starts telling me what to do. He thinks that I'm an idiot behind the wheel and that I make a lot of stupid mistakes."

She doesn't think he drives any better. "I think he goes really, really fast, and I'm sure that someday he's going to kill us both," she says. "And I complain about it constantly. But it's still a little easier for me to take a back seat. I'd rather get to pick him apart than get picked on."

My friend Katie would withstand the abuse. "I like to control everything," she says. "From where we're going to eat to what we're going to eat, to what movie we're going to see, what time we're going to see it, where we're going to see it, where we're going to park. Everything!"

But you can't control everything. So much of life is beyond our control. And to me, that's what makes it interesting. But not to Katie. "I don't like having my fate in someone else's hands," she says firmly. "If I take charge, I know that whatever it is will get done and it will get done well."

I shuffle my feet guiltily. Not too long ago I invited Katie and a bunch of friends out to dinner to celebrate my birthday. It was a control freak's nightmare. Not only did I pick the restaurant and arrange to pick up the check, but Duke also called in advance and ordered an elaborate Chinese banquet. I thought Katie was going to lose her mind.

"What did you order? I have to know," she cried, seizing a menu. "I'm a vegetarian. There are things I won't eat." Duke assured her that he had accounted for everybody's taste. Still, Katie didn't stop hyperventilating until the food arrived.

"I was very pleasantly surprised," she confesses. "And I would trust Duke again."

So would I. Because I'd *never* take control of a party menu.

"I'm sure there are areas where you're the control freak," says Professor Wolpin, "areas where you're more concerned about things than your husband." *Me?* The champion of laissez-faire? "You get very upset if you find something visible to the naked eye on the kitchen counter," Duke reminds me. "And you think you know much better than me what the right shirt for me to wear is."

But I'm just particular. I'm not a control freak.

"A control freak is just someone who cares about something more than you do," Wolpin says.

So what's wrong with being a control freak?

HAVE YOURSELF A MAIL-ORDER CHRISTMAS

I want to live in Catalogueland. Night after night, glossy holiday wish books with wondrous names—such as Trifles, Victoria's Secret, Superlatives, Hammacher Schlemmer, and the Amazing Grace Elephant Co.—breed in my mailbox. Every morning, a new stack appears to open a magic window on a bright shiny world where snowmen never melt and sugar cookies never crumble.

Catalogueland is filled with soignée women who wear black lace body stockings and receive natural Russian Imperial sable capes on the third date, handsome men who have everything except Fishiba, a two-gallon aquarium shaped like a television set, and brilliant but unspoiled children who are thrilled to discover a Hugg A Planet pillow under the tree on Christmas morning.

In Catalogueland, the beef-stick summer sausages (a foodstuff that I would eat only after ten days on a lifeboat) are always freshly made with the finest natural spices. The lighter-than-air fruitcakes (five thousand calories per gram) are baked by adorable, roly-poly grandmothers who bustle around enormous cast-iron stoves in crisply starched gingham aprons. And sharp Cheddar cheese is artistically shaped into bells, stars, and almond logs that have actually lived for years in my refrigerator without spoiling.

Catalogueland is a popular place. "Consumer-product mail-order sales are growing ten percent a year," says Arnold Fishman, president of Marketing Logistics, Inc., of Lincoln-shire, Illinois, a firm that publishes an annual guide to mail-order sales. He tells me that in 1987 consumers spent $43 billion on mail-order products. "The Christmas season prob-ably accounts for forty percent of that," says Fishman, who estimates that there are between two and three thousand Christmas catalogues out this year.

Claire, who already lives in Catalogueland, would like to receive every one of them. "I have an addiction," my friend confesses.

"Do you know what I do?" she asks. "People invite me and my husband over to watch sports. I walk into the house, grab a pile of catalogues that I haven't seen before, and start going through them. The other night, I was into Blooming-dale's for ten minutes before I realized I was being rude. Finally, the wife sat down next to me and said: 'Isn't it great? We don't even have to leave the living room. We can shop from here.' "

Shopping is always pleasant in Catalogueland. You don't have to clutch your purse in questionable neighborhoods. You don't have to endlessly orbit a dimly lighted carbon-monoxide-filled parking garage searching for a space as the relentlessly cheerful piped-in strains of "The Little Drummer Boy" drive you slowly insane. You don't have to stand in line for an hour in the Custom Wrap Department because an irritable salesperson wouldn't give you a gift box. In Cata-logueland, presents are lovingly wrapped with merrily striped imported paper and perky silky acetate bows.

"If something doesn't fit, they take it back, no questions asked," marvels my sister, a self-described mail-order junkie.

"They're much nicer on the phone than they are in the stores."

Laurie continues, "When I leave a dressing room, I don't want those skinny salesgirls whispering, 'That woman had the biggest set of hips we've ever seen.' You may be a size ten, but for all that catalogue operator knows, you're six feet tall."

Shopping in Catalogueland can be a little too convenient. "I ordered a winter coat at three in the morning," says Laurie, who admits that when she's depressed, she no longer reaches for the Häagen-Dazs; she reaches for the Saks Folio. "Sometimes I wake up in a panic worried about what I ordered the night before."

In Catalogueland, needs that you never knew you had can be satisfied toll-free, twenty-four hours a day, at the drop of a credit-card number. Your satisfaction is unconditionally guaranteed (whoever said there are no guarantees in life was not on the L.L. Bean or Lands' End mailing list). So what are you waiting for?

Do you *need* to decorate your car? No problem. Trifles can Federal Express you an artificial fir garland for your car's grille, trimmed with twinkling lights (batteries not included) and a red plastic bow. Do you *need* to frame that two-thousand-piece jigsaw puzzle of Neuschwanstein Castle (which you assembled in a weekend)? Bits and Pieces (The Great International Puzzle Collection) sells Instant Iron-On Puzzle Preserver or Easy Squeeze Puzzle Glue.

Perhaps there's a risk-taking special someone on your list. How about the Neiman Marcus His or Hers, 1988 Cloud Hopper—an eighteen-thousand-dollar one-person backpack hot-air balloon emblazoned with an exuberant cow jumping over the moon (life insurance not included). Or if money is no object (people in Catalogueland seem to have no inhibitions about spending thousands of dollars on things like bejeweled black-capped chickadee brooches that they've never seen), how about surprising your child with a rare

Connemara pony from Ireland, trained by the "world-renowned Lady Jocelyn"?

"Do you want to order it or do you want to know if it's in stock?" asks the operator at P. J. Carroll when I call for details. I ask how much the pony costs. "I have to check and see if it's in stock," the operator says. "What's the item number on that?"

I suggest that she check the warehouse to see if anything is whinnying.

"Can you hold for just a minute?" she asks. Exactly a minute later, she returns and says, "That will be between twelve thousand and twenty-two thousand dollars. It has to come from Ireland, and then a breeder from here will train it for you." Then she asks, "How many would you like?"

"Are they cheaper if I buy by the herd?" I inquire. The operator is not amused.

Maybe Catalogueland isn't all it's cracked up to be. After all, sweaters must be continually shaved with a Super De-Fuzzer to remove unsightly pills. Pepper mills, boxer shorts, toilet paper, even twenty-four-karat-gold-electroplated rulers must be personalized with your initials and/or your pet's picture.

In Catalogueland, closets must be systematically organized with cedar hangers, eight-shelf heavy-gauge vinyl sweater bags, quilted king-size garment bags, and floral hatboxes. Kitchens must be stocked with Electric Pizelle Irons, hand-decorated miniature sugar cubes (with tiny harvest motifs), laundry-size vats of lemon curd, dinosaur muffin/cake molds, and the cathedral steamed-pudding mold.

And everyone in Catalogueland is forced to join the Bakery in Your Mailbox Every Month, the Hickory Farms Gift of the Month, the Popcorn Factory's Snack of the Month, and the Coffee of the Month, Nut of the Month, Gourmet English Muffin of the Month, and Meat of the Month clubs.

Maybe I don't want to live in Catalogueland.

UGLY DOGS
AND THE WOMEN WHO LOVE THEM

P eople can be so cruel. I took my pugs for their morning walk. "Hey, ugly!" yelled a street-corner David Letterman, who wasn't all that attractive himself. I tried to ignore him, but he ran after me. "Your dogs run into a wall?" he asked, laughing uproariously.

Ha ha. I've had Bess and Stella for eleven years. And if I had a dollar for every time some would-be wit asked, "Somebody hit them in the head with a shovel?" (or some equally sparkling variation), I could pay my vet bills.

Still, I shouldn't take offense. My husband assures me that everyone is a dog bigot. "Everyone has his own conception of what a dog is and what a dog should be," says Duke. "Some of them are just wrong."

They certainly are. Duke, for example, believes that pugs aren't "real dogs" because they don't have snouts. "The dog with the snout looks more doglike," he insists. "It's got the sign of dog health—the cold, moist nose—not that mushroom-shaped, leathery knob."

I happen to like the pug nose. "But a snout allows the dog

to really smell the world," Duke argues. "The pushed-in-nose dog comes into the world with sort of a grudge because it can't stick its snout into a really beautiful mass of stinking debris and burrow and enjoy."

People can be so heartless. "Dog discrimination is everywhere," says Matthew Margolis, coauthor of *The Dog in Your Life*. "People who have small dogs don't like big dogs, and vice versa. And with a lot of people, what they grew up with is what they're used to. If it was a good dog, they want every dog to be like that. If it was a bad dog, they hate the breed."

How could anybody hate a pug? "Not everybody likes those liquid sucking sounds they make," Duke points out. "And they snore." (So does he.)

My sister explains that many men are dog bigots. "There are very few little dogs that a man feels comfortable walking," Laurie says. "It's a macho thing. Men go for dogs over four feet tall, the kind who will bring you back dead animals."

But Laurie admits that she's a dog bigot, too. "I wouldn't have one of those bedroom-slipper dogs [Shih Tzu, Maltese, Pomeranian, Lhasa apso] under any circumstances," she declares. "Any dog that you can carry in your pocketbook I find offensive. And as for Chihuahuas . . . I asked my vet what kind of dog he'd get. He told me, 'I'd get a Chihuahua, because when it died, I wouldn't care.' "

Ironically, my sister insists that her basset hound is never the victim of such slurs. "It's totally impossible for anyone to blatantly say that they don't like Elvis," says Laurie. "She looks too sad. Besides, bassets are universally loved because many people grew up with them. They've all seen the Hush Puppy ads."

But you can't believe those dogs on TV. Those dogs talk, play charades, wear dinner jackets, chase a gravy train, or find their way home when they get lost on another continent. And they never seem to stain the carpet.

Recently, Duke and I watched a television special featuring canine heroes. We saw dogs herding flocks of sheep, guiding the handicapped through rush-hour traffic, rescuing earth-quake victims, and pulling sleds for eleven days across the Arctic tundra.

"You notice all those dogs had snouts?" Duke pointed out smugly. I noticed. And I felt the show sold short the crucial contribution to civilization as we know it of the lap dog. "The pug does keep you warm while you're reading," Duke finally conceded.

In a way, I'm lucky to have dogs that aren't taken seriously. My friend Sabina has a huge German shepherd named Shane. "Most people are scared to death of him," she reports. "But Shane's a sweetheart."

I have yet to meet the owner of an attack dog who didn't make this claim. As far as I'm concerned, it's one of the world's great lies, up there with "The check is in the mail." The dog in question could be chewing on a human skull, and the owner will still insist, "Damien's really very friendly. He thinks he's a Yorkie."

Sabina understands people's concern. "German shepherds have the reputation for being killer dogs," she admits. "So people assume that Shane's going to kill them. I like people assuming that." Sabina maintains that shepherds are probably the smartest breed.

She's wrong. "The smartest dog on the scale is the poodle," claims Steven Abrams, a West Los Angeles veterinarian. "And after that comes the brachycephalic dogs—the short-nosed, bulgy-eyed breeds—the Pekingese, boxers, bulldogs, and pugs."

So the pug *is* smart? "They're generally highly intelligent," Abrams says. "I've never talked to anyone who said the breed is really stupid."

Maybe he should talk to my friend Marjorie. She expects a dog to defend her. I think that's asking a lot from a pet. "It doesn't have to be trained to attack," says Marjorie, who owns an extremely protective mutt. "But the dog should growl or bark or chase a threatening person away."

Really? The only thing my pugs would attack is a pizza. Marjorie is amazed. "You're the only person I've ever met who doesn't expect protection from a dog," she says.

Perhaps I *should* expect more from Bess and Stella. A few months ago, my husband suggested that we take them hiking at Joshua Tree National Monument. But the pug is not a trail dog, I explained. The pug prefers to lounge on the sofa and watch TV. "The real dog loves his owner and wants to please her," argued Duke.

To my astonishment, the pugs clambered merrily up the trail to Mastodon Peak. "It's the first time they seem really doglike," Duke marveled when Bess and Stella, wagging their curly tails and panting furiously, finally reached the summit. He patted them both on the head. "I'm very impressed. Maybe we could grow them some snouts."

All BOOKED UP

I'm thinking about converting. I realize that it's a really big step, but I've talked to people who have made it. And they assure me that my life will improve dramatically. I'll be a better person—more confident, more creative, and more effective. All I have to do is surrender my life to a higher power, to the Good Book—the Personal Organizer.

I know it's a little late. For years, millions of Americans have worshiped patented, refillable loose-leaf notebooks. But these three-ring oracles make me nervous. They tell you where to go and what to do—minute by minute—for the next week, month, year, or decade, depending on the model. And there are as many models as . . . well . . . denominations, all promising to fulfill your every need.

"It's my bible," exclaims Kay, a stockbroker who swears by her brown leather Running Mate. "It's with me all the time. I can't move without it." Frankly, I'm amazed that she can move *with* it. The yuppie equivalent to Linus's blanket must weigh a ton.

"I write my theater schedule in it and my notes on paying

bills," Kay says, "and when the kids go to their father and their Scout activities and their doctor's appointments. And my appointments. And lists of things to do each day." Just listening to her makes me feel slothful. "If I ever lost it, I would die," she says. "I wouldn't know how I could reschedule my life."

Many people think that the unscheduled life is not worth living. These never-a-dull-moment types find it comforting to open their Day-Timers, Filofaxes, Write Tracks, and other gospels to the "Today" page and see that every fifteen-minute slot is filled with Places to Go, People to Contact, and Things to Do or Buy. (Stuck with a void, they can always write down "check the book" or "update the book.")

Once, organizers were the exclusive property of bill-by-the-minute professionals. But now CNN reports that they're a $200- to $300-million-a-year industry. Even elementary school students can make sure that they don't miss the big Duck, Duck, Goose game or the power ice-cream-and-cookie networking session with a Dinky Diary Organizer from Day Runner. (Oh, dear.)

Secretly, I would love to be a hyperefficient automaton who never forgets birthdays or holidays, who can find a receipt without turning the house upside down. But I have a weakness for spontaneity. I want to be able to call my friends without making a note in my Communication Log.

"You do have free will," says my friend Marjorie, a Pocket Day-Timer disciple. "You don't have to do everything the book says." She tells me that with her system you carry only one month at a time, "so you can't lose your identity."

I want to believe her. But many people are slaves to their systems. "It makes me more efficient," says Lenny Fagelman, owner of the Filofax department at Fred Segal Melrose. Fagelman, who says, "I don't use my organizer to drive to work," strives for order the way gurus strive for inner peace. He stocks more than four hundred Filofax components, including inserts for keeping snooker records. "It's all function," he insists.

I'm ashamed to admit that for years I've been functioning with just a disarranged Rolodex and a calendar that is usually chosen because it has pretty pictures, not vital information. I make notes in a cheap little notebook that doesn't even have a movable plastic "Today" marker. Or worse, I resort to the Scrap System and jot important details on a used envelope or—if I want to feel in control—a Post-it Note.

I sometimes suspect that the real appeal of the Good Book is that it gives baby boomers a chance to reconnect with the wonder years, when our biggest decision was whether to carry a loose-leaf notebook emblazoned with Fred Flintstone or one featuring Mr. Spock. But nowadays, though most binders still come with the clear-plastic pencil case, our choices are far more complicated.

In fact, I could have been organized months ago, but I can't make up my mind. Should the book be as big as a briefcase or as small as a pocket calculator? (I can also set up shop on a hard or floppy disk, though it would be a pain to turn on the computer whenever I need a phone number.) And my choices go on and on.

Do I want a calendar that has a page per day, two pages per day, a page per week, per month, per millennium? Who cares? And then there's the really big question—What should my organizer be made of? Catalina vinyl? (It's hard to make a commitment to a material I can't identify.) Cowhide? Lamb? Shark? Definitely not alligator, which sells for nineteen hundred dollars.

"My Filofax is reindeer," Fagelman says. Oh, no, not Rudolph. "It's a limited edition," he says. "They recovered the hides from a two-hundred-year-old German shipwreck."

I'm no longer thinking about converting.

THE PERFECT WOMAN

In my next life I want to be perfect. I want to be the kind of woman who can wear a white sweater to a power lunch without spilling soy sauce. Who has only good hair days. Who has never walked into an important presentation trailing a train of toilet paper from her shoe. In this life, no matter how hard I try, I look, well, lived-in.

I bring this up because I just had lunch with my friend—let's call her Barbie—a woman so impeccably dressed and fastidiously groomed that whenever I see her, I feel like I'm wearing the wrong bra. Barbie, a regional sales director for a publishing company, is perfect. She's immune to everyday beauty calamities. Knock on her door at three in the morning and she'll still be flawlessly turned out.

"It's about power," Barbie confided. "If you're a perfectly coiffed business powerhouse, you appear to be all-knowing. It gives you a certain untouchable quality."

I wouldn't know. This kind of perfection is born, not made. Granted, any woman can approach beauty Nirvana, given sufficient time, energy, and cash. But unless you're a natural, no matter how many trips you make to the manicur-ist, hairstylist, makeup artist, personal trainer, and image con-sultant, it still looks like you're trying.

Which, of course, you are. "You can't just go to the store to see what's perfect," laments Claire, who has her act practi-cally together. "You have to read magazines, check out who's walking by. You have to make decisions: Do you want your nails rounded or square? And the lingerie—all those little matching teddy sets. Do perfect women really wear them under their clothes?"

You could spend your whole life hating the born-perfect. Think back to grade school. Remember the girl whose ank-lets were always folded just right? Who returned from recess looking like she hadn't played? I'd be willing to bet that in high school that same girl was head cheerleader, with straight bangs that defied humidity and the ability to apply eyeliner in a moving car. In college she was the one who lost, not gained, the freshman ten.

And today she's the wrinkle-free office paragon, the one with the Ph.D. in scarf tying, the one who never sweats. The one you keep staring at, all the while wondering, does her face ever break out? She never wears the same perfect little suit twice, she never gets ink on her blouse, and her lipstick never smudges when she eats.

Let's face it: A well-honed image is an important profes-sional asset, and most working women have no choice but to try. But there's a big difference between caring about your appearance and being able to control it, as anyone who has ever bent down and simultaneously had her stockings run knows. In fact, beauty maintenance is not unlike a stress test. Take your typical workday. Score fifteen points for every hour in which you manage to look pulled-together. Add bonus points for getting past everyday obstacles: twenty points for public transportation, ten points for inclement weather, forty points for children under five, eight points if you pump your own gas, fifteen points for naturally curly hair, and two hundred points if you have to be in several cities in one week. (If your total score is over 150, drop everything and check into the Golden Door.)

Of course, on the plus side, the pursuit of perfection does provide a delightful diversion from the pursuit of success. It's nice to know that when I'm having a crisis I can get my hair cut or my legs waxed and still be furthering my career. It also helps to remember that no woman is ever perfect enough. No matter how classy and polished she appears, there's always a classier, more polished woman she finds daunting.

So the next time you leave the house feeling out of control because your purse doesn't match your suit and your earrings are faux pearls, consider this: Staying soignée is a full-time job. And who has time for another job?

THE ADVICE SQUAD

If one more person gives me advice, I cannot be responsible for my actions. I went outside to get the morning paper. "You know, you really should cut your hair short, more in the style of today," said a woman across the street whose spiked tresses are dyed a vivid chartreuse.

Why was she telling me this? I wondered, as I nodded noncommittally and went back into my house. It's not as if I asked for her advice. Then again, it's not as if I ask for most of the advice that I receive. Lately it seems as if the world is filled with meddlers who all know that they could run my life much better than I do. These meddlers seem convinced that my life could be a good one, if only someone smart was in charge.

Next, I drove to the gas station. "If I were you, I'd get rid of that car," said an oil-splattered attendant, whom I'd never seen before in my life. I politely explained that I liked my car; it's old, but it never gives me any trouble. "Well, you better sell it before it does," the attendant warned me.

In a way, I didn't blame him for feeling like he could mind

my business. We are living in the era of the busybody. In ancient Greece, if a person wanted guidance, it involved a long, arduous expensive journey to consult the oracle at Delphi. Today, if you want guidance, all you have to do is unplug your ears.

In addition to traditional sources of unsolicited two cents' worth—your mother, your in-laws, and your hairdresser—there are now an unlimited number of amateur and professional buttinskis. A person in doubt has to fight off astrologers, color analysts, credit counselors, career counselors, relationship counselors, closet organizers, image consultants, nutritional therapists, pet therapists, personal shoppers, personal trainers—even channelers who offer to provide spirit guidance from the fourteenth century.

"People want magic fixes," says Carlfred Broderick, a sociology professor at the University of Southern California. "We're living in a society where we send out for help. We have our yards done. We have our plumbing done. We have our cars done. And now people are having their lives done. They would rather find an expert to make all their decisions."

Not me. A short time ago, in a shopping mall a thousand miles away from my home, I succumbed to the sales pitch of a soothsayer who had set up shop next to the escalator. I was in a wonderful mood when I sat down and crossed her palm with MasterCard. Then the psychic went into a trance.

"I see pain and suffering," she began, her voice getting louder and shriller as she ticked off the evils that lay in store for me: illness, heartbreak, betrayal, abandonment. Face after face of escalator-riding shoppers grew grave with concern as they rose through the floor, heard my fate, and then disappeared from view.

"Are you married?" asked the cut-rate Cassandra. Yes, happily. "It won't last," she said, adding that for another ten dollars she would advise me how to lift the curse.

I knew how to lift the curse. I ran away. But other advice is harder to avoid. I pick up the newspaper. Dear Abby is giving advice. Ann Landers and Dr. Ruth are giving advice. I turn on the television. Oprah Winfrey and Phil Donahue are giving advice. Advertisers are giving advice. Celebrities are giving advice. Sitcom mommies and daddies seem to do nothing but give advice.

And this is just the tip of the adviceberg. "Machines are giving advice!" my friend Léon exclaims. She tells me that an electronic message board in her bank flashes dictums like "Get your cholesterol checked!," "Save for a rainy day!," and "Floss regularly!" at her while she's waiting in line.

Pretty soon it's going to be impossible for anyone to make a mistake. Though no matter what you do, there will always be someone or something who can say, or electronically beep, "I told you so."

"Even fortune cookies are getting into the act," Léon says with a sigh. "They no longer say things like 'You're going to come into a wealth of diamond baubles.' Instead, they say to 'be kinder to your friends' or 'listen to your boss.' They're telling me things that I don't want to hear from my mom, let alone a cookie."

Frankly, I would rather listen to a cookie than to self-appointed gurus who ply me with advice that they should take themselves. It seems to be a rule of life that the less qualified you are to give counsel, the more counsel you give.

This afternoon I went to the gym. I had just finished warming up on the LifeCycle and was about to begin working on the weight machines when a generously proportioned woman whose fluorescent-green bicycle pants might not have been her best fashion choice tapped me on the shoulder. It took me a few seconds to recognize Connie, a former coworker, who had put on at least twenty pounds since we last met.

"You really should ride the bike for an hour," said Connie, whose entire workout consisted of buying a T-shirt. I waited for a disclaimer like, 'I realize that I'm the last person in the world who should be telling you this, but . . .' Instead she

imperiously suggested that I raise my weights, do more repe-
titions, and take a longer stretch. "I'm just telling you this for
your own good," she said.

I doubt it. I've noticed that the Connie Syndrome is particularly widespread in the arenas of Romantic Advice, which
seems to be largely offered by the lovelorn, the walking
wounded, and/or folks in the midst of their seventh consecutive doomed affair with a self-destructive abusive psycho, and
Business Advice, which is generously tendered by the un-or-
underemployed.

My husband has an analogy to explain this. "You only
need one foot to be a crutch," Duke says.

As a matter of fact, there is a school of thought that goes,
those who can, do; those who can't, advise. "I've got a friend
who's the wisest person in the world," says Marjorie. "His
own life is a mess, he's absolutely miserable. But all I have to
do is say 'boo-hoo,' and he's on the case. And presto, my life
is better."

But Marjorie asked him to make her life better. And there's
a world of difference between asking for advice and getting
it thrown in your face. I'm sitting in my office, trying to finish
this piece. The telephone rings. "Pardon me, what you really
need are mountain or seashore time-shares," says a phone
salesman. I explain that I am very busy. "Then you really
need a place to relax," he says.

What he really needs is another job, I think angrily. "Let
me give you some advice," I reply.

WHODUNNIT? YOUDUNNIT!

O n a recent vacation I cheerfully devoured a large stack of the latest offerings in detective fiction. Pretty soon, they all ran together. I began to think maybe I could write a mystery novel. Maybe anyone could write a mystery novel. And so in the spirit of *Spy* magazine's legendary "Buddy-O-Matic," a formula for writing buddy movies, I offer Auto-Sleuth.

To create your best-selling mystery, simply choose one of the multiple-choice answers available at each plot twist. And remember, there's no such thing as too many adjectives.

My rising sign was in trouble. It was a *(sweltering / stormy / snowy / freezing / humid)* night in *(Los Angeles / London / Paris / Yorkshire / Fort Lauderdale / Navajo Country / West Covina)*. I'd been looking forward to a quiet evening puttering around my *(flat / trailer / mansion / houseboat / converted mill)*.

I'd been feeling *(moody / gloomy / melancholic / depressed)* since the *(trial / steeplechase accident / divorce / Commission took away my license / love of my life sailed for the Argentine)*. I was about to drown my sorrows in a glass of *(Old Peculier / Plym-*

outh / *Glenlivet* / *Amstel* / *Armagnac* / *club soda* / *Diet Coke)* when the *(phone rang / doorbell chimed / letter arrived / bullet whizzed through the window / dog started barking for no reason).*

It was *(my old pal / the FBI / my ex-whatever / a two-bit punk with a knife in his back / the vicar / Scotland Yard / a stunning redhead).* My visitor was distraught because *(it couldn't have been a suicide / rich aunt Sophie had disappeared / a crazed serial killer was on the loose / it was a frame-up / the star was murdered / a champion racehorse was neutered / someone on the reservation was not in* hozro). They begged me for help.

Naturally, I agreed to take the case. My name is *(Carlotta / Moses / Cordelia / Kinsey / Travis / V.I. / Melrose / Hercule / Gregor / Leaphorn / anything alliterative).* I'm a celebrated *(Navajo / English / French / Belgian / Armenian / other)* sleuth— a *(private eye / barrister / cop / FBI agent / rabbi / lord / viscount / duke / journalist / nosy old lady / classics professor)* who loves a good mystery. I charge my clients *(nothing—I'm paid by the department / nothing—I'm fabulously wealthy / nothing—it's a good cause / nothing—I'm doing a friend a favor / nothing—it's my hobby / thirty bucks an hour plus expenses).*

The next morning, I climbed into my *(VW Beetle / squad car / horse trailer / classic Karmann Ghia / combination Rolls Royce–pickup truck / taxi / Bentley)* and headed over to *(head-quarters / the library / the bank / the paper / the racetrack / the trading post)* to pick some brains. I asked *(the desk sergeant / the receptionist / the head trainer / Rosie / Iron Woman / Pete)* to give me the lowdown on *(the family / the will / the lab report / the corporation / the skinwalkers).* He/she was reluctant, but hell, they owed me *(a big favor / a grand / their life).*

I found out that *(there had been sizable withdrawals at the end of every month / a sonnet was found next to each body / the victim was the town tramp / the kids had been disinherited / the footprints didn't match / there were traces of poison in her feed bag).* On a hunch, I ran the *(license plates / credit card / gun serial number / FAA tail number / AKC registration)* through the computer and discovered that my client had been holding back. Of course,

I knew right away the *(husband / wife / lover / brother / best friend / ruthless partner)* did it, but I couldn't prove it—yet. My chief suspect had been at the *(regatta / Kentucky Derby / Blessing Way / seder)* at the time of the crime and there were dozens of witnesses.

I met up with my *(partner / butler / Siamese cat / octogenarian landlord / friend the economist / friend the ex-earl / friend the Armenian priest)* at an out-of-the-way *(pub / bistro / dive / diner / stable)* I know that serves delicious *(shepherd's pie / lobster à la crème / mash / margaritas / coffee / Indian fry bread)*. My sidekick had been nosing around *(the CEO / the director / the duchess / the psychiatrist / my client)* and had learned that *(the cabinet was always kept locked / the family owned 49 percent of the stock / there was a history of insanity / she was a crack shot / the frozen semen from Secretariat was missing)*. I made a mental note to talk to the *(roommate / postmistress / aerobics instructor / insurance adjustor)*.

But when I showed up at their office I discovered my only lead had been *(shot / poisoned / strangled / hanged / stabbed)* and the cops had the place surrounded. I was so frustrated I had to *(swim / jog / play volleyball / fill my pipe / take a sweat bath)* until I calmed down.

I was headed home when I was *(shot / followed / threatened / beat up / chased / bit / arrested)* by a perpetrator with a *(mustache / foreign accent / tattoo / toupee / silver choke chain)*. I still don't know what hit me, but when I came to I was on *(a houseboat / a Regency love seat / the moors / the Turquoise Mountain / a racehorse)* and a drop-dead gorgeous *(man / woman / thoroughbred / retriever)* was looking at me with grave concern. I was overwhelmed with lust. Unfortunately, I had *(a gunshot wound / a concussion / four cracked ribs / a black eye / two broken legs)* and my rescuer urged me to take it easy. But I insisted on *(walking / driving / staggering / crawling)* home.

Lucky thing. My *(flat / trailer / mansion / houseboat / converted mill)* was being *(searched / torched / rigged with explosives / burglarized / watched / bugged / sunk)*. Fortunately, my *(partner / butler / Siamese cat / octogenarian landlord / friend the economist /*

friend the ex-earl / friend the Armenian priest) showed up just in the nick of time and helped me *(chase / shoot / trap / pulverize)* the intruder. The hooligan didn't want to talk, but a *(knee in the groin / C-note / gun pointed at his back / fix of Demerol)* loosened his lips.

Suddenly, I remembered *(the pantyhose / the insurance hoax / they were twins / we had goose for dinner / the next line from "Paradise Lost")* and I put two and two together. My sidekick went for help and I hurried back to the *(summer house / vicarage / vacant lot / salvage yard)*, where I *(broke in / illegally searched)* and discovered that *(the racehorse / the fetish / the will / the murder weapon / Aunt Sophie)* was about to be destroyed by the crazed *(husband / wife / lover / brother / best friend / ruthless partner)* who was waving a *(gun / bomb / knife / hypodermic needle)* in the air.

Despite my wounds I *(chased / shot / tackled / pursued on horseback / chatted up)* the villain, who then tried to *(shoot / tackle / stab / drug / outride)* me. I thought I was finished, but in the nick of time my drop-dead gorgeous rescuer appeared and distracted the miscreant, enabling me to cosh him with a *(walking stick / poker / gun butt / squash-blossom necklace)*. I was listening to his confession when the police came.

Case closed, I went back to my *(flat / trailer / mansion / houseboat / converted mill)* with the drop-dead gorgeous *(man / woman / thoroughbred / retriever)*, who will *(disappear / die / be accused of a crime / marry me / finally sleep with me / help me clear my name)* in the next book.

YET ANOTHER OUT-OF-THE-LOOP EXPERIENCE

LOTS OF GARLIC
AND NOT ENOUGH INSURANCE

"It's a rare bone infection!" exclaimed the oral surgeon who stuck a needle in my mouth and drew screams. He gave me an hour to get to Santa Monica Hospital for a six-week course of IV antibiotics, thirty hours in a hyperbaric chamber, and surgery.

"What a lucky girl," cooed an admissions bureaucrat as an orderly lifted me on a gurney and rushed me to have a CAT scan. "You have such a good policy."

"You're so lucky," chirped a technician who locked me in a pressurized box and marinated me in pure oxygen. "Some companies wouldn't cover this." By the time I heard this sentiment expressed by the anesthetist, the IV nurse, the dietitian, and the middle-aged lady who dropped by my sickbed to offer me a magazine, I was more afraid of losing my insurance card than I was of death.

I *was* lucky. Not only did I live to tell about this experience, I had this experience while I was working for an ad agency that provided health benefits. A year before Provident Life and Health picked up a hospital tab big enough to buy me a condominium. I was a free-lance writer who chose to insure her car instead of her body. What can I say to defend my priorities? I was young, I felt invincible, and it's illegal to drive in California without coverage.

"Of course you wound up in the hospital; you were insured," scoffed Wendy, a free-lance journalist who claims that her health is the only health insurance she needs. "If you don't have health insurance, you can't get sick," she explained. "It's like car insurance. No car insurance, no accident." I knew better than to argue with Wendy. I hid behind similar logic when I couldn't afford coverage.

On February 15, *The New York Times* reported that the nation's health-insurance industry suffered record losses, at least $1.25 billion, in 1987. I am not surprised. One of my doctors wanted me to try magnetic resonance imaging, an expensive alternative to X rays that produces a high-resolution computer image. "Why should I do that?" I asked. His reply? "I've never seen one."

"When I get sick I do a lot of garlic and I get better," said Wendy.

Maybe I should feed my pugs garlic. I pay the veterinarian on a fee-per-service basis. Bess and Stella lead an enviably stress-free life. They eat vegetarian kibble; they sleep; they walk around the block, on a leash, by the beach where cars are not permitted. Nevertheless, the pugs regularly contract flea allergies, ear infections, and worms when I am having a cash-flow crisis.

Last year I found Bess staggering around the house whimpering. (It had to be serious. She refused her favorite food: an onion bagel.) I rushed her to the animal hospital, where the veterinarian diagnosed a stroke. He eagerly proposed additional tests. "Save my dog," I heard myself cry. "I don't care what it takes."

Twenty-four hours later, after I had paid approximately what it would have cost to put her on the Concorde to Lourdes, Bess was romping on the beach.

Unfortunately, I could no longer afford the premium on

my own health insurance. I shopped around for a cheaper policy, preferably one that would let me choose my own doctor. I discovered that insurance companies want to underwrite a woman with an expensive claim in her past about as much as they want to underwrite a BMW owner who has had his Blaupunkt tape deck stolen three times.

I was quoted a rate. When I was able to breathe again, I said, "Is that for insurance or to endow a hospital wing?" Finally, with misgivings, I joined my husband's health-maintenance organization. It was half as much as my old insurance.

"You get what you pay for," I told Duke after I called for an appointment and got an answering machine instead of the warm, compassionate health professional the slick, handsomely printed brochure promised. *"Hola!"* said the recording at OB-GYN. *"Mi Dios!"* I sighed. My heart sank. Now I know what happened to all those rich, dumb premeds I met in college who went off to the Caribbean for their M.D.'s.

Duke sat me down and calmly tried to reassure me. "You've heard about Type-A people, who are pushy and aggressive."

"The kind who die first?" I asked. (The kind like me who get irritated because they can't make an appointment for a Pap smear?)

"The kind who *used* to die first," Duke replied. "Now they live longer. It's because of the HMOs. The laid-back Type Bs do exactly what they're told. They stay on hold forever and die. Type-A people get the unlisted number of the supervisor and stay alive."

I really tried to be a worthy Type-A wife. I complained when the gynecologist assigned me not to Cedars Sinai, the center listed in the slick, handsomely printed brochure, but to a tiny hospital that even my doctor friends had never heard of, situated in a graffiti-splattered downtown neighborhood. I let the supervisors know I was aware of the state regulations governing the HMOs. But it's been six weeks, and I still can't get an appointment for a Pap smear.

Maybe I should go see Bess's vet.

BABY BORES

It is a truth universally acknowledged that a married woman in possession of a good job must be in want of a child.

However little known the feelings or views of such a woman may be (to further paraphrase Jane Austen), this truth is so well fixed in the minds of others that she and her uterus are considered as the rightful subject of general public inquiry. Or, as my grandmother recently put it when she called to wish me a happy thirty-fifth birthday, "So when are you going to have a baby already?"

I do not blame Grandma for trying to get me pregnant. She, after all, is upholding a traditional role. But lately she seems to have allies everywhere. I go to the movies and Diane Keaton has a baby. Molly Ringwald has a baby. Ted Danson, Steve Guttenberg, and Tom Selleck have a baby. Pee-wee Herman seems to be on the verge of having a baby.

And *The Star*, my authority on these matters, is crammed with diaper-to-diaper coverage of real-life celebrity accouchements: Princess Caroline's and Caroline Kennedy's, Fergie's and Demi Moore's. Even Diana Ross, at forty-four, just had a baby.

"So why aren't you having a baby?" my grandmother repeats.

Fortunately, she hasn't read the newspapers today or she would ask me why I am the only woman in my generation who *hasn't* given birth. The National Center for Health Statistics reports that a "slight increase in fertility of women in their prime childbearing years resulted in an estimated 3,829,000 births last year, the most since 1964."

If anything, this figure seems low. It seems that I have received at least this many birth announcements and/or invitations to baby showers. In fact, if the birth rate gets any higher, I will have to start a sinking fund at the Stork Shop to cope with the financial burden of the baby-boom echo.

"There's no such thing as a cheap baby gift," I recently told a friend. "Everything under twenty dollars is flammable."

"It's an investment," said Connie, who had just returned from her third baby shower of the weekend. She gave the mother-to-be a twenty-nine-dollar infant carrier, but now she feels guilty that she didn't spring for the sixty-four-dollar interchangeable car seat/carrier. "Your return is what you get when you get pregnant."

"What are you waiting for?" Grandma asks me.

I don't know. It certainly would make me more popular at parties. Everywhere I go, everyone is talking about breast-feeding, amniocentesis, epidurals, child-care classes, and baby-sitters. And everyone seems to have a baby, which they take everywhere.

"The adults just stand around watching the babies interact," says Wendy. "One jumps in and dabs a face. Another jumps in and straightens the little hat. It's like a grown-up circle game."

I think it is wonderful that so many couples are having children. But I also think that if these couples really want to persuade me to have a playmate for their newest family member, they should repackage their pitch. As it stands now: I go to visit the new baby. Generic new mother is invariably exhausted, nervous, brain dead, fat, flat broke. Her hair looks terrible, her house looks worse, and she tearfully confides that she hasn't had sex in a year. And then she asks, "Why don't you do this, too?"

"It doesn't get easier when you wait too long," says Grandma.

Unfortunately, she read that *Newsweek* cover story on miscarriages, so she has a new worst-case scenario with which to scare me into motherhood. According to *Newsweek,* the risk of miscarriage "rises with the mother's age." I try to look on the bright side. Last year, the same magazine reported that women in their thirties have a better chance of attracting a lightning bolt than a husband. Many bolts later, these same women generated a contradictory trend/cover story. At least so far, I have been spared a "very special infertility episode" of *ALF.*

"Everyone always wants to get into the horrible stories about people who can't," laments Claire, whose mother-in-law calls daily and makes biological-clock ticking sounds. "Then they tell you the horrible adoption stories. And you sit there thinking that you better go home and get with it or you're going to be up a creek."

"Are you trying?" Grandma pries.

I am trying not to lose my temper. But people won't leave me alone. I have actually had total strangers come up to me at business luncheons, look at my wedding ring, and ask why I am not pregnant. Frankly, I do not think that this is an appropriate opening gambit. I prefer anything—even "What's your sign?"—to "Are there scars on your Fallopian tubes?"

But the hallmark of this baby boomers' Baby Boom, which should be rechristened the Baby Bore, is graphic public disclosure of what used to be considered private parts. Infertility, everything from slow-moving sperm to the morning's basal temperature readings, is now casually discussed over dinner. And after dinner, if the couple has defied the odds and actually managed to conceive, they proudly offer to show me close-up color videos of the birth.

This is not my idea of after-dinner entertainment. As far as I'm concerned, the only thing worse than watching such a film is starring in one. Nobody is going to point a camera between my legs while I am giving birth.

"Doesn't your husband want children?" Grandma asks me. Why doesn't she ask my husband? Why doesn't anyone ask my husband?

They all say, "We don't feel *comfortable* asking your husband."

So why do they all feel comfortable asking me? Or, in Grandma's case, *telling* me.

"We have to name a child after Grandpa," Grandma wails.

The guilt factor involved in denying a seventy-five-year-old widow a great-grandchild named after her beloved husband is considerable. Still . . .

"I cannot name a child Irving," I tell Grandma.

DIRTY LINEN
IS NOW SMALL TALK

"**I** hate buffets; I'm bulimic," Maxine remarks casually, as if she's admitting that purple is her favorite color. We are standing in the buffet line at the Westwood Marquis Hotel, an unlikely choice for a confessional.

What is the etiquette here, I wonder helplessly. Am I supposed to ask how long she's been vomiting, though the fact is that I don't want to know? Maxine is a colleague I occasionally meet for coffee. My stomach recoils with sympathetic nausea. "Thank you for sharing this with me," I stammer.

Maxine smiles and divulges that she's taking Elavil to control her binges. Then she says, "Let's get something to eat." She loads a plate with pasta primavera, Caesar salad, and shrimp wrapped in bacon as I look on, bewildered and aghast.

Later, halfway through brunch, she hurries off to the ladies' room, where she remains for half an hour. Maybe her contact lenses are scratchy, or she got her period, or dysentery, I speculate, wanting to give her the benefit of the doubt, a doubt she removes when she returns. "I had to get rid of the quiche," she says, ready for dessert.

Judge not, that ye be not judged, I scold myself. Maxine is battling what is now termed an "eating disorder." These are common, but not as common as what I would like to term "confession disorders."

"What was I supposed to do?" I ask my husband that evening. I feel guilty for revealing a secret, but I can't keep secrets I can't handle.

"You're supposed to help her, honey," he responds.

I am not a therapist. I can't help most people who reveal their deep, dark secrets, particularly people I barely know. There are limits to what I want even my closest friends to tell me, not because I lack curiosity or fear intimacy, but because it could warp our friendship.

Bette tells me a man who took her to *Tristan und Isolde* tested positive for AIDS antibodies. "I haven't slept with him yet, but I want to," she confesses over lunch. Then she asks, "Would you?"

"Are you out of your mind?" My respect for her judgment drops faster than the stock market.

"I really admire him for being open," she argues. "And it's safe if we use condoms, don't you think? I want your honest opinion."

Nobody ever wants your honest opinion. People who throw unpleasant facts in your face fully expect approval as a reward for being open. Bette is begging for reassurance that she is doing the right thing. She wants me to offer up a similarly wretched detail from my past to validate her decision. The best I can offer is an emphatic: "I love you. I don't want you to die."

"You're overreacting," she complains.

I can't blame her. Nothing (and this includes impotence, infidelity, manic depression, past lives, plastic surgery) is shameful anymore. This is the golden age of full disclosure. Actors, authors, athletes begin comebacks with front-page confessions about their "chemical dependencies" (isn't anyone embarrassed to be a drug addict?), followed by television coverage when they check in at the Betty Ford clinic.

And it trickles down to ordinary life. Lately, everyone I meet behaves as if they're on a talk show and the interviewer has just asked them—"Just between us"—for the up-close-and-personal truth. What used to be regarded as airing your dirty linen in public has come to be regarded as small talk.

I call an editor to thank him for sending me a reprint. "I wasn't that efficient when I was a junkie," he replies. I ask my housekeeper to sweep under the bed. She answers, "I've made a political decision to be a lesbian." Take a plane from Los Angeles to New York, and the odds are better than even that a total stranger in the next seat will say something like "I'm having an affair with a Catholic priest" before the plane crosses the Mississippi.

If it isn't a total stranger, it's even worse. I arrive in Connecticut to spend a warm family Christmas with my friend Cathy. She meets me at the train station with the news that she is pregnant. "But don't mention this at dinner," she warns. Charles, her boyfriend, is in the kitchen basting the turkey, but that doesn't stop Cathy from highlighting the current conflict: Charles, she says, "wants me to have the child and ruin my career"; her mother wants to have a grandchild, Cathy wants to have an abortion. "What would you do?" she asks.

"See a therapist," I insist. Don't tell me about it. Just tell me when it's over.

I run into Bette at an art opening. She throws her arms around me and discloses that after a few months of torrid safe sex with Mr. HIV-Positive she ended the relationship. She wants me to fix her up with an attractive man she spotted at my house. She assures me her AIDS test is negative.

Enough about Bette. I have a confession I want to make.

THE ART OF THE DEAL

How many words do you want to read today—200, 300? This piece is supposed to be 850 words. But let's make a deal.

Don't want to bargain? Neither do I. Yet, lately it seems as if the world has become a big bazaar. Maybe it's the recession, but price tags everywhere have come unglued. On Main Street in Santa Monica, where I sometimes shop, it used to be that I'd pick up an item for a closer look and a supercilious clerk would say, "Five hundred dollars," and I'd put it down. Now, as soon as something catches my eye, the supercilious clerk chirps, "I can give it to you a little cheaper."

Don't get me wrong. I have nothing against lower prices. I just don't like to haggle. Once a price starts fluctuating, I know I can't win. Someone—anyone!—is bound to get a better deal. And what fun is buying something for $300 that used to be $500 when tomorrow it's going to be $160?

Lots of fun for some people. "I like to bargain better than I like sex," says my sister-in-law Robbie. "When I get a good deal, it makes my whole week." What's a good deal? "A seventy-five-percent-off sale—that's a bargain. Ten cents on the dollar—that's a bargain. Of course, then I say, 'I love it, but can you do a little better on the price?' "

I wouldn't have the nerve. I'm never sure when dickering is appropriate. It used to be something you did only on vacation. If I go to a picturesque stall in a foreign land and an older woman sitting behind a pile of straw hats demands two thousand pesos or won or some other oversized currency that has a guy with a mustache on it, then I know I'm supposed to say, "Fifteen hundred." But now people dicker everywhere.

"I was behind this woman in the checkout line at the supermarket," my grandmother says, "and the cashier tells her, 'That will be one hundred sixty-eight dollars and forty-two cents.' And this woman says, 'I'll give you a hundred.' " She was up to $125 when Grandma left the store.

Of course, sometimes you have to bargain just to stay even, like when you're trying to get any five rooms of carpet cleaned for the coupon price of $24.95 while an abusive representative keeps warning you that the steam cleaning is absolutely useless without the color brighteners, Teflon coating, and preconditioning (none of which are included).

"There's always an angle," my brother, Bobby, says. "That's the root of all bargains—the unknown. Like I bought a four-hundred-dollar suit for two twenty-five. I thought I got a great price, and then they clobbered me on alterations. Such a deal. Nobody could have walked out with that suit unless he was six-eleven and didn't want finished bottoms."

And to think I called my brother for some bargaining tips. I wanted a wall built in my yard and had been taking bids. My lowest bidder, a contractor from Tonga in the Friendly Islands, measured and said his price was one thousand dollars, "but for you, nine-fifty." I didn't know what to say.

"Tell him you'll give him five hundred dollars," Bobby advised. "If you want a good price, you've got to be ridiculous." I couldn't be that ridiculous.

My husband agreed that I had to negotiate. "I don't think they have a word for *fixed prices* in the Friendly Islands," Duke said. "Tell him eight hundred dollars, and he'll settle for eight-fifty." And he did. But why couldn't he just ask for that? "Because then he thinks people will feel cheated if they don't get it for seven hundred dollars," Duke explained.

Nobody wants to feel like a sucker. And I suppose that a lot of folks would look at my nice new wall and fret that they could have gotten it for less. Not me. I have this principle about bargaining called the Mexican Blouse Theory. It goes like this: You're at a booth in Tijuana. You see an embroidered peasant blouse that costs twenty-five dollars. You rant and rave for forty-five minutes until the *señora* agrees to part with it for three dollars. But ask yourself: Do you really want a three-dollar blouse?

"Do I really want another brass Aztec calendar?" says my friend Doug. "No, but if I can get it for five dollars, what the heck?" He sees bargaining as a competitive sport at which he excels. "It has all the advantages of exercise. Your heart gets pumping. You raise your voice. You pace, you pound, you wag fingers."

That is not my idea of a pleasant shopping experience. And neither is this: "You must be willing to walk away," Doug says. "It's the basic rule of bargaining. If you can walk away, you can't lose."

Last year, my husband and I were in Hong Kong, home of the adjustable price tag. I fell in love with an adorable pair of shoes. I was ready to buy them, but then Duke, who likes bargaining in a foreign country because it's one of the few social interactions possible when you know only twenty words of the language, decided to get me a better price. I watched in horror as he and the salesman bickered over thirty dollars HK.

"Let's go," Duke said, leading me away from my beautiful shoes. "It's an act," he whispered. Luckily for him, the salesman ran after us and met our price.

Then the most incredible thing happened. I'd be happy to tell you about it.

Just make me an offer.

WHEELS OF MISFORTUNE

There is no escaping Car Hell. The other day I walked out
to my parking space expecting to drive to the gym. A behe-
moth van was parked three centimeters away from the
driver's side of my Mazda and I couldn't get in. No problem,
I thought, as I circled to the passenger's side and inserted my
key in the lock.

But there *was* a problem. With a car there is always a
problem. The passenger door wouldn't open. I trudged back
to the house and informed my husband that I was in the midst
of yet another automotive crisis.

"The lock's just jammed," said Duke, who understands
cars. "I can fix that."

"Don't bother," I replied. "It's better this way." If I can't
get in my car, then I don't have to drive it. As far as I'm
concerned, the only good thing about driving in Los Angeles
is that it saves you from taking the bus.

Dante with prescience structured his hell very much in the
architecture of a contemporary subterranean parking structure ("Remember your color and level"). Car Hell is the

psychological equivalent of Dante's *Inferno,* a vast, multi-leveled, bottomless pit of increasingly unpleasant, increasingly expensive car-related experiences. In my opinion, there is no such thing as a pleasant car-related experience in Los Angeles; Car Hell, like death and gridlock, is inevitable.

The Department of Motor Vehicles reports that in 1987 in Los Angeles County there were 6,057,648 registered cars and 5,404,200 licensed drivers. On any given day, at any time, many of these drivers will find themselves in Car Hell. Some will have flat tires, some will pay five dollars to stack-park at the Hollywood Bowl, some will try to get financing for a new car, some will have to go to traffic school, and some will be rear-ended at a red light while they are putting on their makeup. But none will be very happy.

"When I look at my checkbook ledger, every single expense is car-related," my friend Wendy says. "I have come to the realization that all of my problems seem to be manifested in cars. They say that people live for their cars in this city because they have such high payments, but I have two junk heaps."

It doesn't really matter what you drive. The road to Car Hell is paved with Honda Prelude owners begging their insurance companies to pay for their fourth stolen steering wheel and Mercedes owners on the verge of a nervous breakdown because still another runaway grocery cart dinged their car door, necessitating still another six-hundred-dollar Glasurit paint job. True, it may be less stressful to be stuck in rush-hour traffic on the 405 Freeway in a $185,000 Rolls-Royce Corniche convertible, but consider the stress of finding a safe place to park it.

"People only live in Car Hell because they believe that they are what they drive," argues Doug, who drives a Honda. "All this tension in traffic is caused because people think the car is an extension of them. You're in stop-and-go traffic and you're terrified to make a turn. You don't want to get hit."

Of course you don't want to get hit. A collision automatically sentences you to the depths of Car Hell: Body-Shop Hell and worse, Insurance Hell. Insurance premiums are now so high that when someone smashes into you, the big concern is no longer, "Are you hurt?" but rather "Do you promise that you won't report this to my insurance company?" And even if the state supreme court upholds Proposition 103 and approves the 20 percent rate rollback, you will still have to find a company left in California that will condescend to write you a policy.

There's always something to worry about when you own a car. If the car works, you worry about how it is working. And if it doesn't work, then you worry about how you're going to fix it.

"You ask twenty people what's wrong with the car and you get twenty different answers," Wendy says. "You look in their eyes and you search for truth. But I don't think that truth and auto mechanics go together."

This is especially true if you're a woman. I realize that there are women who can and do rebuild carburetors, but I am not one of them. (In my opinion, lying under a car covered with grease is simply another form of Car Hell.) Last month, my car wouldn't start. I called in my first-string automotive troubleshooter: my husband. He tried to give it a jump. The car still wouldn't start. He diagnosed that the car needed a new starter and made me an appointment with Morales Auto Electric, whose estimate for the job came in $150 cheaper than the one from my second-string automotive troubleshooter: the Mazda dealer.

So, I called my third-string automotive troubleshooter: the Auto Club. Its tow truck arrived an hour later. A brute splattered with oil and tattoos insisted that the car just needed a jump. "My husband already tried that," I said.

"My cables are bigger than your husband's," the brute said.

I knew better than to argue about that. I let him put his cables on my terminals. The car still wouldn't start. So, I told him where he should tow it.

"If you're smart," he sneered, "you'll let me tow it to my garage."

If I were smart, I would have insisted that my husband stay home and deal with this creep. Instead I did the next best thing. "My husband won't let me take it to anyone but Morales," I said. It was not this liberated woman's proudest moment, but it worked.

"When I left my husband, I lost everything," Wendy says. "He was a Volvo mechanic."

But even the most mechanically skilled person cannot avoid the fiery pit of Car Hell—the Department of Motor Vehicles. I do not understand why we even bother to elect government officials to run this state. The Department of Motor Vehicles runs California.

Recently, I had to renew my driver's license. I called the Department of Motor Vehicles to make an appointment. I was put on hold. Twenty-two minutes later, an operator came on the line and begrudgingly scheduled me in.

I arrived on time at the DMV in Santa Monica. I waited in the "Appointments Only No Wait" line for ten minutes only to learn that I was not on the schedule. "You can wait in the regular line if you want," the clerk said.

The regular line was the length of the Space Mountain line at Disneyland. I assertively insisted that they honor my appointment. And what was my reward? The surly clerk punched my driver's license number into the computer and declared that he couldn't renew my license because there was a warrant out for my arrest.

"How can there be a warrant?" I asked. "I haven't even gotten a ticket."

"The computer says that you committed a moving violation five years ago," the clerk insisted.

I could not believe that I might be arrested at any moment because I was alone in the Diamond Lane at 3:05 P.M. in 1983. I remember paying the ticket, but I couldn't prove it to the DMV because I don't save five-year-old canceled checks. Still, all that it took to clear my record was a drive downtown to Traffic Court, a two-hour wait in the warrant line behind a mob of misdemeanants who looked like the lineup for the Freeway Killer, and $174.

Fortunately, the DMV will take a check. In fact, they don't even bother to make sure it's good. They always know where they can find you.

Does anybody have anything good to say about the DMV? "I think that our image has improved drastically over the past three years," says Bill Gengler, DMV spokesman. "We're making very positive steps."

What positive steps? He tells me that the department now has a computer that keeps track of licenses and registration (somehow I find this more frightening than comforting), that employees go to school to "learn things like customer relations," and that the driver's test is now given in twenty-three languages.

"If they call for an appointment, then we will go and find an interpreter to give them an oral test," Gengler says. "And incidentally, we do the same thing for English-speaking people too, if they're illiterate."

How many drivers are illiterate? "We're probably talking three to five percent," he tells me. I begin to sweat. Then he says, "Just because someone can't read doesn't mean that they can't drive."

There is no escaping Car Hell.

BACKFIRE OF THE VANITIES

"**N**obody's perfect," proclaims a recent cover of *Harper's Bazaar*. Hope springs eternal, I think, eager to discover "what to wear if you are too tall, short or heavy." Ever the slave to beauty, I quell my suspicions that this is another ruse to sell me something and turn to page 82, where Aphrodite's secrets will be revealed.

Fooled again! The imperfections under consideration are those of such disfigured wretches as Paulina Porizkova (sharply defined bone structure), Kim Alexis (a thin top lip), and Cheryl Tiegs (too tall). Suddenly, I'm depressed. If these are flaws, I'm a walking disaster.

But not to worry. A beauty addict can always find some new, revolutionary beauty fix on the horizon, especially if she's willing to fork over a couple of months' salary. Women (and men) are no longer paying even lip service to the concept that beauty comes from within. They now know that beauty comes from investments in French manicures, shiatsu pedicures, herbal body wraps, custom-blended makeup in a personalized seasonal palette, twenty-five-hundred-dollar

Chanel suits, daily workouts with a personal trainer, and a few nips and tucks by a plastic surgeon.

Still, whatever you do is never enough. Recently, for example, I invested the equivalent of a week's groceries in a facial. For twenty minutes I lay sweating in a thick cloud of steam, my skin encrusted with gritty, lime-green pore cleanser. Then the cosmetician smothered me with a wet towel, covered my eyes with tea-soaked cotton, and began assaulting my cheek with a sharp instrument. Finally, I lay motionless for half an hour while an enzyme masque removed a layer of skin.

Afterward, I basked in the satisfaction that one part of my body was under beauty control—for a glorious second. Then my beauty policewoman scowled. "You really should be using our revitalizing neck cream," she warned me.

Neck cream? This was new. So far this year, people have tried to sell me eye cream, lip cream, day cream, night cream, foot cream, hand cream, and breast cream. Will ear cream be next?

"You can't win," says my sister. "You could spend twenty-four hours a day, seven days a week on your appearance, and you would still miss some critical beauty maintenance."

Laurie is right. I religiously go to the gym three times a week. Surrounded by grunting would-be Mr. Universe manqués, I lie upside down on a slant board and pump ridiculous amounts of weight with my feet. Then I ride the Life-Cycle for half an hour and finish with twenty minutes of stretching.

And I still feel as if I'm shirking. After all, there are people who go from the LifeRower to the StairMaster to the tread-mill to the Versa Climber to the free weights, and that's not even counting the classes that feature muscle conditioning with huge rubber bands, six different "impacts" of aerobics, Aerobic Slimnastics, Jazzercise, and yoga.

"I don't do gyms," scoffs Laurie, who believes that I'm

beauty-obsessed. "I don't need a personal trainer. I have a dog. I pick her up occasionally. She weighs forty-two pounds; that's as close as I get to Nautilus. I run her around the block a few times. She goes one way; I go another. It's resistance."

Sometimes, I can't believe that we were raised by the same mother. My beauty addiction began in the womb. "When I went to the hospital to have you, I wore an exquisite night-gown and a matching peignoir," my mother recalls. "And I had beautiful white mules with high heels and little bows, and of course, my hair was all fixed. I looked like I had stepped out of a magazine. I went into the labor room, and the nurse said, 'Where do you think you're going in that? It's see-through.' "

"When Mom had me, she went into labor at the Dairy Queen," Laurie says. "That's the difference."

Nevertheless, my sister recently jumped at a chance to be the model for a beauty makeover for a women's magazine. "It was a nightmare," she says. "I went in looking about as bad as I could. I rolled out of bed. I didn't brush my hair, which is not that unusual. I hadn't slept in a week. I thought I looked plenty bad enough, but they wanted to make sure that the circles under my eyes really showed, so they darkened them in for the 'before' picture."

Next, they photographed her in the same complexion-dissolving light that's usually found in department-store dress-ing rooms. As for the "after" picture: "I spent an entire day having people fuss over me so I looked perfect," Laurie laments. "I was in the beauty shop for five hours."

The bottom line? "I did find out that, with enough makeup, I could look like an anchorwoman," she says. She estimates that it would cost her three hundred dollars a month, plus an additional ten hours a week, to duplicate this look. "Of course, if I were an anchorwoman, it would be worth it," Laurie says. "And I could afford it."

Curiously, many people believe that they can't afford *not* to look like an anchorperson. More curiously, not all of these people are women. The other day, I ran into my friend Jeff at the hairdresser's. He was smocking up for a conditioning shampoo and trim. "Your looks are something you have to maintain in this society," says Jeff, who spends his working day locked in an editing room with a Moviola. "I have an advantage over people who are less good-looking, so I work to keep the advantage."

But where exactly does he draw the line? "I know guys who go to a tanning salon, and I think that's over the top," he says. "I don't get my nails done or get facials. I don't see the need. That seems more like a luxury than a requirement for beauty. If I was on vacation in a spa or a resort and that service was offered, I might indulge. But I think plastic surgery is obscene."

My friend Doug disagrees. "I'd have a face lift in a minute," he says. "If my jowls were sinking, I'd go to Beverly Hills and have it taken care of." Why? "I feel that I look better when I look younger," he says. "And when I feel better about myself, I'm more creative. I don't want to turn it into a business decision, but it's that important."

"I think I'd try just about anything," says my friend Katie, who is about to give up on her regimen of mail-order cactus moisturizers and drive to Tijuana to buy Retin-A over the counter. "I don't draw any lines. The object is to get rid of the lines." Katie does confess that she prefers to avoid anything that causes pain, unless she is knocked out.

Speaking of being knocked out . . . A few months ago, my beauty bibles reported that au courant eyes would be shadowed and lined in rich shades of purple. So I made my semiannual pilgrimage to the cosmetics counter. There a lacquered makeup artist expertly smudged my eyelids with a palette of dusty, smoky, and downright dirty plums.

"See how natural this looks," she gushed, as she coated my lashes with navy-blue mascara. "It really brings out your eyes." It also brought out my checkbook. Forty-five dollars later, clutching a small bag filled with two tiny boxes (I didn't spend enough to rate the free gift), I left the store. Shortly thereafter, I ran into a friend. "Are you and your husband getting along?" my friend asked.

"Of course," I said, widening my perfectly shadowed eyes. She seemed unconvinced. So did the next person I ran into. And the next. I couldn't understand why everyone kept asking about the state of my marriage. Then I returned home.

"Were you in an accident?" my husband asked. I shook my head. "Don't tell me you got into a fight," Duke said. I shook my head again. "Then where did you get the black eye?"

Fooled again!

BRAZEN NEW WORLD

I wish I could get rid of these vestiges of shame. They seem to be holding me back. Day after day, I see other people breeze through life unhampered by manners, promises, or common decency. And I am filled with wonder.

It's not just a matter of having a lot of nerve. These folks do outrageous things and then, if you call them on it, they're completely unabashed. They either look bewildered and shrug or they accuse you of picking on them. I never know what to say except maybe "Where do I go for lessons?"

Recently, for example, I was in my car, waiting to exit a crowded underground parking structure. Without warning, the driver in front of me put his car in reverse and rammed my bumper. The impact shook me up a little, but what really unhinged me was that this squirrelly looking guy got out of his car, cursing and shouting, "You moron, this is all your fault!"

Gosh, and I was kind of expecting him to ask if I was OK.

I politely pointed out that his car had moved and mine had not. But he just raised his voice a few more decibels. I actually felt guilty for inspecting my car for damage. Not that it did me any good to find any. I asked if he was insured. "None of your beeswax," he snapped.

What was the correct response? Liar, liar, pants on fire?

I don't know why I was staggered by his gall. Shame is not a hot commodity anymore. Secretaries declare that their boss is in a meeting while in the background you can hear him hissing, "Lose this call." Unblushing triathletes in giant jeeps park in spaces for the handicapped, claiming, "just for a few minutes." Lithe blond nymphets roller-skate in string bikinis, and if a guy so much as gapes, they spin around—offended! And then there's Hollywood.

But "dating is where the shameless really shine," insists my sister, Laurie. "People will say the most unbelievable things, and they don't even wince."

Laurie recently met an attractive man on a train going to New York. As they chatted, he revealed that he'd just graduated from college. "He told me it wasn't because he was young," she recalls, "but because he took time off from school when his father died, to help his mother with the money. I thought he was pretty noble."

So she went out with Joe College—once. "At dinner, he mentioned something about visiting his parents," Laurie continues. "I said, 'Oh, did your mother remarry?' And he said, 'Why would you think that?' I said, 'Because you told me your father was dead.' And he said, 'Oh, well, I just said that because I figured I'd have a better shot at your going out with me.'

"He didn't even feel bad when I caught him," Laurie marvels. "He was proud that the lie worked."

The Shameless are very goal-oriented. They'll do anything to get what they want. There's no favor too big for them to ask, no loan small enough for them to repay. To see them in action is to be struck dumb with fascination, wondering, *How could they possibly do that?*

"A guy I know comes to me and says, 'I've got a million

dollars to invest and I want you to draw up a portfolio,' " says Paul, a Beverly Hills stockbroker. "I spend a weekend working out long-term and short-term investments. He listens to my suggestions and doesn't say a thing."

Paul figured it was a wash. "Three months later," he says, "I bump into the guy at a party. He comes running up to me all excited and says, 'I don't know how to thank you. I took all your suggestions and gave them to my broker, and we're making a fortune.' But wait. Then this guy asks, 'You still have that box at Dodger Stadium? I could use two seats for Friday night's game.' "

Why am I surprised by such audacity? Look at our leaders. Politicians have always been shortchanged in the shame department, but lately it seems as if they've hit record lows.

When *I* break a promise, usually on some relatively minor thing like not returning someone's call the same day, I feel bad. It never occurs to me to issue, as President Bush does, a statement to tell the person that I've welshed. On the other hand, I've never promised millions and millions of people something while I was seeking the most responsible position in the country. Maybe that's the difference.

Or if I were the mayor of a nation's capital and I was videotaped in a hotel room coming on to someone other than my spouse and smoking crack, I would probably admit that I had made a mistake somewhere along the line. I'd even apologize. But the Shameless never apologize.

The other night I was driving down Melrose. I was stopped at a light when suddenly my car was rear-ended—hard. As soon as I could breathe again, I pulled over. A woman wanted by the fashion police for the abuse of bicycle pants got out of the car and lambasted me for making her late for dinner. "There's nothing wrong with your car," she howled. I wanted to grab my neck, cry whiplash, and call out my mad-dog attorney.

I wish I could get rid of these vestiges of shame.

LET'S CALL THE
WHOLE THING OFF

Take my telephone—please. The love affair that began when I got a powder-blue Princess phone for my sixteenth birthday is on the rocks. After spending the happiest years of my life hand in hand with my receiver, blissfully gabbing with friends and, for that matter, strangers, I want to call the whole thing off. My phone and I are still living together, but it's just not the same.

"You can't live in L.A. and hate your phone," says Wendy, who is madly in love with hers. "That's like living in New York and hating the bus."

I really do want to save our relationship. But my phone won't give me any space. Every time I turn around, I am urged to commit to yet another telecommunications breakthrough that promises to keep me perpetually plugged in— car phones, picture phones, mobile phones, fax machines, pocket pagers. When will someone sell me *privacy*?

Still, I'm afraid to make a break. All my friends will side with my phone. "I can't wait until they invent a wrist phone," says Wendy, who is calling from her bathtub. "I don't wear a watch, but I'd wear a phone. Just imagine—wherever I go, my number would go too. It might be a little annoying when I'm with people and I'm talking to my hand, but still, I think it would be great."

Sounds like hell to me. My phone used to be Mr. Nice Guy, but lately he's developed a cruel streak. Once, I was gently invited to reach out and touch someone. Now, I'm threatened with warnings about what will happen to my life, my family, and my career if I refuse to join the interconnection revolution.

I switch on the television. Two women executives are sipping white-wine spritzers. One is gloating over the other's failure to get a big promotion because she chose an inferior office-communications system. The gloater has the inner smile that comes with the right equipment. Even the Yellow Pages have become menacing and guilt-inducing. "I tried to let you know, but there was no answer," says the pitch for call-forwarding thoughtfully repeated every few pages, along with equally shame- or fear-provoking plugs for three-way-calling, speed-dialing, and call-waiting.

My once-obliging phone has become far too demanding. Guests arrive at my house for dinner and, instead of bringing flowers or wine, they are accompanied by a slew of forwarded phone calls. Just when it seems like old times and I'm having a heart-to-heart with a friend, the moment is spoiled by a call-waiting beep. "How are you?" has been officially replaced with "Can I put you on hold?"

But I shouldn't be offended. "People just can't stand unanswered questions," explains Chaytor D. Mason, a USC associate professor of human factors, a field that deals with the psychological aspects of the work environment. When you know there's a call waiting, "your interest and fear grow magnificently second by second," Mason says. "No matter who you're talking to, you're going to put them on hold." And is there a better caller on line number 2? No, says Mason: "You invariably get a guy trying to sell you gold shares."

I could use gold shares. My formerly humble telephone has developed expensive tastes. I long ago gave up trying to understand the luxuriant profusion of surcharges on my phone bill. And those costs don't even include the phones.

Recently my bedroom extension died. I went to the phone mart to buy an inexpensive red Trimline phone without a memory dialer, intercom, clock radio, answering machine, or coffee maker. I would have had better luck finding a pair of tin cans with a string.

However, I did discover that for the right price (high!) I could own a work of telephone art: a football helmet, a cabin cruiser (complete with foghorn ringer), a grand piano, a pair of lips, a red spike-heeled shoe, a trout, Mickey Mouse, a dozing Garfield (who opens his eyes when you pick up the receiver), and Quacky, a mallard decoy.

"He's one of our most popular models," exclaimed the salesman. "Instead of ringing, he quacks." If anything quacked at me at seven in the morning, I'd shoot it. The salesman then tried to sell me on the virtues of a mobile phone: "You can make a call from the middle of a field."

What am I supposed to say? "Hi, Mom, I'm in the middle of a field, so I thought I'd give you a ring. Whoops, gotta go, the cow has to call her broker." Still, "people are now willing to spend thousands of dollars to maintain a sense of control over the world," says USC's Mason. "As far as they're concerned, the more information per second, the better."

As far as I'm concerned, my phone is trying to change me into a control freak. And I'm not the only one who feels the pressure. Today, even gardeners have beepers. What kind of crisis do they need to respond to—a sudden aphid infestation? Mason explains: "A lot of people who aren't anybody will buy a car phone or a beeper just to feel important. It's the same sense of control people feel when they strap on a thirty-eight. They aren't planning to kill anybody, but they feel more powerful."

I refuse to get in a power struggle with my telephone. I opt for a temporary separation. I turn off my ringer and let my machine take my calls. And what do I miss? Not a three-picture deal at Columbia. An automatic voice trying to sell me aluminum siding. A heavy breather who leaves an obscene message. Three business associates I called months ago who now merrily announce that we are playing telephone tag. And a couple of calls from my friend Monica, who's been too busy to get together for weeks.

Amazingly, she knocks on my door the following morning. "Why didn't you call me back?" she wails. A thousand excuses cross my mind: I left town without my answering-machine remote control. Her line was busy, or, better still, there was no answer. I was in a dugout canoe going up the Amazon. Unfortunately, state-of-the-art phone technology negates all of these rationalizations.

"Maybe your machine is broken. Or you accidentally called my computer's line," suggests Monica, who wants to give me the benefit of the doubt.

I don't deserve it. I deliberately broke the first commandment of our accessibility-obsessed society: Thou Shalt Not Miss a Call. "I had a fight with my telephone," I confess.

"Sounds serious," says Monica. "Why don't we talk about it over lunch?"

We are halfway out the door when my phone rings. I lunge for the receiver like one of Pavlov's dogs. "Wait a second," I tell Monica. "I've got to take this call."

THE NOUVEAU POOR

"**P**overty stinks," Bette exclaims when we meet at a faux-Nantucket seafood house in Santa Monica. Is she comparing herself with illegal aliens or the Rockefellers, I wonder. She is wearing a three-hundred-dollar orange and purple quilted satin jacket over a four-hundred-dollar crushed velvet skirt.

"You look like a million dollars," I point out, leaning over the bulkhead of the lifeboat-cocktail table.

"I only made eight hundred dollars last month," Bette continues. "I got so depressed I went shopping. And I just happened to strike up a conversation with a shopkeeper who just happened to need someone to shoot a catalogue. She can't pay me in cash, just clothes. Good, huh?"

"Does your landlord accept designer sportswear?"

Bette reveals that her boyfriend liked the new outfits so much he invited her to share his house rent free. "You'd be surprised how much money you save wearing expensive clothes."

I'd be shocked. A few years ago I worked in advertising. In addition to an ability to tap-dance verbally around product defects, the job required high credit limits at Ann Taylor, Saks Fifth Avenue, and Neiman Marcus.

"How can you save money on clothes you have to take to the dry cleaners?" I ask. (What do dry cleaners actually do besides charge fifty dollars for wrapping a white linen suit in a plastic bag in such a way that you can't see the note that reads, "This stain could not be removed"?)

"Nothing succeeds like the appearance of success," she giggles. Then the waiter arrives with the bill. She starts biting her French manicured nails. "Do you have any money?" Bette asks nervously, passing me the five-dollar check. "I'm broke."

Let economists insist that we are not in a recession and note that unemployment is at an all-time low. It still seems that half my friends are nouveau poor. Some lost important jobs; some lost the desire to have important jobs; some lost money in the stock market; some just moved to New York. But all these ambitious, well-educated, once well-heeled professionals are clinging to a lifestyle they no longer have the means to support.

These arrivistes into arrears economize by letting their hundred-dollar highlights grow out, dropping the cleaning service, and canceling expensive health-club memberships. (Would aerobic walking be in vogue if people could still afford Jazzercise?) In Los Angeles, Volvo station wagons, turbo Saabs, even Benz convertibles are going unwashed— unsimonized!—and can be observed skulking outside Pioneer Bakery's discount outlet. Pedigreed pugs, salukis, great Pyrenees, and their sheepish owners line up in city parks for cut-rate vaccinations.

Happily, though, the shabby genteel are developing new coping skills. For example, Lisa, formerly middle-class, lowered the cost of living by becoming a devotee of the fine arts. "If you work as a broker you need two-hundred-dollar shoes and a Brooks Brothers suit," she informed me. "But as an artist you have credibility wearing five-dollar dresses from the

Salvation Army, beat-up sneakers, old jeans, or all black so everything matches."

Further details of la vie bohème, 1988: "Last night, I went to the City of Angels Brewery. You should see this place. It's architecturally divine, and for seventy-five cents I got a taster of beer and met the hippest people. Tomata du Plenty was there and Tequila Mockingbird. Then I rolled right along to a series of art openings, all of which served free food and wine. You should come with me sometime."

"I can't handle Tequila. Let's go to the Getty."

"Perfect," Lisa says. "For a buck fifty we can see two thousand years of beauty."

Wendy, on the other hand, earnestly insists she's not nouveau poor, she's one of the landed poor. For years she's been living in an apartment that rents for $550 a month on an income of about $1,000 a month. The apartment, a hundred feet from the beach, is easily worth more than half of her income (if only for the sublet value when she travels). "Banana Republic's having a sale," she reports when I catch her roller-skating down the boardwalk to a beachfront café for her morning croissant.

"Did you get anything?"

"I got jealous."

Of course Wendy, an actress turned journalist, has the kind of looks that can make a horse blanket and a pair of boots from army surplus look like something out of a Ralph Lauren ad. She stays trim on a low-cost diet of croissants and popcorn. "I don't want to be rich," Wendy says, "because I can never be rich enough to make a difference."

But most of the déclassé tighten their fraying Judith Leiber belts and wish for the good old days when it didn't matter how much Maud Frizon shoes, movie tickets, or a six-pack of Diet Coke cost. Like the newly sober, they regard people who still have what they do not with disdainful suspicion. "Everything that I really want becomes as meaningless as a gold swizzle stick," says Mary, a writer riding the crest of a slump.

Buoyed by an inherent sense of entitlement, they cling to the hope that insolvency is just a temporary setback.

Comforted by artifacts from a former life—the compact-disc player, the sterling flatware for twelve that you can't sell for three hundred dollars but you can insure for three thousand—the nouveau poor wait for their ships to come in again. This sets them apart from the real poor, who have reason to believe their ships have sunk.

Now if you'll excuse me, I have to get down to the dock.

OFF THE INSIDE TRACK

Where does this *loop* everyone keeps talking about come from? It reminds me of those mysterious circles from outer space that television stations short of news are now finding in cornfields. "They form at night when nobody is looking," an investigative reporter recently explained solemnly on camera.

Why not? Every morning I read the newspaper and learn the latest high-level loop scoop. James Baker is in the loop. General Dugan got kicked out of the loop for leaking loop poop. President Bush is always in the loop except when the loop is doing something unfortunate, like writing blank checks to S&L operators, at which point he is temporarily unlooped.

As for me, my answering machine just has messages from my dry cleaner, copy editor, and grandmother, none of whom were seeking my opinion about a major offensive in Saudi Arabia. The cleaner did want to know if I'd assume responsibility for laundering an embroidered white blouse. Does that make me a player?

Of course, the loop is a lot bigger than the power circle in

Washington. It's bigger than the power circles in every major city combined. The loop has to be at least the size of the Equator. Because almost everybody wants to be in it.

"I worship the loop," says my sister, Laurie, a publicist who eats, sleeps, and breathes inside information. "The loop is power. It's knowing what's going to be on the front page of *The New York Times* two days before it happens. It's getting a jump on things." She puts me on hold for the fourteenth time in our phone conversation. "This might be a call that puts me even further into the loop," she explains.

Gosh, and last night I had yet another humiliating out-of-the-loop experience. I was at a screening, the film was late in starting, and a woman behind me was getting frantic. "If this doesn't begin soon, I'll miss the Steven Wright special," she complained.

Forgive me, Steven Wright, but I didn't know who you were. I go to bed early, so I'm out of talk-show loops. I'm not hooked up, so I'm out of the cable loop. I actually had to utter "Steven Who?"—a cardinal sin in the Age of Information.

"It's tough to be in the loop when you're a free-lancer," Laurie says smugly. "You're like the little house on the prairie."

I think it's better that way. Many people spend an awful lot of energy playing a cutthroat version of "Here We Go Loop de Loo"—getting in the loop, staying in the loop, bumping another person out of the loop. Sure, the rewards can be amazing. But no matter how good you get at the game, there's always someone more on top of it than you.

"The loop is a circular argument that keeps what goes around from coming back around," David says.

"Wondering if you're out of the loop is a big pastime in corporate America," says Doug, who did hard time in an advertising agency. He tells me an "absolutely true story" about a Paranoid Group Head (P.G.H.) who became loop-obsessed.

"The president of the agency sends out a memo to a bunch

of people," he recalls. "And in the distribution list some people have asterisks next to their name. At the bottom it says, asterisk, 'group head.' Only P.G.H. doesn't have an asterisk. And he panics. He's sure he's falling down on the job. He walks around the office asking everyone what we think having no asterisk means. We say it's probably nothing, but if he really has a problem he should ask the president.

"Finally the paranoia is too much for him. So he asks. And the president plays it perfectly. He says, 'It's just a mistake.' Now P.G.H. knows he's out of the loop. If you have to ask, you are."

Maybe the loop is like a computer virus that keeps making copies of itself until it fills up the whole memory. There must be zillions of loops: the Literary Loop, the Ex-Hippie Loop, the Society Loop, the Industry Loop, the Hairdresser Loop, the Fitness Loop, the Art Loop—all the way down to the In-law Loop. Pretty soon we're going to run out of loop-holes.

"If you're trying to be in the loop, you suffer anxiety all the time," says Marjorie, who is super-connected. "Anything I see that leaves me out seems to be worth penetrating." Well, almost anything. She does admit that the Private School Loop seems to be more of a noose.

"I don't have a lot of time to devote to working for my son's school," Marjorie says. "All the parents participate in certain activities. And if you're not in the loop, you go there and drift around doing odd jobs and see that everyone is friends except you. It's like re-creating your own school years. Still, if I went to all the meetings that would get me in that loop, I'd never have time to see my kid."

Where does the loop come from?

Why should I tell you?

CINEMATICALLY CORRECT

"I'm Batman," said Laurie when she called last month from New York—or should I say Gotham City? This way lies madness, I thought nervously. And that way lies the movies.

"I don't have a lunch box or underwear or anything with a bat on it," my sister assured me. "But I do walk around saying, 'I'm Batman.' I love the way he says that in the movie. And it's a really great icebreaker at parties."

I'll bet. Lately, it seems as if there's no life outside of the movie theater. People used to talk about cheating on their diets, or who was sleeping with whom, or sports or politics. But now, every conversation seems to revolve around films and videos.

"This is the hottest year in Hollywood since television came along and ended the first great epic of movie-going," says *Times* film writer Jack Mathews. "Hits are generating hits." Somehow, I suspect that peer pressure is generating the hits. But Mathews suggests that it's a matter of convenience. "There are now thousands of multiplexes in malls," he says. "People go to see something that's hot. They're there and they can't get in, so they go see something else."

Anything else. Duke and I sat through *Great Balls of Fire,*
Ghostbusters II, Indiana Jones and the Last Crusade, and *Star Trek*
V before we finally drove all the way to Monterey Park to
hear the magic words "I'm Batman."

"It's tacky to admit that you've seen anything with a
Roman numeral in the title," my sister warned me. "Or
anything with Sly Stallone. Or *Uncle Buck.*"

But whatever you see, you can never see enough. There's
no keeping up with the movies these days. Just when you
think you've seen them all, there's a fresh crop of new releases
that you must see, right away, whether you really want to or
not. If you don't go the first week it opens, people are on to
the next film.

"You're not hip until you've seen certain movies," said
Laurie, who was on her way to see *sex, lies and videotape.* "I
can't function in an office setting without having seen it."

I know how she feels. My friends started raving about
When Harry Met Sally . . . weeks before it was even released.
"You've got to go to a screening," they insisted. I was sort of
embarrassed to admit that I wasn't on any screening lists—the
ultimate humiliation in Los Angeles—but I promised to see
the film as soon as it opened.

This was easier said than done. First, I had to persuade my
husband to go. Whereas I have a weakness for romantic
comedies, Duke prefers obscure, badly subtitled foreign films
in which men and women with mustaches suffer without
redemption, preferably in a bleak industrial city with no
name. After a spirited negotiation, I agreed to sit through
Little Vera and Duke agreed to sit through *When Harry Met*
Sally . . .

That left us with the problem of finding a seat. So desperate
was I to see this movie and thus be able to hold my own at
a dinner party, we actually went to Westwood on the weekend (which is as close as you come to going to hell). The good
news: We found a parking space. The bad news: The line for
the movie seemed to go from the theater to our parking

space, which was six blocks away. And the movie was sold out.

In fact, the movie was sold out the next two times we tried to see it, even though we showed up an hour early. Not only did we spend twice as much time outside the theater as in, but by the time I finally saw Billy Crystal and Meg Ryan, I had already heard almost every line that came out of their mouths. Still, I'm glad I saw it. Now I know what those strange noises coming from the next booth in the deli are. And my social purse has some small change. "Having seen a movie is like a social coin," explains Carlfred Broderick, chairman of the sociology department at USC. "The more you see, the more currency you have. In fact, I've rarely heard anybody say, when asked, that 'we didn't see that.' They may have lied. But it's just not the thing to admit."

Of course you don't admit it. People judge you by your ticket stubs. My sister, for example, informed me that it was "politically incorrect" to see *Batman* before I saw *Do the Right Thing*. "Do you want people to think that you care more about a man in a mask than racial tension in Brooklyn?" asked Laurie.

Not only do you have to see the right movie, you've got to have the right opinion of the movie. "There are films like *Dead Poets Society,* which you're supposed to love," says my friend Josh. "I didn't. But it's not worth it to force the issue. If someone says they adored *Parenthood,* do you say, 'piece of garbage'? They look at you like you're not a very nice person. They wonder whether you hate kids. On the other hand, try to love *Weekend at Bernie's*. They'll probably never let you sit in Morton's again."

Paradoxically, movies are supposed to be a "safe" topic of conversation. "Movies are the equivalent of 'Nice day today' or 'Boy, is it hot,' " says USC psychology professor Jerald Jellison. "It's a subject guaranteed not to offend a lot of people. And it's something that everyone knows something about. We may not know the neighbors up the street. But movies are something that are widely shared."

By adults and children alike. "I usually go to a movie if it's a really good movie and my mom says I can," says my friend Sam, who's eight, "though we usually only go about three or four times a week." But not to worry. Whatever Sam can't see, his friends see for him. "We tell each other parts of movies," he explains. "Like, there's a part of *Jason Takes Manhattan* where a really famous boxer is hitting the killer. And the boxer's head goes flying off. That's one my friend Megyn shared with me."

I'm looking for a friend to share a movie with me. "You've got to see *The Adventures of Milo and Otis*," said my sister. But at this point, I still hadn't seen *The Abyss* or *Cookie* or *Casualties of War*. "It's about a pug and a kitten," Laurie said about *Milo and Otis*. She knows that I consider the pug to be the crown of creation.

I would do anything to see a movie with a pug star. Well, almost anything. "I'll see the pug movie if you see *The Burmese Harp*," said my husband. I learn that this is the story of a group of Japanese stragglers in Burma during World War II who are going slowly mad. "The cannibalism scenes aren't that graphic," Duke said. "What do you think?"

"I'm Batman," I replied.

PRICED TO KILL

Where can I get the price gauge in my brain recalibrated? It used to be that I'd see an item, a mystic number would appear before my eyes, and I'd know how much the item cost. And usually I'd be pretty close, unless it was something wildly unpredictable, like auto parts. But lately my mystic number bears little resemblance to reality.

Maybe it's inflation or just a stab of social conscience. But I'm in a constant state of sticker shock. I make a simple cash transaction, like buying a small Diet Coke at the octoplex, and the cashier says something incredible: "That will be three seventy-five, plus tax." And all I can do is shake my head and wonder: Is that in American dollars?

Recently, while I was shopping, a pair of canary-yellow silk suspenders patterned with tiny circus strong men caught my eye. How strange, I thought, but I knew my husband would love them. I figured they'd set me back fifty dollars, tops.

"It's a limited edition," the clerk said, unlocking the glass case. It had never struck me that braces were a collectible, but she quoted me a three-figure sum that I recall as my monthly rent on a one-bedroom apartment not that long ago.

What could I possibly say?—except maybe: Hey, I'll take eight pairs.

I've never been accused of being cheap, or even thrifty, unlike my husband, who views any purchase over two digits as a catastrophe. Still, for the price of those suspenders, I could buy two hand-painted silk ties to hold up Duke's pants, put the ties on a plane to Phoenix, and have cash left for dinner. But friends say that it doesn't pay to think that way in these days of the twenty-five-cent gum ball.

"What about vitamins? What about bottled water?" asks Monica, who balks "on moral and ethical grounds" at paying two dollars for six ounces of Evian. "In order to be healthy, you've got to be rich. What about doctors' bills?"

Please spare me. Six months ago, I broke my foot. Duke took me to an emergency room. If it had been *The Price Is Right,* a Vanna White clone would've gestured through the curtained examining room, while an announcer shrieked the details:

"Twelve exquisite ice cubes for the reusable ice pack, a handsome leg splint, a complete foot X ray, a precision pair of adjustable aluminum crutches, and an authorized signature on a hospital release form by an unseen physician who graduated from God-knows-where in the Caribbean. This showcase package can be yours—if the price is right!"

I bid two hundred fifty dollars. But when I got the bill, I heard Bob Barker's voice booming in my head, "And the retail value is seven hundred sixty-two dollars!"

Why was I surprised? Nowadays, the price is never right. Even a high salary can't protect you, though it certainly doesn't hurt. Sticker shock is all relative.

Claire, for example, just bought a house. "I complained to the electrician about having to replace all the wiring," she says, "and he asked, 'Well, what do you expect for a quarter of a million dollars?'"

Actually, with home improvements, it's not sticker shock—it's sticker cardiac arrest. Take the time Duke and I decided to do something about our yard. Enter Fran, a talented landscape architect with whom I spent a delightful hour walking around the neighborhood, pointing out my favorite flowers and trees. Fran used enchanting words such as *arboretum* and *grove* until I was willing to fork over everything we had—well, up to one thousand dollars.

"A complete landscape goes for between fifteen thousand and seventy-five thousand dollars," she said. I began to hyperventilate.

"What's she going to plant," Duke asked later, "the Tree of Life?" Normally, with sticker shock, even if I had the money, I couldn't justify spending it. But I'm still dreaming about that grove.

Marjorie suggests I quit thinking about prices. "I don't know what anything is supposed to cost anymore," she says, "because nothing is consistent. And that's how they get away with it.

"A chocolate-chip cookie is now a dollar fifty," Marjorie says. "There's probably a whole generation of people who don't know that it isn't supposed to cost that. To them, it's just what a cookie costs. It's like Weimar Germany. Next year, we'll have a wheelbarrow to go out and buy twenty-six-thousand-dollar cookies."

But it's not just a matter of prices being high; some prices seem ridiculously low. Durable items such as a toaster oven, a blow dryer, or a computer modem are cheaper than a teeny bottle of moisturizer. Of course, try to get these appliances fixed—then acute sticker shock sets in.

Happily, there is a cure. "Once you've lived in New York, it's almost impossible to ever suffer sticker shock again," says Laurie, who just moved to Chicago from Manhattan. "Once you pay a hundred dollars for a haircut, it completely desensitizes you."

Hmmm . . . New York is cheap compared to Tokyo. Maybe I should take a trip. By the time I get home, my grove might seem like a real bargain.

A CUSTOMARY CHRISTMAS

Standing around the piano singing Christmas carols? Trimming the tree with popcorn garlands? Eggnog? Fruitcake? Big family dinner? Let's get real.

I'm sure that lots of folks revel in these seasonal traditions. I don't know how many, but I can guesstimate from the zillions of catalogues hawking red-velvet dresses, honey-baked hams, and table settings decked with holly. Still, for many of us the holidays are marked by other rituals—the kind you never see on a greeting card or the Care Bears' Christmas special.

"One of our holiday traditions is going to Toys 'Я' Us and having a nervous breakdown," my friend Marjorie says. "It's so crowded, people actually crash their carts. You never go until it's too late, and you're going for the thing they ran out of the day before. It's Hell 'Я' Us."

I wouldn't know. From Thanksgiving to New Year's, I avoid any store bigger than my living room. I can't feel goodwill to men if I'm being attacked by a swarm of harpies spraying bad perfume.

Still, friends tell me that going to the mall can be an

important holiday ritual. "Fred hates to pick out my presents," Claire says. "So a couple of days before Christmas, when the stores are packed with people and there's not much left, he takes me on a forced march and asks what I want. Then he has me turn my back while he charges it and hands me the package to carry home."

The media would have us believe that holiday customs are delightful and pleasant, all play and very little work. But many Christmas activities seem designed to maximize stress. Who could possibly remain cheery after cutting out and baking fifteen dozen sugar cookies or outlining a two-story house in twinkling colored lights (and that's after you untangle the cords)?

Actually, anything you do in December is difficult. "I don't celebrate Christmas," says Katie, who is Jewish. "I send cards, and that's basically it. But every year I search high and low to find a general card that's right for every religion. And then I have to find Hanukkah cards for my family. And then, if it's for a mixed marriage, I have to find something in between."

You can drive yourself crazy trying to please everybody. Or just drive.

"Both Elise's family and my family are freeway-close," Rusty says. "And my parents are divorced, plus we have two sets of living grandparents, not to mention aunts and uncles. So that's three or four houses we have to visit and two or three others that aren't mandatory, but we'd lose a lot of Brownie points if we didn't stop by. Every November, we start this informal dickering where we kind of strike deals."

Maybe he should consider getting an agent. "For ten years, we've had an asphalt Christmas," he says. "We've done stuff like drive to Riverside for a Christmas Eve party, open presents, drive to Palos Verdes, spend the night, open more presents, see the cousins in Huntington Beach, and then drive to Thousand Oaks for Christmas dinner. Every year we say we should get on a plane and go to Mexico."

I say go for it, but you can't go by me. My most sacred holiday ritual is to leave town. This is a legacy from my Jewish father, who found it less stressful to take three kids on vacation than to explain why we couldn't have a tree. I grew up convinced that there was no such thing as Santa because if there was, I would have seen him Christmas Eve from the window of the plane.

Luckily Duke doesn't mind giving up his cherished holiday tradition—going to the octoplex, spending the day switching theaters. "I've spent several happy Christmases doing that," Duke informs me. But I prefer a total escape from holiday reality.

My sister understands. "Christmas is the time to fight," she says. "In the stores, people are fighting about how much to spend on Aunt Myrtle. At home, they're fighting about who's going to put the toys together, who's going to wrap the presents. I've even yelled at people because they don't have enough Christmas spirit."

Funny, every December Duke and I have the same argument: What time should we leave for the airport? "The airlines just tell you to be there early to express their control," he says. But I hate to feel rushed.

So I have developed another tradition—I lie about our departure time. Last year, Duke thought our flight to Bali left at eight P.M. (and mind you, we didn't have seat assignments yet). He came home from work around seven-fifteen, blithely finished packing, and then, on the way to the airport, stopped at the bank to get some money. "Admit it," he said, when we finally arrived at LAX and found the usual Christmas crush. "The plane leaves at nine, right?"

"Wrong," I smiled. "It leaves at ten."

"I guess I underestimated you, honey," Duke said. He doesn't know it, but this year he's going to underestimate me again. So I'm going to have a happy holiday. And I hope you do, too. Any way you celebrate.

THE DAY ONLY AN
ACCOUNTANT COULD LOVE

I knew I was in trouble when I walked into the office and saw the framed photograph of his Porsche Cabriolet Carrera. Joel, my longtime CPA, had recently moved from an unpretentious office over a health spa to a power suite in a high-rise glass cube. I was somewhat comforted to see that the walls were still festooned with perma-plaques and he hadn't thrown away his "Accountants Do It with Numbers" coffee mug. But once-chubby Joel, now whippet-thin thanks to Jenny Craig, had clearly become A Player.

I sat nervously chewing my cuticles as he scrutinized my 1099 forms. "I can't believe you get paid this little for writing articles," he said, as his fingers beat a rapid tattoo on his calculator keys. "I don't mean to be derogatory or anything," Joel added hastily. "But this is subexistence."

I realize that very few people leave their accountant's office feeling cheerful. But I began to wonder why the yearly confrontation is so unpleasant. In all fairness, I hired Joel for his financial skills, not his diplomacy. As my sister put it later when I called, crestfallen: "You want sensitive, see a psychiatrist."

Not that Laurie is fond of the priests of the Ides of April either. "They terrify me," she said. "They look incredulous, like, how could you make such stupid investments? 'You didn't save the receipts?' You're back to being six in the principal's office."

Actually, it's worse. Going to the accountant is like the Day of Judgment. No matter how scrupulously I prepare, I'm doomed. There's always some oversight—you can't be too rich or too organized—and the accountant, the living manifestation of a guilty conscience, is more than happy to point it out. And not only must I pay him to make me feel inadequate, I must pay taxes, too.

Money is a sensitive topic of conversation. It's tricky enough to broach with one's spouse without getting into a meltdown argument, let alone a comparative stranger who boils every trauma in life into a deductible or nondeductible sum. Besides, "People don't go into accounting because they have great people skills," my sister noted.

But come April, there you are, spilling your guts to robo-CPA. "You'd almost rather have them watch you have sex than go through your finances," said my friend Monica. "They know how many times you've been divorced. They know your medical operations. 'What's this bill for a sex change? Oh, we can add that in all right.'"

Are we all being phobic? I called the California Society of Certified Public Accountants and gleaned this ray of hope. "Accounting does take a lot of good interpersonal skills," said spokeswoman Jane Herzog. "And one of the movements in the profession is away from the death-side manner toward people-oriented managerial skills that in the past weren't necessarily required."

"Who said that?" scoffed Joel, my CPA, when I called to see if he was up to speed. "It's propaganda. What they really have seminars on are things like 'How to Deal with the Stress of the Tax Season.'" What's stressful about accounting? "The client who brings in the shoe bag and is slow to pay."

Actually, I would find it a strain to be the person everyone blames for their financial mishaps. Though I suspect accountants make so much money because people want to put the onus on somebody else.

Joel assured me that he has plenty of people skills. "I can read the body language," he said. "The squirming in the chair, the fidgeting, and when they get the number and it's not the number they're expecting, they go nuts. It's a traumatic experience. I offer people alcohol to ease their pain."

Speaking of pain, Joel was surprised to hear I was hurt by his crack about my subexistence income. "I think we have a good enough working relationship for me to give you a little motivation," he said. "Otherwise, I might have said it afterward, but not to your face."

I had to give him credit for honesty. And he was very helpful. He suggested that I increase my income by filling a serious void on TV. "There are no sitcoms about accountants," Joel complained. "Why don't you write *L.A. CPA*? It could be like *L.A. Law*. I could be the Arnie Becker character."

I was imagining a television lineup filled with shows like *CPA Dad, Spread Sheet,* and *Police Accountant* when Monica called. Her husband has found a way to factor all human emotion, judgment, and involvement out of taxes. "Our return is being done by MacInTax," she said smugly.

There's only one thing more frightening than going to the accountant: going to an IRS audit with a floppy disk by my side.

FUR SURE

I've made a politically incorrect decision. And it's all my mother's fault.

A couple of months ago I needed surgery. The day before I went to the hospital, Mom arrived from New York. My husband and I picked her up at the airport. "Wait until you see what I brought you," she whispered excitedly as Duke strained to hoist her bag into the trunk of the car.

I expected something frivolous. Mom believes that the best way to cope with adversity is to improve your appearance— or as she puts it, "the worse the operation, the nicer the peignoir." She'd already Federal Expressed me a trousseau's worth of lingerie and enough cosmetics, skin elixirs, and hair potions to stock a small drugstore. Still, I was astonished when she unfurled a large fuzzy bundle that looked like Smokey the Bear. "It's a fur coat!" I exclaimed.

"A ranch mink," she said proudly, helping me into an elegant full-length coat with vintage rhinestone buttons. "I knew it would cheer you up."

I wanted to be revolted, but I found myself stroking the

sleeves. When I put it on, I felt uncharacteristically glamorous, like I was back in 1940 and I was headed someplace fantastic—El Morocco or the Copacabana—anywhere but UCLA Medical Center. Suddenly my fear of not coming out of anesthesia the following day dissipated: I had to live to wear the coat.

"Just what you need in Southern California," Duke said, rolling his eyes.

I ignored him. I'd secretly coveted a fur since last winter when I went to New York on business and got caught in a snowstorm with only a trench coat for insulation. There were so many pelt-garbed women sauntering down Madison Avenue it looked like the teddy bears' picnic. Even my editor friend Margot, not an uncaring person, wore a three-quarter-length mink with pride. "It's the only thing that's ever kept me warm," she said. "I basically decided if someone messes with it, I'll rip their heart out."

It wasn't the sort of thing I would ever buy for myself. And Duke would be more likely to buy me a space shuttle. But I was pleased to accept it as a gift of love from my mother, and I thanked her profusely. "You really shouldn't have," I added, pro forma.

"Oh, I didn't buy it," Mom said, explaining that it originally belonged to an elderly relative who was suffering from severe Alzheimer's. As my mother put it: "She doesn't know her name. She'll never miss the coat."

I forgot about the coat too, for a couple of weeks, until I was home from the hospital. Then I showed it to my sister, who was visiting from Chicago. "I'd never wear a fur," Laurie said. "There's something about them that gives me the creeps. I have this nightmare the animals are going to come alive and kill me."

What could I say? I don't eat meat or chicken. I don't buy makeup that's tested on bunnies. I wouldn't dream of wearing a seal or a leopard, or a cute cuddly Disney creature or an endangered species. But I don't have much sympathy for

minks, which I believe are members of the Fashion Phylum—
an unheralded classification of the animal kingdom that includes oysters, snakes, alligators, and other beasties that look
better on your body than on the ground.

"Minks are mean, voracious, unpleasant little animals,"
Duke conceded. "The parts that aren't fur are mostly teeth."

"My friend Caroline has a mink coat," Laurie said. "I call
it Roger. I'll call yours Max."

I decided to put Max and my social conscience in cold
storage for the summer. Duke dropped it off at Leonore's,
a fur outlet in Beverly Hills. He came home with a receipt
and a disturbed look on his face. "All those generations of
poor trapped creatures giving their all just to make a woman
happy," he said.

"You mean the animals?" I asked.

"No, the husbands," he replied. "The poor males got
caught doing something they shouldn't have and bought the
coats to make amends."

The next day Leonore called and suggested I have the coat
cleaned. She invited me to come in and try it on, in case it
needed repairs. I wasn't sure how committed I was to my
mink, but I figured it couldn't hurt to pay her a call.

The small shop had barred doors, like a cage at the zoo, and
inside Leonore, a vivacious Angela Lansbury lookalike, was
tending a herd of minks, nutria, lynxes, sables, muskrats, and
broadtail fashioned into stoles, shawls, capes, jackets, boleros,
strollers, throws, scarves, hats, muffs, and fur-lined raincoats.
I expected the air to be thick with bad karma, but instead it
was buzzing with the elated vibrations of satisfied customers,
most of whom had emblazoned their names or initials in the
various wraps.

"It's a very happy time for women when they come in
here," said Leonore, whose family has been in the fur business
for sixty years. Eight years ago she started selling used coats
out of her house, and today she has over 250 items ranging
in price from fifty dollars for a fur neck piece to six thousand

dollars for a black willow mink coat. Ninety-eight percent of her customers are women, who buy or rent the coats as rewards for themselves. "Furs are luxurious, they're beautiful, they make a woman feel pampered," she explained.

Sure enough, when she helped me on with my coat, I was filled with delight. Leonore beamed with approval. "The only thing I'd do is update the sleeves and put in larger shoulders so you can move around," she said. To give me a better idea of what she was talking about, she brought out a similarly styled sheared black muskrat ("mink's first cousin") with large yellow Bakelite buttons. "Try this."

I was mortified to discover that I liked that coat too. In rapid succession, Leonore wrapped me in a Russian broadtail jacket, a white mink stole, and a silver fox bolero. I didn't start to get squeamish until she draped a handmade basket-woven mink shawl with a familiar-looking fringe over my shoulders and explained "when they make coats they have lots of tails left over, so they use them for a fringe." I drew the line at a fox boa with a feral, alert head and rhinestone eyes.

Still, I decided it couldn't hurt to get the sleeves on my coat remodeled. Leonore assured me that contrary to what certain friends had told me, the minks weren't skinned alive. "Of course not," she said. "That would hurt the fur. They don't feel a thing. They just go to sleep."

When I got home, my sister, Laurie, called and announced she was getting married in Chicago this winter. I figured it would be a good opportunity to wear my coat. "On Michigan Avenue you see furs on everyone," she said. "No one thinks twice and no one throws paint. The paint would probably freeze."

Just then, Sophie, my pug dog, came bounding up to greet me. I eyed her shiny coat and hoped that nobody out there was wearing a pug jacket. "I won't give you a hard time if you bring the coat," Laurie promised.

I wonder if I'll have the nerve.

part 5

GUIDED BY MY MANTRA, "RUN AWAY"

A VIEW LIKE
YOU GET FROM GOD'S LAP

If it's Tuesday, it must be Zermatt, I decide as I awake between clean, crisp Swiss linen to a blast of clean, crisp Swiss air. I stagger from my bed and close the window on yet another picture-postcard view. It's too early to admire the scenery—I've been admiring Swiss scenery for a week now, and the one thing I've learned is to pace the oohs and ahhs so I don't get bored.

Today is the fifth day of my Barnett Special Swiss Alpine Tour, an adventure foisted upon me by my travel agent, who feared I might need company after ten days alone in Italy. Actually, a single woman is never alone in Italy; there is always a handsome man in expensive shoes willing to ply you with Campari. But since I had planned to just wander the Alps smelling edelweiss, it didn't seem like a bad idea to wander in style. My only trepidation was that I'd be wandering in style with a Golden Age tour from Miami, but the travel agent swore this would not be the case.

And he was right. The seventy-year-olds are from South America. None of them speak English, so I am spared the inevitable hype about their grandsons, but unless I count Ursula, the super-organized tour guide, I am totally isolated.

And how much time can I spend smelling edelweiss?

Still, Switzerland is quite the luxurious prison, so I can't complain. I switch on the Jacuzzi in the ultra-deluxe bathroom of my ultra-deluxe cell in the Hotel Schweizerhof and pour the Dead Sea Salts under the faucet. And the minute I break the seal on the bottle, a computer magically adds ten dollars to my tab. Just part of the Swiss national effort to bleed tourists of cumbersome traveler's checks.

And you don't really mind. You're so pampered and cozy, you lack the will to object. Leave worldly woes at the border; enter Cuckoo-Clock Land confident the trains will be prompt, the meals will be hearty, the eiderdown turned down precisely at seven-thirty. Pick a town, any town; they're all the same. Pretty alpine view, pretty chalets with geranium-laced window boxes, pretty streets with pretty stores selling pretty trifles. Music boxes that play "Lara's Theme," pocket knives with corkscrew, golf tees, scissor blades, tea towels emblazoned with the history of cheese.

And cow bells—large, small, brass, silver, monogrammed, plain. And watch shops, ski shops, sausage shops. Nothing you really need, but one can only stand so much natural splendor. So you hike and shop, or ski and shop, or yodel and shop, or ride the funicular up the Jungfrau and shop, or just check into your hotel and shop.

The Swiss don't give you much of a choice. Pick a hotel, any hotel, they're all the same. Your room is clean and climate-controlled, with a view like you get from God's lap.

Let's say you're thirsty and you would like a glass of wine even though it's late for room service and the shops are closed. You're tired, on the verge of despair, almost willing to eat fondue at the Folkloric Restaurant where you blow the Alpine Horn for twenty francs . . . then your eye zooms in on this cute little refrigerator cleverly disguised as a night table. (To leave a plain refrigerator out is garish, which is not the Swiss way.)

Then you recall, through your hunger pangs, that the concierge handed you a little key when you checked in. And wouldn't you know it, that cute little key opens that cute little refrigerator, and inside there's everything you feel like eating or drinking.

So you pour a glass of Riesling and toast Swiss practicality, and the computer magically adds ten dollars to your bill. And that efficient computer keeps right on magically adding as you chase the wine with Diet Cokes, a bag of toasted almonds, a cup of yogurt, and two oranges. Pretty soon you've run up a bill big enough to feed you on Crete for a week, but who cares? You're too relaxed and cozy to worry about anything more strenuous than buying a watch.

Which is what I did yesterday, for excitement, in Montreux, after a quaint horse-and-buggy ride left me near brain-dead.

I slither from the tub, limp and ready to sleep like the Dead Sea Salts package promised—the perfect energy for a scenic train ride. Yes, today is the highlight of the tour—a seven-hour trip on the Glacier Express to Saint Moritz. This ride is supposed to stop the heart and rival Disneyland for sheer excitement (which probably means it's like sitting in a little boat listening to little dolls sing "It's a Small World After All").

It can't be worse than touring the Brienz cuckoo-clock factory.

After a quick stop at the candy store in the lobby for a couple pounds of Gummi Bears (Gummi Bears grow here), I trot over to the train station. Ursula counts and recounts her tourists, their luggage, and their seats on the train, and her eyes grow wide. The unthinkable has happened, there has been an error (didn't the Swiss outlaw errors in 1642?), and our Special Alpine Tour's special train car is two seats short.

Ursula is tall, dark, tweedy, and unflappable, but today she looks worse than she did when Señora Hernandez left her goat cheese on the bus overnight. I immediately offer to sit in another car, both to spare myself the tedium of staring at my tour mates and to spare Ursula the embarrassment of asking me for a favor.

The Swiss hate to ask anyone for a favor.

Ursula and I roam until we find seats next to two handsome mountain climbers with a flask of homemade wine they're more than happy to share. The bright red narrow-gauge train climbs over Furkpass, following the upper Rhine Valley across the Alps.

After three slugs of wine, Ursula is as carefree as a young mother whose child just started nursery school. She tells me about her failed marriage to a Barnett bus driver who had the unfortunate habit of sleeping with the rich widows he transported.

"You can't trust bus drivers," she sighs, and the Glacier Express drops down to the valley near Andermatt, then up through the Oberalp Pass.

At noon, Ursula trudges off to escort her charges to the dining car. She promises to bring me my tilted souvenir wine glass since I don't think I can stomach a three-course meal when I'm moving. I drink some more wine, fall asleep, and dream through a thousand panoramic views . . . until Ursula's agonized shout of "Oh, no, I've lost the tour" jolts me awake. Ursula begins screaming at the conductor in the four official Swiss languages—German, French, Italian, and Romansh. The conductor looks humble. I sense disaster.

Swiss conductors never look humble.

But he has no choice. It seems he detached the wrong cars when the Glacier Express hit the Albula track. The tour car is headed to Saint Moritz; our car is racing toward Chur, a town even the Swiss deem dull. Ursula wrings her hands. "It can't be, it can't be," she mutters, incapable of believing the Swiss railroad has led her astray.

When we arrive at Chur Station, we are forbidden to leave our car. (The conductor wants no witnesses for the prosecution.) We hang out the window as he crawls over to his boss, a rosy-cheeked man who looks like he's carved out of a dried apple. Our conductor is led into the station and slinks back thirty minutes later to inform us we get a free drink and will not have to pay extra to get to our destination. So great is his shame, we all feel guilty for complaining about the five-hour delay and thank him profusely for our complimentary beverage.

Ursula joins me at dinner in the cafeteria where I'm listening to a math professor from Bern explain why logarithms are wondrous tools of life.

The train pulls in after midnight. Ursula is fast asleep. She murmurs, "Where are we?" as I collect our bags.

"Don't worry," I tell her. "If it's Wednesday, it must be Saint Moritz."

LA TIERRA SIN BAÑOS

"**K**nowing when to leave may be the smartest thing that anyone can know," I whistle as I toss a suitcase full of shorts, T-shirts, diaphragm jelly, sunscreen (numbers 5 through 29), and water-purification tablets into the trunk of the car. Duke and I have been living together four months and the one thing we agree on is we need to get away.

Two hours later a man in a dirty glass booth waves us casually into Mexico, like we are entering a parking lot, not another country. (Across the divider, cars destined for the United States are stalled for miles.) Duke studies a map as he drives along the Avenida Revolucion looking for the *carretera de cuotaital* (toll road) to Ensenada. "We'll spend the night in Puerto Santo Tomas," he says.

"Great," I say, forgetting countless domestic quarrels that resulted from his making plans without consulting me. Geography was never my best subject. Duke, on the other hand, is a walking atlas who speaks fluent Spanish (my knowledge of which is limited to "please," "thank you," and "How much does it cost?"). It seems in my best interest to make an effort to get along.

I close my eyes as he accelerates to pass a large truck impeding our progress on the two-lane Transpeninsular Highway (the first commandment of long car trips is Thou Shalt Not Criticize Another Person's Driving).

"Excuse me, if you see a bathroom, could you stop?" I ask timidly (you should never stop a man who is trying to make good time). Duke agrees, but two hours go by. The closest thing to a ladies' room is an abandoned tire in the middle of a sand dune.

"La tierra sin baños," laughs Duke. "The land without bathrooms." This is not my idea of a joke.

"Just go up on that cliff," he sighs, and I suddenly understand the concept of penis envy. (It is difficult enough to unsnap a lace teddy in the privacy of a stall.)

After a dusty ride over the unpaved side of a mountain misleadingly marked as a small road on the map, I am starving. Duke parks in front of an idyllic resort—a cluster of cottages fifty yards from the beach. It has painted tile, it has a view of the ocean, it even has toilets that flush—it doesn't have a restaurant.

Duke is never happier than when he's in the middle of a crisis. While I am calculating how much weight I will lose, he magically finds a fisherman with a spare corvina, builds a driftwood fire, constructs a grill from green sticks, and cooks dinner. I am wildly aroused (men only act this way in Barbara Cartland novels), but he falls chastely asleep (the way men act in Zane Grey novels).

The next day we drive nine hours through the Vizcaino Desert (the car isn't air-conditioned), with nothing but saguaro cacti for company. It is one hundred degrees when we arrive at Bahía de Los Angeles, an ugly fishing village on the Gulf of California. An old Mexican woman drags herself away from her satellite-dish television set and shows us a large hotel room that would be air-conditioned if the generator weren't turned off.

"Don't worry, honey," says Duke. "She'll set up cots so we can sleep on the veranda." This is not my idea of a romantic evening (not only does the veranda face the main street, it is ten feet from the town's only cantina), but the room is so hot the hot-water faucet actually works. I jump into the shower to get wet enough to benefit from the cooling properties of evaporation and slip into the nightgown I was saving for a special occasion. Then I walk outside and see there are now four cots and hear two strange men bid me good night.

Duke promises if we leave at dawn and drive all day we can spend the weekend in Mulege, an even more charming fishing village. I have never enjoyed an experience that begins at five A.M. and this one is no exception. At ten o'clock Duke decides to take a nap. I do not drive a stick shift well, but I manage two hundred miles without making a mistake. Unfortunately, Duke awakes at the precise moment the gears grind.

"You've wrecked the clutch," Duke mutters, and takes the wheel. I stare out the window at a road sign featuring a car plunging over a side of a cliff. This seems a more pleasant fate than being trapped in a man's car I broke a couple hundred miles from civilization.

By the time we get to Mulege I am ready to murder the first person I see. She is a tall, leggy blonde wearing nothing but a long wet T-shirt, and she is screaming, "Duke, Duke," as I walk into the hotel lobby and find my boyfriend in her arms. "I can't believe I ran into you," she squeals.

"Honey, this is the funniest thing," Duke says, introducing the blonde as K.C., a "girl who used to live next door." (Half the reason I'm on this trip is to escape from a neighborhood filled with attractive "girls who used to live next door.") This one is enjoying a second honeymoon with Jack, an ex-boyfriend who took her on a fifteen-hour bus ride from Tijuana to woo her back (not my idea of a persuasive argument).

"We should have taken the bus," says Duke wistfully, as we walk through a marsh to a place K.C. recommended for romantic atmosphere.

Paco's Restaurant is attached to an RV park. It looks like a Mexican version of Trader Vic's. There is a sombrero on the wall, feather flowers, and a glass jar with a sign that reads, PUT A DOLLAR IN FOR GOOD LUCK. Paco himself leads us to two padded vinyl kitchen chairs around a linoleum table. The entire room is filled with these tables and chairs.

"My God, this is the Dinette Set Graveyard, spoken of by the old hunters," says Duke. He empathizes with the brave little chairs who, drawn by mysterious instinct, drag themselves down the Transpeninsula Highway under the eyes of circling vultures. Paco takes our order, then he moves to the center of the room, clutching a guitar. This is more like it, I think, reaching for Duke's hand.

"This is the show. Don't worry, your food is coming," says Paco, and he begins to strum. I will settle for "Guantanamera," even, "La Cucaracha." "Hava negila, hava negila," sings Paco.

Knowing when to leave may be the smartest thing that anyone can know.

NEXT YEAR,
ANYWHERE BUT JERUSALEM

A big hello from the Holy Land—home of Herod's Tomb, the Knesset, and the Wailing Wall. It's a warm, sunny day in Jerusalem. Wish you were here instead of me?

Me, too.

What's a nice Jewish girl like me doing in a place like this? Discovering latent religious zeal? Visiting ancient shrines? No, I'm hiding in a hotel room because I'm afraid to stroll the streets. It's not the kidnappings, car bombs, or Uzis that scare me. It's the guilt. How do I feel guilty? Let me count the ways . . .

The FB *Paloma* sailed into Haifa early Rosh Hashanah morning. My boyfriend, Duke, and I rushed to the deck for our first look at the Promised Land. "Oh, look, Duke, Israel." I fought off my urge to hum "Exodus." Duke scanned the shore for a bus stop. "If we clear Customs by ten, we can catch a bus to Tel Aviv, find a hotel, go to the beach—"

A loudspeaker drowned out his itinerary: "Due to the Jewish holiday, no passengers will be allowed to disembark until sundown."

The purser was negotiating with an Israeli dock official. I sidled up to a ship's officer to glean information. "Excuse me, my boyfriend and I want to take a bus to Tel Aviv—"

"There aren't any buses today. Don't you know it's a holiday?"

I felt guilty. I haven't set foot in a temple since my brother's bar mitzvah.

The purser almost managed to convince the Israelis to let us disembark after morning services; but just as he was about to secure our release, an angry mob of German tourists stormed the deck. A tall blonde who looked like he'd been hiding in Buenos Aires since 1945 pushed to the front of the crowd. "You can't do this to us!" he screamed at the Israeli. "Who the hell do you think you are?"

I felt guilty agreeing with the Germans.

Twelve hours later Duke surrendered our passports to a Customs official. "Are you married?" We shook our heads. "Well, what exactly is the nature of your relationship?" "She's my girlfriend," said Duke. "We've been traveling together."

The Customs official looked at me like I'd been turning tricks on the dock.

I felt guilty for getting divorced.

I walked into a snack bar and ordered a Diet Coke. "What's the matter with you? Don't you like sugar?"

I felt guilty for preferring Nutrasweet. I walked up to a fruit stand and asked for two apples. "That's *all* you want?"

I felt guilty. I wasn't starving.

I walked into a bank to change money. I dutifully handed the clerk a traveler's check and my passport. She handed me a form. "Now what do I do?"

"It's a receipt. You should *know* these things."

"I'm sorry, I just got off the boat."

"Well, push your way to the front of that line." I walked to the back of the queue. The clerk shook her head, took a deep breath, and slammed into two old ladies, one rabbi, and a sleeping hiker. A moment later she triumphantly produced my shekels. "Don't you have any chutzpah?"

I felt guilty for being nice.

Duke and I walked up Ben Yehudah Street in search of a cheap ticket back to Los Angeles. We got four different quotes for the same El Al scheduled flight.

"Don't you have airfare regulations in Israel?"

"You have something against getting it cheaper?" asked the travel agent.

Duke patted my back as I dejectedly trudged away from the counter. "What's the matter, honey?" he said.

"I *hate* this country!"

I felt guilty for being negative about the Homeland.

"You're just tired. Let's find a hotel. I'll go for a swim; you'll go for a walk; we'll both feel better." We checked into a quaint hotel by the sea. The manager gave Duke the key. "Is there a double bed?" I asked. "What do you need a double bed for?" asked the manager.

I felt guilty for desiring comfortable sex.

Duke disappeared into the Mediterranean. I trotted into the Sheraton Hotel to buy postcards. The minute I left the lobby, a man grabbed my thigh. "I want you. How much?"

I didn't stop to haggle; I kicked him and ran. Lost and sobbing, I flagged down the first woman that passed by.

"Please help. A man just attacked me."

"You shouldn't have shown fear."

I felt guilty for expecting any sympathy.

Duke consoled me over dinner. "I hope you crippled him for life."

I felt guilty for not being violent enough.

Duke gently steered me through the Jerusalem bus depot. He deposited me and the luggage on a bench in the sun. "I have to go inside and get a map. Will you be OK alone?"

I felt guilty admitting dependency.

An Israeli soldier tapped me on the bum with his machine gun. "Want to be my girlfriend?"

I began to shake. "Leave me alone!"

An Israeli woman watched me as I picked up my suitcases. "You know what your problem is? You see machine guns as threats. You should see them as decorations."

I stormed into the bus depot to find Duke. (Things are bad when you have to seek refuge in a bus station.) I grabbed his hand and refused to let go of it. "You know what the problem is, Margo? You're the only one around here with red hair."

I felt guilty for not fitting in.

So here I am, lying in our room at the King David Hotel while Duke is off on business. I am happily reading Robertson Davies's new book, waiting for room service to bring me lunch. Outside my window, a beautiful, ancient city beckons. I shouldn't let these people get to me. I should be out exploring.

I feel guilty for feeling guilty.

UNHAPPY CAMPER

"Camping? No, thank you." I begin to scratch imaginary bug bites the minute my husband suggests checking into the Los Padres backcountry with an Insolite pad and a large marmot-down sleeping bag. This is not my idea of a relaxing summer vacation.

"Your idea of roughing it is a Motel 6," Duke says, laughing.

Let him laugh. I refuse to feel guilty because I choose to sleep in a bed. I have a Golden Eagle National Park Pass and a collection of Sierra Club Trail Guides. I hike. I climb mountains. But I view camping as an exercise in masochism.

Recently, I was merrily ambling down the Bright Angel Trail in the Grand Canyon, encumbered by only a canteen and a Swiss army knife (the model without the can opener and fish-scaler blades). I passed a German tourist trudging uphill with about sixty pounds of state-of-the-art camping gear strapped to his back. "How far are you going?" he gasped.

"The Three Mile Resthouse." Far enough to take in a few

million years of rock formations and close enough to get back to the El Tovar hotel in time for dinner.

"You should go to the bottom," he insisted. "I've been there ten days."

"No, thank you." I would rather be french fried than carry this man's load up a one-mile vertical incline. And he was traveling light. Arnold Schwarzenegger could not haul all the stuff that I would require to make myself comfortable for ten days.

"You're missing the beauty of the Canyon experience," he said as he reluctantly dragged himself back to civilization.

What was I actually missing? The chance to wake up in the middle of the night and wonder: Was that noise: a) a rabid ground squirrel? b) a bubonic plague–infected ground squirrel? c) a foraging bear? d) a psychopathic killer?

The chance to squat behind a bush, gingerly balancing a packet of toilet paper which, true to my wilderness oath, I have vowed to pack out with me? The chance to rinse off my diaphragm in an icy mountain stream teeming with giardiasis protozoans?

No, thank you. Camping destroys a relationship even faster than a trip to Mexico. Sure, it sounds romantic, the two of you alone in the forest like Adam and Eve, but how good is sex going to be when there's fauna in your lingerie and your partner hasn't showered or shaved for days? Worse, the dynamic is such that a man struggles to prove that he's as macho as his forefathers, while a woman struggles to prove that she looks attractive without makeup.

"It's not that bad," argues my friend Claire. "Once I realize that I can't go home and screaming doesn't do any good, I enjoy it. I take my down comforter and my pillows and lots of books."

In a backpack? "I don't walk," she scoffs. "You pull the car up and they assign you a campsite, usually something named Squirrel Cove or Deer Glade—combinations of country words. You get this little flat area for your tent so you don't have to worry about sleeping on bumps. I have the trunk nearby, it's like having a closet. The good places even have electrical outlets so you can plug in your blow dryer."

Claire calls this car camping. I call this sleeping in a parking lot. For the money you spend equipping yourself for this pseudonatural experience—Patagonia wilderness wear, charcoal starter, half-dome tent, battery-powered television—you could check into a rustic room in a historic national park hotel.

If there are any left. On May 26, *The New York Times* reported that George Frampton, president of the Wilderness Society, announced at a news conference that "motels and hotels and that kind of thing should go outside our national parks."

"Oh, no," Duke says. "The lodge is becoming extinct."

I am deeply concerned. For almost a century this delicate and often quite beautiful endangered species has raised the spirits and gladdened the hearts of millions of weary wanderers. The authenticating sign of civilization is being able to run a hot bath. The Romans knew it. The Japanese knew it. The only people who don't know it are in the Wilderness Society.

I decide to explain it to them. I call Nobby Riedy, assistant director of the California/Nevada region of the organization.

"I don't find it a hardship to go in the natural environment and sleep on a foam pad in a tent," he says. "It allows me to escape from the city and the noises and the hectic life."

"I'm very glad there's such a thing as pristine wilderness where human intrusion is kept to a minimum," I quickly assure him. "I pay taxes to keep it there. I vote to keep it there. And I do my part to keep it pristine by staying out of there."

"Early in the morning is when most of the animals are active—birds, and deer and raccoons," he says. "You can see reptiles, mountain lions, and bears if you're lucky."

I tell him: "Some people don't want to deal with wild animals early in the morning. Some people don't want to deal with anything more strenuous than room service."

"I respect that," Riedy says. "A reporter at our press conference misunderstood our position. The most likely candidates for relocation are not necessarily the places where visitors sleep, but the shops and other add-ons."

"I really didn't need to buy an official Grand Canyon professional-model slingshot," I concede.

"A beauty parlor, to cite just one example, should not have been built in the heart of Yosemite. What do people need a beauty parlor for?"

"It's sort of a female tribal ritual," I reply. "After a grueling day in the wilderness a woman sometimes needs to reassure herself that she's really not turning into Lucy the australopithecine ape girl."

"You mean going to the beauty parlor is restorative for a woman?" he marvels. "Like when a man goes fishing?" I feel like I have just given Smokey the Bear a cigarette. Then he says, "Maybe we should keep the beauty parlor."

"Wait," I say. "Maybe I should go camping."

ROOM WITH A VIEWPOINT

"**S**o where are we staying?" I asked my boyfriend, Duke, when our plane touched down in Hērákleion, Crete. I envisioned a secluded white villa by the sea with round-the-clock room service and bouzouki music.

"I don't know," Duke said blithely as we elbowed our way past throngs of Dutch tourists, touts offering us a cheap deal on a rental car, and the odd donkey. "We'll find some place."

"You didn't make reservations?" I stammered, trying not to sound judgmental. I'd never gone anywhere without a hotel reservation—preferably a hotel reservation confirmed in writing. But Duke believes that reservations cramp the true wayfarer's style. He prefers to head off into the blue horizon, certain that confidence and ability to adapt will find a suitable nest.

Of course we had yet to agree on what a suitable nest looked like. We hadn't been traveling together for very long. Two days before, I was in Zurich, wrapping up what was supposed to be a two-week holiday in Italy and Switzerland—a holiday that I was taking alone, because Duke, after six months of dating, couldn't decide if he was ready for a joint vacation. But while I was fending off the advances of handsome men in expensive Italian shoes, Duke magically overcame his resistance.

The concierge at my charming little three-star hotel on the Limmatquai was aghast. "You can't check out," he said. "Your room is prepaid through tomorrow night."

"My boyfriend just called," I said gaily. "He wants me to meet him in Amsterdam tomorrow morning."

"I can't give you a refund," the concierge said, showing me a voucher written in the four official Swiss languages. But a voucher has never stopped a woman in love.

"Keep the money," I said. Suddenly I was seized by a premonition. "Just let me take a towel." I know better than to steal plush towels from posh hotels, especially in Switzerland, where towel theft might result in an arrest at the border.

Twelve hours later Duke met my towel and me at the Amsterdam train station. After a romantic streetcar ride to the Leidesplein past a landmark four-star Art Deco hotel where, for a brief moment, I actually imagined that we were staying, my boyfriend led me up the rickety stairs of a seedy lodging that didn't appear to have any stars.

The old-fashioned room had large double windows that overlooked a canal. But . . . "The bathroom is down the hall," said Duke. "It's very continental."

I'd rather not be on that particular continent. I don't like to grope down an unfamiliar dark corridor in the middle of the night. On the other hand, I was far too glad to see Duke to complain. "It's very romantic," I lied.

"Here's a towel for the shower," said Duke, offering me a scratchy cloth the size of a dishrag that looked like it used to be a shirt.

"No, thanks," I said cheerfully, unpacking my premonition.

The next morning Duke announced that he was taking me to Crete. All I actually knew about Crete was that the Minotaur used to live there, but I was more than happy to go. And I would have been more than happy to stay, if we could find a place to stay.

Around midnight, after Duke had endlessly orbited the narrow crooked streets of Hērákleion searching for economical accommodations, I spied a modern hotel with a Class C listing. Duke reluctantly trudged into the newly renovated lobby.

"They have a room," I said.

"Can we see it?" asked Duke. I'd never asked to see a hotel room in my life, but then again, my travel agent is even more particular than I am. The on-site inspection revealed a spacious air-conditioned room with a double bed and a private bathroom. It even had decent towels. "Let's look around some more," said Duke.

Look around? The room was twenty dollars, including breakfast. We were only staying for one night. "We'll take it," I said firmly. Afterward, Duke pointedly told me about the good old days when he used to stay in the youth hostel. I felt too guilty to tell him about the good old days when I used to stay at the Ritz.

My heart swelled with hope the following evening when we drove into the picturesque port of Seteia. There we were, feasting on patates tiganites and taramosalata, holding hands under the stars at a scenic taverna overlooking the harbor. *"Panda me yia!"* Duke said, as we clinked glasses of retsina. "May you always be happy."

Happy? "I feel like I'm in Harlequin Romance Heaven," I sighed breathlessly. At any moment I expected Duke to fall on his knees and propose marriage. (Actually, I had to wait another eight months.) Instead, he proposed that we ask the owner of the taverna if he had any rooms where we might spend the night.

The last thing I want to do on vacation is be a guest at someone's house. A taverna is out of the question. "We're not going to spend a lot of time in the room," argued Duke.

Spiros led us upstairs to a dusty chamber conveniently situated above the crowded bar where fishermen were quaffing ouzo. ("You're welcome to use the bathroom in the bar," said Spiros.) The room had large double windows that overlooked the Sea of Crete. The ceilings were adorned with murals of sea scenes; delicately rendered dolphins, sea foams, and octopuses danced around the cornices. "It must be pre–Greek Revolution," said Duke.

"So is the mattress," I said. But Duke couldn't resist. Since it was only five dollars a night.

"Can I borrow your towel?" he asked the next morning when he decided to take a refreshing dip in the harbor, since there was no running water.

"Dream on," I snapped. I was tired of being a good sport.

"This is Harlequin Romance Hell?" Duke asked, laughing. But he seemed to understand. Because when we arrived at our next destination, near the village of Pitsidia, he suggested that we check into a quaint, secluded hotel on top of a hill. The room had large double windows with a panoramic view of a lush valley blanketed with wildflowers, and beyond that the Libyan Sea. But . . .

This time the room was simple and clean, with a private bath, clean sheets, and hot water. The towels were smallish and thinnish, but progress had clearly been made. "If you'd prefer, there's a luxury resort by the beach," said Duke.

"No, this is perfect," I said in all sincerity. At last in harmony, we spent three idyllic days there; exploring the ancient Palace of Phaestos and the Roman ruins of Gortyna, playing volleyball on Matala beach, and sipping sweet wine on the hotel terrace as the sun set over the carob trees. Then a fierce wind sprang up.

"This happened to Odysseus too," said Duke. " 'While the wind of the north shut everyone inside—even on land you could not keep your feet, such fury was abroad.' "

I would have been more impressed except that my contact lenses were killing me. "How long does it last?"

"Homer says about two weeks. At least." said Duke. We agreed that it was time to leave. So did everyone else in the hotel. A battle royal was in progress when we went to check out. The manager had accused a German tourist of stealing one of the hotel towels. The German snorted in disgust, threw down a two-thousand-drachma note, and stormed out.

Duke studied our bill. "What's this two-thousand-drachma charge?" he asked.

"A towel is missing," said the Cretan.

I searched the room. I searched the car. I couldn't find the flimsy towel. And Duke was absolutely certain that he had brought it back from the beach. "It's a scam," Duke decided. "He was counting on another good week before the end of the tourist season." Duke refused to pay. He and the Cretan began a heated negotiation.

I hated to spoil a perfect vacation. I unpacked my faithful Swiss towel, which was now gray from use. "Here," I said. "Take this towel." The Cretan looked astonished. *"Adio,"* I said cheerfully.

EUROPE ON
FIVE HUNDRED MILES A DAY

"**A**re we there yet?" I sigh as we drive through the lush countryside of the Verde Minho region of northern Portugal. I'm in no mood to appreciate the picture-postcard view. It's been nine hours since we left our pension in Santiago de Compostela, and I'm extremely carsick.

"Not much further, honey," says my husband, Duke, whose idea of a relaxing vacation is to drive five hundred miles a day—preferably on a narrow, twisting, erratically paved road through a range of mountains featuring unexpected appearances by wildlife and cattle. I brace for collision as he simultaneously studies the map and passes a dump truck overflowing with large rocks.

Today's excursion was billed as a leisurely scenic drive into Portugal, with a possible stop at Barcelos, an ancient town on the right bank of the Cávado River that the Portuguese government tourist guide and Michelin agree is famous for its brightly colored handicrafts. "We can buy some *azulejos,*" Duke cajoled, knowing I'm a sucker for any form of folk art.

"Not another Laceville," I groaned.

Yesterday's excursion was billed as a breathtaking ride along the picturesque *rías* of the Costa del Muerte to Camariñas, a Galician fishing port that the Spanish government tourist guide and Michelin agree is renowned for its handmade bobbin lace. "We can buy a tablecloth," Duke promised.

After a four-hour journey on a narrow byway clogged with ox carts, women carrying haystacks on their heads, and farmers on Vespas dragging immense hoes, we finally arrived at Camariñas. We discovered neither the Plaza Mayor filled with busy lacemakers nor the *artesianas* selling the exquisite handiwork that the guidebooks promised. An extensive search did reveal one wizened *pallillera* bent over her bobbins, counting stitches. But all she was selling were doilies.

Still, part of the charm of a driving vacation is that you never know exactly where you'll wind up. And you do get to see a lot of places, which you get to leave instantly, if they turn out to be tourist traps.

"It's a really *nice* doily," Duke reminds me.

Far be it from me to come between a man and his rental car. The highway has turned into the last frontier. The instant my husband climbs behind the wheel of his rig (for this trip a Volkswagen Polo) and heads out into the Great Unknown, he turns into an indefatigable adventurer, whose mission is to explore every square inch of wherever we happen to be. We've been motoring around the Iberian Peninsula for two weeks, and he has yet to feel the urge to stop moving.

Of course, sometimes he doesn't have a choice. This morning, for example, we were supposed to cross the Minho River from Spain into Portugal. The plan was to drive over the bridge at Túy. Unfortunately, the bridge was closed, because of a traffic accident. "How can the bridge be closed?" muttered Duke, who tends to take roadblocks personally.

An image flashed before my eyes: an aggressive Spanish driver in an ancient Seat delivery van attempting to pass a wide-load truck hauling half a forest's worth of logs casually laced together with trash-bag twist ties. That Spanish driver was probably related to the man with pesetas in his eyes who was operating the ferry boat near the tiny town of Tomino, where all of the bridge traffic was detoured.

That ferry operator was the only happy man in the vicinity. Cars from all over Europe were backed up for miles. Curiously, men from all the world had the same reaction to being delayed while they were trying to make good time. They leaped out of the driver's seat cursing in French, Castillian Spanish, Galician, Portuguese, German, Italian, and Arabic, shook their fists in the air, then opened and slammed shut the trunk of their cars a few times to alleviate their frustration. Meanwhile, women from all over the world sat placidly in the passenger's seat reading their bibles, the Michelin guidebooks, as a platoon of cars from Portugal drove by into Spain.

A few moments after they passed, Duke hit his forehead with his hand. "We should have counted the damn cars coming off the ferry," he groaned. "Because then we would have known how many cars fit."

This isn't anything that would have occurred to me in a million years. "Relax," I said. "We're stuck here for at least two hours."

But Duke couldn't relax. He leaped out of the driver's seat cursing in English, shook his fist in the air, and marched down to the river to take control of the situation. The middle-aged German driver of the Mercedes in front of us immediately became alarmed.

"Are you sure that you can manage alone?" Herr Benz asked me. There wasn't much to manage, as the line of cars wasn't moving, but I assured him that I did in fact know how to drive a stick shift. He seemed unconvinced. "What's your husband going to do down there? Drive the boat?"

"He's probably counting the cars driving onto the ferry," I replied. "And the cars in the line ahead of us. And then he's probably going to time the crossing."

Herr Benz's face fell. "Oh, that's very smart," he conceded, berating himself for failing to think of it first. "Let me know the results," he said.

Twenty minutes later Duke reappeared, muttering arithmetic under his breath. "Four loads, two hours," he said.

"Oh, good," beamed Herr Benz when he heard the news. "My wife was afraid that we wouldn't make it to the Algarve in time for dinner." Frau Benz rolled her eyes at me and patted a giant thermos.

Was he out of his mind? It was noon. Granted, he was driving a 238-horsepower, fuel-injected V-8, but the Algarve is at least 465 miles south. Still, I know better than to underestimate a driven man's capacity for long distances. Or to second-guess the pilot, even if the fuel-gauge needle seems to be developing an attachment to the letter *E*.

"We can go at least a hundred more miles," my husband assured me on one such occasion, when we were in Israel. We were long past the last service station on our way south to Eilat, after climbing to the fortress of Masada, when I suddenly noticed that Duke had turned off the air-conditioning and had dropped his cruising speed to a mere eighty kilometers an hour. "We're doomed," he said, staring glumly at the fuel gauge.

We were in the middle of the Arava desert. Sunset was fast approaching and with it the beginning of Yom Kippur, when all of Israel would close for twenty-four hours. I began to pray.

Miraculously, we ran out of gas in the parking lot of our hotel. "Thank you for not saying 'I told you so,' " Duke said. He promised he would never again drive in the desert with less than half a tank of gas. If only he would promise to stop for lunch.

"So where are the handicrafts?" I ask when we finally arrive in Barcelos. It is a rather dour and ragged small city, with none of the light and charm of the coast town of Viana do Castelo, where we'd rushed through a cup of coffee in order to make it here.

While Duke blandly studies his map (which I'm ready to burn), I waylay an apple-cheeked old woman who looks like a cookie jar. *"Ha artes manuals?"* I ask, in my best effort at Portuguese. To my astonishment, the *senhora* smiles, bobs her head, takes me by the arm and leads me to a nondescript brick building, then disappears before I can say *"Muito obrigado."*

Inside, it's handicraft heaven. There are two floors crammed with embroidered tablecloths, hand-painted tiles, woven wall hangings, rag rugs, fanciful papier-mâché sculptures, and vivid-colored cockerels (the town's symbol) in wood, clay, and yarn. And all of these treasures are remarkably inexpensive. "I can't believe that you found this place," I exclaim, giving my driver a hug.

"Are you sure you're going to be able to carry all this stuff?" asks the clerk, interrupting her weaving to take our traveler's checks.

"We'll just put it in the trunk of the car," says Duke, looking at his watch. "If we hurry, we'll make it to Póvoa de Varzim by sundown."

ROAD WARRIORS

"**M**aybe I'll swim with the whales tomorrow," my husband says. Is he out of his mind? I wonder. How will I bring his remains back to his parents? I wonder. What am I doing in this dark, far-from-immaculate hotel room in Ciudad Constitucion in Baja California?

What I'd hoped would be a romantic Mexican holiday is turning into the relationship equivalent of that automotive endurance classic—the Baja Torture Test. Travel broadens the mind, but it also broadens the differences between even the most compatible couples. For example, my husband's wayfaring fantasy role model leans toward Amundsen mushing his huskies toward the South Pole, while mine is more like Cleopatra lounging on her barge floating majestically down the Nile.

We are not the only mates with travel conflicts. "I throw running clothes, a pair of jeans, and a change of underwear into a suitcase, and I'm gone," says my friend Don. "Meanwhile, Linda is calling Bekins. She won't go anywhere without the whole closet."

Claire won't even pack. "Fred and I don't travel well," she declares. "I only like to go places where they speak English so I can be in control. And he likes to venture out into The Great Unknown and be lost. There's nothing I hate more than that."

Maybe Claire should talk to Joseph A. Broger, a Pacific Palisades travel agent who routinely acts as a marriage counselor. "The artistry of my job is to ferret out disagreements in the first interview, long before the first reservations are made," he explains. "I let both parties have their say, and then I try to find a travel feature that satisfies both. It's not as difficult as it seems."

Recently he saved a couple from marital hell in the Himalayas. "She was dead set to go on a trek in the high mountains of Nepal," Broger recalls. "And he just didn't want that. So I found a situation where there was a short, very easy walk of about four days rather than the two-week march. She's happy because she gets the exposure she was looking for. And he's happy he doesn't have to walk so much."

Unfortunately, Broger didn't plan our trip. I had no objections when Duke suggested that we go see the California gray whales wintering in Bahia Magdalena. But I naïvely assumed that the whale-watching expedition he had in mind was a pleasant day cruise aboard a large, bright and shiny white boat with an observation deck, free margaritas, and maybe even a snack bar.

I was wrong. "I'm going to find a fisherman," Duke announced as we drove into Puerto San Carlos along a dirt road littered with broken Corona beer bottles and overturned rusting car hulks. He stopped by a ripped tent fronted by a colossal mound of scallop shells. I watched in horror, anxiously chanting my travel mantra, "Be a good sport," as he negotiated with men who didn't look like staff members of the Princess Cruises line.

"It's all set," Duke reported happily when he returned to the car. "Ramiro will take us out tomorrow morning in his *ponga.*" What's a *ponga*? "I don't know," Duke admitted. "But don't worry. It'll be fun."

One thing you learn when you're traveling with your mate is that your definitions of fun may not be the same. Annie and Jeremy recently returned from a monthlong vacation in Europe. "It wasn't a let's-go-visit-the-museum trip; it was more a cows-in-the-country trip," says Jeremy, who planned the journey. "But Annie mostly wanted to buy shoes. We hit every shoe store in every city in Europe. She was looking for the perfect pair of black flats. She never found them."

"He hated to shop," Annie agrees. "He liked going down streets that went to nowhere." But not exactly to nowhere. "The area had to be listed in his bible, the Michelin Guide."

Not surprisingly, Annie and Jeremy are no longer living together. "When two people go off on a trip *before* they get married, it's a good bet they'll either get married or it will be the end of the relationship," says psychologist Gary Emery, director of the Los Angeles Center for Cognitive Therapy. "When you're traveling, there are so many reasons to get negative."

Like what? "In normal day-to-day life, there are not that many decisions to be made," Emery says. "But when you're traveling, there are countless decisions: where to buy a stamp, where to make a phone call, how to talk to the desk clerk. And every decision is a potential conflict."

Don't I know it. Take the other night in San José del Cabo. We pulled up to a luxurious beach hotel, after a "relaxing" seven-hour drive, during which a kamikaze vulture narrowly missed our windshield. My heart swelled with hope as the bellhop showed us a sunny, spacious room with an ocean view, a deep bathtub, and no strange stains on the king-size bedspread. "Let's look around some more," Duke said. "We can do better."

Better? We wound up in a subterranean closet with a sink in the shower and a view of two water heaters. "Give me one good reason that we couldn't stay in that beautiful place," I shouted.

"I once stayed there with someone else," Duke confessed. Maybe he *should* swim with the whales tomorrow.

But the next day the air is too cold and the sea is too rough for swimming. However, it doesn't stop us from boating. I grit my teeth as we climb into what looks like a heavily patched bathtub with a motor. There are no life jackets or oars in the boat. "Be a good sport," I chant as my husband instructs Ramiro to get as close to the whales as he possibly can.

Still, I have to admit that seeing a gray barnacled fluke rising gracefully over the waves ten feet away is a breathtaking experience. "Honey, thanks for bringing me here," I say sincerely. "Where are we going next?"

Duke puts his arm around me to stop me from shivering and asks, "Would you mind if we checked into a romantic hotel on the beach?"

TRIPPED UP

I love my husband, but I want to go with Joe. In four days, Duke and I are flying to Indonesia. Our plane tickets were purchased months ago, but our itinerary is still up in the air. My husband, an intrepid pathfinder, wants to get as far off the beaten track as possible and wing it. I'm all for adventure, but this makes me very nervous.

I wouldn't be nervous going with Joe. He realizes that a vacation is more relaxing when the destination doesn't require prophylactic antimalarial drugs. He understands why I'd feel more secure knowing that there's a bed waiting for me when we finally arrive in Bali after a twenty-four-hour ride on a sold-out DC-10. But my husband likes to push the envelope. "It's not a twenty-four-hour flight," Duke argues. "It's just twenty hours."

Years ago, I went with Joe—a.k.a. Joseph A. Broger—a meticulous, courtly Swiss travel agent who looks like the Elf King. I met him when Duke, then my boyfriend, couldn't decide if he was "ready" to take a joint vacation. Maddened by his indecision, I marched into the first travel agency I could find. There sat Joe, virtually entombed behind stacks of tour brochures. "Can you get me out of the country by the end of the week?" I asked.

Joe took care of everything. He delicately advised me not to go to Venice ("In your romantic situation, I couldn't recommend it"). He found the inexpensive flight to Zurich and the berth on the TEE to Florence. He booked the quaint *pensione*. All I had to do was dramatically announce that I was leaving and board the plane.

Joe arranged for one of his representatives (apparently he has a worldwide elf network) to magically whisk me through Customs. And he managed to alter my unalterable ticket when Duke, ever unpredictable, suddenly arrived in Europe for a romantic reunion on the day before I was scheduled to return home. I never sweat the details with Joe.

Then I got married. "You don't need me anymore," Joe said reproachfully, after a few frustrating attempts to help Duke plan our honeymoon in Spain and Portugal. "Your husband prefers to make all of the arrangements himself."

I couldn't argue with that. My mate actually *enjoys* studying guidebooks, contemplating atlases, and calling shady travel consortiums looking for the world's cheapest flight. He believes that he alone will discover the hidden treasures.

In all fairness, he usually does, though not without getting us into a pickle (often involving a shortcut that only looks good on a large-scale map). But Duke likes chaos—almost as much as I like order. "What you travel for is to shake up your life," he says. "Otherwise, you might as well save your money and rent a travel video."

Secretly, I long to be a carefree vagabond. And if we were going anywhere in the United States or Europe or even Mexico, I wouldn't have panicked. But we're supposed to arrive in Denpasar during peak season—along with a zillion summer-vacationing Australians. And even Duke acknowledges that we "might be" looking at a potential problem.

"Say it ain't so, Joe," I cried.

"Your husband can get away with winging it in Spain," Joe said smugly. "But here he's going to have a problem."

"No problem," said Duke, who had just figured out Plan B (for bad). We'll get off the plane when it stops to refuel at Biak, an oil port that is also the historic site of "The Sump"—a cave system where thousands of Japanese soldiers were burned alive during World War II. "There's a two-engine prop flight from there to Lake Paniai, in the highlands of New Guinea," he continued. "It's supposed to be beautiful. But there are no tourist facilities."

I love my husband, but I'm going with Joe. I just called and begged him for help. "Don't worry, Margo," he said. "My representative in Jakarta will handle all the arrangements." I thanked him profusely.

"You benched me and sent in Joe?" Duke says. "You expect me to sit on the pine while Joe makes the reservations?"

I'd feel guilty, but I'm too busy packing. My husband gives me a hug. "Listen, honey, after we rest up in Bali, there's a local boat that can take us to . . ."

NO CRATER LOVE

It's amazing the crazy things you do on vacation. Duke woke me up before dawn. "It's time to climb the volcano," he said. I could hear the little voices pleading: "Stay in the hotel. Get a cold drink. Relax. Read a book." But I didn't want to miss The Experience.

We were on a small island in east Indonesia called Bandanaira, the fulfillment of my husband's yen to get off the beaten track. There are five cars on the island, no phones, no hot water, and no innerspring mattresses. Across the lagoon, we could see Gunung Api, another tropical island, whose only amenity is a picturesque volcano, complete with fresh lava and a plume of smoke.

One night we saw a film of the 1988 eruption. Highlights included a mushroom cloud, rivers of molten lava running into the sea, and a mass evacuation to the nearest safe refuge— 150 miles away. This was unsettling enough, but then the owner of our hotel asked, "Who wants to climb Gunung Api?" Anyone who makes it becomes an honorary citizen.

I had no desire to risk my life to become a member of a

primitive island whose hazards included not only volcanism but typhoons, tidal waves, earthquakes, and, until recently, slave insurrections. But Duke thought that it would be "fun" to get a view. I should have let him go without me.

I would have let him go without me. But then he uttered those fatal words: "You can't do it, honey. It's too hard." Immediately, my ego went into overdrive. There was no way I was going to let him be the star of our vacation slides.

The speedboat landed on the shores of Gunung Api at five-thirty A.M. Even though I've never had a positive experience at that hour in my life, I was optimistic. Three other guests were making the climb, along with two guides. I was relieved to see Martine, a cheerful Australian chain-smoker in penny loafers. "If she can do it, I can do it," I confidently told Duke.

I got a little nervous when her eighteen-year-old brother, Luke, turned out to be a mountain racer who was going for the speed record. He bounded into the thicket like a deer. Then, to my dismay, Martine ground out her cigarette and loped out of view. "She's only twenty-three," Duke reminded me.

Still, I didn't worry until I realized that I was in for a 2,198-foot straight vertical ascent (666 meters, the number of the devil in the Bible, appropriately enough.) There were no switchbacks, no convenient shoulders with gradual slopes, not even a clearly marked trail. The air temperature was eighty-five degrees and rising. Humidity: ninety-five percent.

Bruce, a soft-spoken third-grade teacher transplanted from Santa Rosa to Java and the winner of the Thirty-Something Sensitive Guy Sweepstakes, suggested that I lead what was left of the pack. "Just set your own pace," he said reassuringly as I crawled along on all fours, clinging to vegetation that I prayed wouldn't be uprooted. Branches whipped back and lashed my face as I desperately struggled to avoid the three sizes of loose rocks: the small ones that got into my shoes, the medium ones that bounced off my ankles, and the large ones, which threatened to snap off my ankle.

"You're doing fine," Bruce said.

"You're never going to make it," said Duke, barely fifteen minutes into the climb. "I'll take you back." I didn't want to give him the satisfaction. But I didn't want to die either.

"Remember the story about the Little Engine That Could?" Bruce said. " 'I think I can. I think I can.' "

I didn't think *I* could, but suddenly Alden, the friendly Bandanese guide in the traditional Bandu mountain footwear—bright yellow flip-flops—scurried ahead of me and gave me a hand. With his help, I began to make steady progress.

"I'll get you a gold volcano if you get to the top," Duke said.

I got to the top. Luke was there, smiling triumphantly. He'd set a new record: forty-eight minutes. Martine was enjoying a cigarette. Me, I inhaled the reeking volcanic acids. I saw sulfur blooms on hot rocks. I felt no joy, wonder, or pride, only a keen sense of imminent danger. "And *you* missed the five-hundred-foot sheer drop into the caldera," said Duke, who'd viewed it precariously from the unstable lip.

I wish I'd missed the trip down, which was even more treacherous than the ascent. One false step would bring a three-hundred-foot slide into a thorn bush—if you were lucky. When the ordeal was finally over, I embraced my mate. "Thanks for not saying 'I told you so,' " I said.

"Thanks for helping me save face," Duke said. "If I'd had to keep up with Luke, I'd be in intensive care." Duke then suggested that we spend the rest of the day lying motionless on a secluded beach.

It's amazing the crazy things you do on vacation.

TWO PUGS IN A JEEP

The pugs didn't look very happy. My husband and I were on vacation, driving around southern Utah—Dixie, they call it—with Bess and Stella, my twelve-year-old pugs. We were meandering toward Zion National Park, and Duke had decided to take "the scenic route," a winding unpaved road through a wild series of gorges past Grosvenor Arch and Cottonwood Canyon. In the back of the jeep, the little dogs were ricocheting off the luggage and the wheel wells like pachinko balls.

"We're lucky they don't get carsick," I groaned. (I had been carsick twice already and believe that four-wheel drive was invented as a marketing tool for Dramamine.) Considering that we were driving along the edge of a cliff, it was also good that the dogs didn't feel the urge to explore the front seat, unlike my sister's basset hound, Elvis, who once wedged herself on the accelerator in a Manhattan traffic jam.

"The pugs love to travel," I said just before the journey began. This may have been an overstatement. Granted, Bess belted out an exuberant series of yips when she noticed that

Duke was carrying her bed out to the car along with the luggage, and Stella hopped on the front seat and refused to go back in the house.

But I didn't have to satisfy their wanderlust. It just beat the alternatives: leaving them alone with an apathetic pet sitter who only wants to watch VCR movies or boarding them at the vet, the definitive lose-lose situation. Not only am I racked with guilt at the thought of my "children" locked in a cage without so much as a sofa for comfort, but when I finally go to pick them up, I am also confronted with a sizable bill. With boarding fees, preboarding shots, and postboarding treatment for the inevitable kennel-related ailment, it seems cheaper to check them into a nice motel.

Of course, it's not always easy to find a nice motel where they're welcome. Earlier in this trip, for example, my husband and I drove to Bryce Canyon to see the spectacular maze of pink chiseled cliffs. I wanted to stay at the Bryce Canyon Lodge, which the guidebook described as a picturesque historic lodge inside the national park with rustic guest cabins with gas fireplaces. The price was right, and there were vacancies. But the guidebook clearly stated: No Pets.

"The pugs can always sleep in the car," said Duke, whose idea of a dog is a collie or a shepherd. He's suspicious of pugs because they have a giant sense of entitlement and they don't have the inclination to dart into underbrush on the trail of quarry. "And they don't respond to their own names," he adds.

Actually, I think they know their names, they just choose not to react. "What's in it for them?" I retort.

I reminded him that his wards were elderly lap dogs. Chastened, he drove to a gigantic motel outside the park, complete with tacky, ersatz Western town. The parking lot was lined with German tour buses.

"Pets, no problem," said the desk clerk. "We'll put you in one-oh-five. Around the back. Behind the Dumpster."

"I should have put them in the kennel," I muttered as we

trudged dejectedly into a charmless room with gold shag carpeting covered with enigmatic stains and smells. My husband immediately started sneezing. "It's the allergy barn," he said.

The next day, after a brief debate over whether the pets could be concealed, I threw myself on the mercy of the manager of the Bryce Canyon Lodge. I assured him that Bess and Stella were small, quiet, and housebroken (the three big lies of pet ownership), and he graciously let us stay in one of the historic rustic cabins.

Shortly thereafter, my husband insisted on taking the pugs on a hike from Sunrise Point to Sunset Point on the Rim Trail—the only trail in the park where dogs are permitted. "They'll love it," he said. But Bess really didn't want to go, and a small demonstration of altitude sickness—a swift swoon, a gasping "ahwk, ahwk," a spasm or two—did the trick. "The pug is malingering," Duke said as she writhed on the ground. But I scooped her up and rushed her back to the cabin, where she recovered instantly and spent a pleasant afternoon dozing in front of the fire. "A Lab would never do that," Duke said scornfully.

I sensed he was a little hostile because he had to sleep with the dogs, something he refuses to do at home. Bess and Stella have a repertory of slumber-disturbing behavior including pathetic whimpering, liquid-sucking sounds, and the restless shuffling and clawing of nails across the wood floors, which my husband recently called "irritating almost beyond comprehension."

Fortunately, he wasn't there the time I took them to Palm Springs and forgot to drag along their twenty-pound sack of special vegetarian dog food. I substituted high-protein, high-fat fast-food cheeseburgers, which made them so wired that they chased each other around the room all night.

Bess and Stella were also not model transcontinental fliers, even though their vet prescribed tranquilizers that he swore would last at least twelve hours. I slipped the pugs the drugs in a wedge of Brie, paid the fifty-dollar-a-pet airline charge, and nervously checked them through. Six hours later, when we landed at Kennedy International, my blood froze as I heard Bess, from halfway across the terminal, howling like Cerberus, demanding to be released from her Sky Kennel.

Most pet problems can be solved with a little ingenuity. We made a brief stop in Las Vegas on the way to Utah from Los Angeles. Duke wanted to look around the Strip. Initially, he suggested leaving the dogs in the car in a casino parking lot, with the window open a crack, but then he considered the odds of burglary with the luggage and the stereo in plain sight in a canvas-top jeep guarded by two pugs, one of whom was sleeping. "Worse than craps," he mused, "worse than blackjack, even worse than the slots."

I found a factotum who was willing to do almost anything to get us into the casino. For a red chip, he jumped at the opportunity to watch the pugs—and the luggage. Stella opened her rheumy eyes hopefully. "Go back to sleep," I said firmly. "You've been checked."

Traveling with pugs might be more fun if we were going someplace like Paris, where a pair of attractive lap dogs lends a grace note to an outfit and is welcome everywhere, even in restaurants. Or if we were visiting relatives, where a pet can be a handy conversation piece. But in the wilds of Utah whenever I walked them, I found myself looking over my shoulder to see if I was being trailed by coyotes or a circling hawk.

When the car stopped at Coral Pink Sand Dunes State Park, Duke lifted the pugs out the back window and let them settle to the ground. Stella waddled over to the side of the road and squatted on a cactus. Ever the city dog, Bess waited expectantly for me to get her leash and take her for a real walk, but Duke wanted her to run free, like Elsa the Lioness. "I've never seen dogs so unaware of their environment," he said. But we were both surprised. Bess and Stella plodded gamely up the trail to the dunes. The coral sand was warm and soft, and they were filled with an uncharacteristic joie de vivre.

"They're frolicking like real dogs," Duke said. He took pictures until he ran out of film. Then he pointed to a curious braided track in the sand. "Sidewinders," he said hopefully. "Very poisonous. When it gets a little hotter, they'll come out and start hunting."

Maybe the kennel is worth the money after all.

UNHAPPY TRAILS

Sometimes you hit it off. Sometimes you don't. I had a really strong feeling that Patsy didn't like me. But what could I do? She had on the only saddle with stirrups that were short enough to fit me.

Boy, and I'd hoped that this half-day trail ride through Bryce Canyon National Park would be an adventure in which I'd finally get to shine. Horseback riding is one of the few forms of recreation that I'm better at than my husband. For a week Duke and I had been hiking through Utah's scenic wonderlands, and I was tired of trying to keep up with him.

But there I was, being tortured by a four-legged prima donna. Patsy used to be the lead horse, ridden by experienced cowboys—the Star. Recently demoted, she nursed a poisonous hatred for the other horses. I clung to the saddle horn as she gave Blondie, the mare behind us, a swift kick.

She had no love for her new class of riders either. She balked. She rolled. Worse, she spoiled a great opportunity for me to prove that I was brave.

My husband, a former Boy Scout, is fearless in the Great Outdoors. He dreams of sailing a small boat to Tahiti. He swims in Santa Monica Bay. But I, an all-time urban dweller, tend to be a little cautious.

Inevitably, I get cast as the phobic spoilsport. For example, a few days earlier, we hiked the Emerald Pools Trail in Zion National Park. We were at a scenic spot near the lower pool, where we had to walk across a sandstone cliff. My blood froze as Duke ambled off the beaten path and up to the precipice to admire a view like the one you get from God's lap. "Honey," he said excitedly, "come here."

I remained as glued to the trail as lichen on rocks. The National Park Service had posted a large sign: DANGER— CLIFF. SLIPPERY SANDSTONE. UNSTABLE ROCK EDGE. And just in case you miss the point, there's a little drawing of a hiker plunging to his or her doom.

"The sign's just an attractive nuisance," Duke scoffed. "It's perfectly safe."

If I had a dollar for every time he's said that, I could take an enormous insurance policy out on his life.

Not that Duke was taking any chances on the Bryce Canyon horse trail. He made sure of that at the corral. A casting agent's vision of a cowboy was assigning horses and mules, asking about riding experience. "Do you have one with an automatic?" asked Duke. "I can't drive a stick."

He wound up on Jenny, a sturdy, surefooted, sweet-tempered Tennessee mule with long, aristocratic ears and a résumé that included a stint at the Grand Canyon. Meanwhile, our guide, Binky, a buckaroo who looked and acted as if he'd done time at the Wild West Stunt Show at Knott's Berry Farm, gave me the petulant Patsy. "Like Patsy Cline," said Binky. What were her hit songs? "Crazy"? "I Fall to Pieces"?

It was not a good sign.

Along with a posse of tenderfoots, we descended through Bryce Canyon's breathtaking labyrinth of fantastic red rock formations with fanciful names. Binky pointed out Queen's

Garden, the Cathedral, Seal Castle, and Naked Woman. "Only one I see around here," he joked.

Duke rode in front of me, placidly snapping pictures as his mount plodded along as smoothly as an escalator. I tried to appreciate the scenery. But I was busy obeying Binky's orders: "Don't lean, don't scream."

The horse trail, which drops one thousand feet, is narrow, steep, and windy, with hairpin turns. The animals are trained to walk near the edge, to give you a better view. (Who needs that good a view?) My husband says that I'm afraid of heights, but that's not true. What I'm afraid of is falling.

Patsy sensed that instantly. With her glory days behind her, she had little reason to live. Why not take a tourist with me? she thought. Patsy shimmied. She shied. She craned her neck over the brink, looking for the perfect spot.

"Don't jump, Patsy!" cried Binky, and then he burst into merry laughter. Duke focused his camera and told me to smile. I didn't know which one of them I wanted to kill first.

For the record, I'm not a blazing coward. I stayed calm in Death Valley when Duke lost the dirt road up to Dantes View from Amargosa and we wound up in a blind canyon. "There's nothing to worry about," said my ever-resourceful mate. "We can always set fire to the spare tire, and they'll find us."

I knew he'd get us back on track. The spare tire was new.

"Turn, Patsy, turn," Binky yelled as my horse lurched to the brink again. This was getting old fast.

Forty Binky guffaws later, we arrived back at the corral. "If you enjoyed the ride, tip the guide," he coyly hinted. I tipped him anyway.

By then, Duke and Jenny were so chummy that I half-expected them to run away together. He stroked her flanks and bid her a fond farewell. I would have patted Patsy, but she bared her teeth.

Sometimes you hit it off. Sometimes you don't.

THE THEME-PARK KINGDOM

'm not usually one to complain about any development in tourism that increases my chances of finding a decent bathroom. But I'm a little taken aback by the transformation of a country into a theme park. I realize it happens everywhere, but Thailand has elevated marketing to an art form. My husband and I spent three weeks traveling around the realm recently, and I still can't decide what was more spectacular—the scenery or the proliferation of tourist facilities.

Disneyland is divided into Frontierland, Fantasyland, Tomorrowland, and Adventureland. The Thai equivalents are Trekland (in the north, with its popular attraction, the Golden Triangle—Opiumland), Beachland (from Pattaya to Songkhla), Sexland (Patpong in Bangkok), and Ruinsland (the fallen cities of Sukhothai and Ayutthaya).

"Actually, there's Riceland too," Duke said, speaking of rice production, which was the leading source of revenue until 1987, when it was replaced by tourism. "They haven't figured out how to market it yet."

It's just a matter of time. The Thais are committed to

sanuk, a word and philosophy that means having fun. To augment their visitors' pleasure, they have turned their country into the safest exotic place one could possibly go. Little is left to chance. Wherever we ventured in the picturesque magic kingdom, we were presented with a set menu of marvelous experiences displayed in a photo album and so deftly packaged and tirelessly promoted that it took determination to do anything on our own initiative except sign over our traveler's checks.

Duke, the great explorer, found this difficult to accept at first. He reconnoitered the northern city of Chiangmai (Trekland!) certain he would uncover some hidden treasure that millions of visitors had overlooked. Instead, he discovered that every third shopfront was a travel agency touting tours of the temples, jaunts to handicraft factories, orchid ranches, butterfly farms, and elephant extravaganzas. The streets were lined with giant placards advertising the main attraction: HILL TRIBE TOURS, 2, 4, 7 DAYS and CHEAPEST TREKS IN TOWN (just what I'd want to economize on) and WE GUARANTEE TREKS WITH NO OTHER VISITORS.

"They probably dress them up in outfits," my husband said skeptically of the hill people. And this was before we saw the Meo and Karen tribeswomen at the Night Market selling fanny packs and sofa cushions.

Duke was sure we could see Chiangmai without a guide, and he flagged down a *tuk-tuk,* a rickety three-wheeled, lead-breathing cart. "Wat Chedi Jet Yod," he said, pointing to the shrine on the map. The driver frowned and named an exorbitant sum, "One hundred baht" (four dollars). Then I had an inspiration.

"Handicrafts," I said. The driver beamed and pulled out the ubiquitous photo album and pointed to the shopping tour. "First Wat Chedi Jet Yod," I explained. "Then handicrafts. Thirty baht." The driver demurred for a moment and then agreed. I'd been tipped off that the drivers received a bounty for every tourist dropped at the outlet doors.

"Maybe he'd have taken twenty," Duke said. But he was clearly impressed. The driver concealed his impatience as we toured the temple, a ruined fifteenth-century structure with beautifully eroded bas reliefs of Buddha set high into redbrick walls. I bought my nomination for the world's best religious-shrine souvenir: songbirds in bamboo cages, which I got to release for forty cents, a Buddhist's way of improving your karma. I pondered what would happen if the birds wouldn't fly away and I was stuck with them, but they soared out of the cage instantly.

We then zoomed off down the road to a five-mile stretch of factory outlets selling Thai keepsakes: carvings, celadon, umbrellas, silk. In the leather plant we discovered skilled craftsmen executing the ancient workmanship handed down from King Rama II: rack after rack of faux Vuitton, Gucci, St. Laurent, and other name-brand purses. The gold paint on the interlocked C's was still wet on the quilted bags with chains. "It's Maison de Knock Off," Duke said.

Actually, it was Pays de Knock Off, the world capital of cultural piracy, judging from the mind-boggling array of er-satz designer sportswear and counterfeit cassettes available everywhere. I kept expecting someone to offer me a bootleg of *Godfather III*.

Not that the package tours were all bad. On one memora-ble occasion, in Chiangmai, we signed up for a day trip that featured elephants and rafting. First, we went to a butterfly farm where I saw a beautiful monarch inching out of its translucent cocoon. And after the miracle of birth, we were led to a gift shop where we could buy families of butterflies mounted and framed. At our next stop, the elephant pageant, a group of them demonstrated their lumberjack skills, build-ing a wall out of logs. This was incredible; then again, so was the "Currency Exchange" van that was parked outside.

The highlight of our tour was an elephant ride through a jungle. I felt as though I had stepped out of the pages of Kipling. Each of the giant creatures had a *howdah*, a bench, strapped on its back, where we sat ten feet off the ground, while a thirteen-year-old mahout rode on the elephant's head.

"I wish I could ride on the head," Duke said as our thirty-year-old elephant, Bo Sidur, the largest in the herd, waded through a river. Before I could say, "Are you out of your mind?" he had unhooked the safety chain and was climbing into the power seat. Soon the mahout was on the ground snapping pictures and I was on a two-and-a-half-ton animal that was climbing up a steep hillside path under the nominal direction of a grinning kid with a stick and my lunatic husband whose résumé as far as I knew did not include elephant training.

"Feel like a maharani?" asked Duke.

"I feel like a large life insurance policy," I replied.

Actually, once the terror subsided, it was lots of fun. Perhaps too much fun, because the episode reversed my husband's longstanding policy to avoid all organized tours. Which was how I wound up on a slow boat from Phuket to Ko Phi Phi, an island off the southwest coast. Every hotel, guest house, restaurant, food stall, travel agency, and taxi stand in Phuket was peddling a Ko Phi Phi expedition. The guidebooks promised an unspoiled tropical paradise with luminous coral reefs, emerald waters, and deserted beaches. I had my doubts, but Duke can't resist any destination with snorkeling.

"You'll love it, honey," he said when he bought the tickets, even though he knows I'm not an enthusiastic swimmer.

"Have a life jacket, honey," he said after we boarded, handing me a tatty one, which I promptly used as a seat. "There's only four of them on the boat."

For three hours I huddled in the corner of a small cabin (in fact a bare deck with a roof over it) on a packed ferry that reminded me of a polyglot ship of fools. There were at least 150 travelers crammed on board; mostly French, Germans, and Italians in iridescent beachwear who, oblivious to every health warning, were sprawled on the deck chain-smoking, devouring sweets drenched in coconut oil, anointing their bodies with tanning oil (SPF: Minus 5) eager to disembark and catch some serious sun. And ours was just one craft in a mighty tourist armada.

After a long hot voyage, we disembarked and discovered not the enchanted desert atoll that the guidebook promised but a scenic paradise right out of Disney, with bungalows, hotels, restaurants, shops, and even competing travel agencies. A bevy of enterprising local women ran down the beach to give us the traditional island welcome: "Manicure?," "Pedicure?," "Massage?"

"Well, it was remote once," Duke said, twirling his goggles. A guide with a major crush on his bullhorn herded us into an enormous open-air dining room for our fixed lunch: lukewarm seafood soup, squid salad, and fried chicken—the perfect meal for right before a swim. Duke, of course, ate hearty and then hurried down to the beach to snorkel. I remained calm, even as I overheard my husband tell another swimmer, "Sure, there are sharks in these waters."

I was walking on the beach when a boy with a gibbon on his shoulder grabbed my arm. "Wanna buy a ruby?" he asked. This wasn't my idea of a personal jeweler. The kid pulled out a box of precious stones, "Sapphire? Emerald? Diamond?"

I pointed toward the sea. "Go talk to my husband," I said.

TRAINS, PLANES, AND TUK-TUKS

I love to travel, but I don't like getting from place to place. My idea of a fun form of transit is the Transporter from *Star Trek*. Occasionally, my particles might get scrambled and I'd wind up in a time warp. But it would be easier than a lot of other things.

Recently, before the war, when tourism was still in flower, my husband and I were in Thailand. "Honey," Duke said, looking up from his guidebook, "there's a lot of places we could see if you'd take the bus."

I rolled my eyes. Unlike my mate, who hops aboard anything that moves, I have certain prejudices regarding, for example, buses, which I detest. From Switzerland to Santa Monica, to ride a bus is to wonder how you're going to die. Will a show-off driver attempt a fancy passing maneuver on a one-lane mountain highway? Will you be dropped at a mugger-friendly stop? Or will you catch a virulent strain of flu?

"You'll take the bus when they have staterooms," said Duke, who has bused around Mexico and who occasionally takes the RTD to work even when his car is running. I tried not to feel guilty. I've gone on lots of disagreeable conveyances.

Take the twenty-hour trip from Los Angeles to Bangkok in the coach section of a sold-out 747. It was a little disconcerting when we discovered that the ground crew hadn't vacuumed since the last transpacific haul and that my vegetarian meal had disappeared. Still, I didn't flinch, not even when I found out that the woman in front of me was wildly susceptible to airsickness.

I was prepared. I've been flying since I was a child and I know how to cope. I take food, I take books, and most important, on intercontinental trips, I take a sleeping pill. I see no advantage to remaining conscious. I live for the day my doctor agrees to put me in a temporary state of hibernation like a black bear so that I can be checked through.

I also wouldn't mind a mini-version to get me over a ride in a Bangkok *tuk-tuk*—a flimsy, lead-spewing golf-cart type of vehicle that zips around in traffic that makes rush hour on the 405 seem light.

My blood froze the first time my husband let an air-conditioned taxi go by and flagged down a *tuk-tuk* instead. Following a spirited negotiation in Thai, Duke agreed to a fare of eighty cents, and a moment later we were sitting at tailpipe level breathing sweet-smelling carbon-monoxide fumes while our driver performed a 360-degree spin into oncoming traffic.

"Every street is a one-way street, his way," Duke said with growing respect. He added that if it really bothered me, we could always take the bus.

Well, at least the *tuk-tuk* was quick, unlike the *songthaew,* a small pickup truck with three benches that is favored in rural areas. We shared it with thirty or forty people, livestock, and the catch of the day. In Thailand there's no such thing as too crowded. On one memorable expedition, I sat downwind from a basket of eels. "I like trains and boats best; you can walk around," Duke admitted later.

I'd like them too if he was talking about the bullet train or the kind of ship where the main thing to remember is that you don't dress for dinner on the first night out. But my husband can't resist a Third World transportation bargain.

Another day, we took a train from Bangkok to Ayutthaya, the capital of old Siam. It wasn't the air-conditioned second-class express with assigned seats that I'd been promised but rather a sweltering fourth-class commuter with little elbow room and lots of stops.

Vendors swarmed aboard and forged through the aisles peddling the usual snacks: chicken-on-a-stick and dried squids, fastened *en famille* with their tentacles dangling from a curious point-of-purchase display. It cost us each sixty cents to go fifty-three miles. We got what we paid for.

"Maybe we should have taken the three-hour boat ride," Duke said. But I hadn't forgotten the five-hour junket to Ko Phi Phi on a ferry with 150 travelers, four life jackets, and a squat toilet.

For the record, there are many forms of transit I remember fondly: the long-tailed boat down the Pai River to the Burmese border, the bikes we rode around the ruins of Sukothai. The ox cart, the river raft, even the elephant, which is another story.

But it always came back to the bus. Finally, Duke suggested a day trip from Bangkok. I reluctantly agreed to take a "motor coach," provided that it was air-conditioned and I wasn't stuck on it for more than two hours. We went to Bang Saen, a beach sixty-five miles away.

To my immense relief, the bus was clean and not too crowded. Granted, a guy in the seat behind us was sniffing furniture polish, a child howled for half an hour, and the scenery highlights included billboards that said DEVELOPMENT COMING SOON. But it was tolerable. Possibly too tolerable, because when we got to Bang Saen terminal—a cardboard sign surrounded by dried-banana vendors—Duke was in a vile mood. "Enjoy the ride?" I asked brightly.

"I hate buses," he replied.

SORRY, NO HABLO ESPAÑOL

I am not wired for foreign languages. Perhaps I was born with the wrong plug, because six years of high school and college French made a very faint impression, and despite numerous trips to Mexico my Spanish is limited to a few basic expressions and the first two verses of "La Bamba." On the other hand, my husband can have a dinner conversation in French or Spanish, make small talk in Russian or German, bluff Italian, and bargain in Thai.

"I'm just a dilettante," Duke says, which only makes me feel more inadequate. "I can barely follow this." He gestures toward the television, where he is honing his skills watching *Nuestra Belleza* ("Our Beauty"), a Spanish-language beauty pageant.

False modesty notwithstanding, traveling with an accomplished linguist can be sort of a strain, as I was reminded (again) on a recent trip around the Yucatan. Duke tends to avoid destinations where English is widely spoken—it takes away some of the fun—so as soon as our plane landed in Cancún, a staggeringly Americanized resort, he proposed we head for the hinterlands. He rented a beat-up Volkswagen Beetle with two switches, one for the lights and one for the flashers, while I was still rifling through the Berlitz phrase book trying to figure out how to say, "Excuse me, does this car have brakes?"

I tried to look on the bright side. Having a multilingual mate means I always have an interpreter. But the downside is I am never in control. Take the afternoon in Tulum, for example, when my husband drove down a dirt road past the tenth-century Mayan fortress-city and parked in front of a dilapidated colony of huts along the beach. I watched helplessly as Duke dragged El Director away from grooming a fighting cock and engaged him in a spirited conversation, the only words of which I understood were *"no hay electricidad"* (no electricity) and *"no agua caliente"* (no hot water).

"No, gracias," I said politely. Duke ignored me. He adopts a different personality with every tongue. It's like touring with Sybil. In French, he's François, a sophisticated charmer; in Russian, Dmitri, a soulful intellectual; but in Spanish he's Paco—the epitome of Latin machismo. Paco demanded a tour of the hut. It was a filthy space with no windows, moldy sheets, and impressive specimens of native bugs. *"No, gracias,"* I repeated. *"Cuánto?"* he asked. (How much?) I resorted to the international throat-slitting gesture and walked back to the car.

"I was seeing what I can get for you as a concubine," Duke joked later.

I dislike being at anyone's mercy. So before the trip I sent away for a revolutionary language-instruction system based on accelerated learning experiments done in Bulgaria. According to the brochure, specially arranged baroque music could enable me to learn Spanish at five times my normal speed. One alumnus claimed to have mastered the entire three-cassette basic traveler's course on the plane. (It must have been a very long flight.)

I figured I'd become bilingual in the car. Duke was speed-

ing along the jungle road from Tulum to Cobá when I put on
the first cassette. I was directed to visualize myself on the
seventh floor of a rainbow-colored building with a special
silver escalator and descend smoothly through the spectrum
until I reached my main inner level—where learning would
be effortless. I got as far as the vivid blue third floor when
suddenly the car bounced like a basketball and my head hit
the ceiling. We had run over a tope, a giant Mexican speed
bump.

"I slowed down as much as these brakes would let me,"
Duke said. A bunch of bilingual local children stuck their
hands through the window and cried, "Dollar, dollar."

When my heart stopped pounding, I continued down the
special silver escalator until I arrived at the luminous ultraviolet first floor. Strains of Pachelbel's Canon tinkled in the
background as I was instructed to breathe out and in with
four-second pauses and repeat phrases like *"Escríbalo, por
favor"* (Write it down, please) and *"Dónde está la embajada de
Canadá?"* (Where is the Canadian Embassy?).

I almost got it, but then Duke did the unthinkable—he
passed a Mexican bus driver, which roused fighting blood.
The huge bus belching black smoke was instantly on our tail,
close enough to make me think we might soon be one of the
many shrines to deceased drivers along the road.

Actually, one of the expressions I learned did come in
handy the next day in Uxmal when Duke suggested that I
climb up the Pyramid of the Magician, a towering Mayan
temple. *"Dónde está el elevador?"* I jested. (Where's the elevator?) My husband fearlessly bounded up the steep narrow
stone steps. Against my better judgment, I dragged myself one
step at a time toward the summit, fighting off waves of ver-
tigo, clinging to a grab-on chain for dear life. The view from
the top wasn't worth the effort.

Paco was entertaining a giggling young señorita dressed in
traditional pyramid-climbing garb—black lace bicycle pants,
a spandex halter, and high heels. *"Dónde está el elevador?"* he

said, as if he had thought it up himself. Then he saw me. "Honey, do you happen to remember the Spanish word for wife?"

I did. My language skills dramatically improve when I'm in a pinch. A couple of years ago, in Java, a local guide was helping me down the slope of a volcano at a breakneck pace. Without thinking, in flawless Bahasa Indonesia I cried, *"Pelan-pelan"* (Slowly, slowly).

And then there was the Spanish phrase I mastered when Duke proposed what seemed to me a dubious swim in a gray-whale nursery off the coast of Baja: *"Ayudame! Mi esposo fue comido por una ballena"* (Help, my husband has been eaten by a whale).

Still, back on the special silver escalator, I was progressing at my usual glacial speed. No matter how many times I practiced a simple phrase like *"No hablo español"* (I don't speak Spanish), it vanished from my memory instantly, like a drawing done on a child's magic slate. Duke winced at my every utterance as if I were mangling his native tongue.

Or, worse, he succumbed to the expert's temptation to show off. After we toured the ruins at Sayil, I ventured a cheerful *"Buenas tardes"* to a salesman hawking sisal hammocks.

The vendor seemed pleased, but Duke one-upped me with a little Mayan, which he had learned from a bellhop in Uxmal. Naturally, the vendor was impressed and regarded me like a simpleton when I said, *"Adiós."*

Ironically, left to my own devices and a Berlitz phrase book, I can usually manage with gestures, the words for "please" and "thank you." (In Italy, all you have to be is female and the language barrier completely disappears.) I've yet to be in a store where the words "traveler's checks" or "credit cards" were not understood, and I can haggle in any language with the help of that universal bargaining tool—the pocket calculator. I just can't do anything fancy.

In Uxmal we checked into a quite beautiful, not inexpensive colonial hotel that had seen much better days. After three room changes we decided to check out. For half an hour Paco carried on a heated negotiation without lapsing into English, the only word of which I understood was *"demasiado"* (too much).

It turned out that they wanted to bill us for half the room rate. Paco miraculously talked them down to ten percent. I was truly impressed.

"If I used English, I'm sure I could have gotten another five bucks back," said Duke, who conceded his language skills may have turned them off. "Sometimes, it just doesn't pay."

I don't know. I'm looking at a brochure for a state-of-the-art foreign-language cassette training program. It promises that I will be able to pass the Foreign Service's first level of achievement in Spanish in one month. The course costs as much as a plane ticket to Mexico City, but my friend Monica, who is very quickly mastering Japanese, swears I'll get results.

Por qué no? Why not?

GUIDEBOOK GAMES

How did Columbus find his way to America without a guidebook? I can't leave home without at least two heavy tomes for cross-referencing. From the moment I land on foreign soil until I return, my life is controlled by an author I've never heard of, who for all I know considers a hot shower to be as superfluous as a silver toothpaste key.

Left to my own devices, I prefer to heed the advice of Suzanne, my travel agent, whose definition of a dump is fairly congruent with mine. But my husband only trusts what he reads for himself. A guidebook addict, he devours them the way others gobble mail-order catalogues. Weeks before we left on a recent trip to Ecuador, he'd scrutinized three different books and mapped out an itinerary, while I was still working up the nerve to finish the lengthy sections on health warnings and inoculations (ironically, the one part he refuses to take seriously).

"They just put those in to take up space," said Duke, who complains that I travel with more drugs than a Rexall. Ever cautious, I went to the doctor and got prescriptions to combat

almost everything the book said we could contract and teta-
nus, gamma globulin, polio, and yellow-fever shots too. My
sore arm wasn't the only irritation caused by the printed page.

We flew into Guayaquil, a muggy, crime-ridden port with
a malarial air and nervous residents who looked as if they'd
just stepped out of a Fellini film. Suzanne had advised that we
check into the Gran Hotel, which was safe, reasonable, and
had good coffee, but Duke consulted his book and chose a
"top end" selection on the riverside walk, the Malecón. I was
less than enthusiastic because in Chapter One the author had
revealed that he traveled with a tent.

Writers of guidebooks tend to fall into two categories. Half
are Robin Leach manqués who recommend private barges up
the Thames and exquisite little Alpine hideaways that cost
four hundred dollars a night. The others are Peace Corps
alumni who believe big old buses are more fun because of all
the passengers getting on and off with their livestock; who are
wowed by any accommodation more luxurious than a
thatched hut. My husband favors the latter variety.

Sure enough, we wound up in a sleazy, overpriced joint
with dank carpeting, a broken lock, and two soldiers with
shotguns stationed in front of the lounge guarding a bat mitzvah.

The next morning Duke proposed that we fly to Loja, a
small town in the southern highlands. "We can rent a cabin
in Vilcabamba," he said, speaking of a remote village in the
southern highlands known as the "valley of longevity" because inhabitants live to be over one hundred. "The book
says it's just a two-hour bus ride from Loja."

Guidebooks are loaded with off-the-beaten-track destinations, which frequently require a life-threatening, sick-mak-
ing boat, train, and/or bus journey that I'd just as soon skip.
Fortunately, luck was with me. The airline schedule had
changed since our guidebook was published (funny, so had
the museum schedules); there was no flight to Loja that day,
so instead we went to Cuenca, an attractive colonial city on
the River Tomebamba.

It was pleasant walking around the cobbled streets, but I was on my guard. The guidebook had warned about a known rapist who asked females to write letters for him to nonexistent friends. He was described as a short, dark, pudgy man, a description that matched 60 percent of the male population. I didn't meet him, but I did meet The Devil on Calle Larga.

Duke had just struck a deal with a taxi driver to take us to see the Inca ruin of Ingapirca. He was congratulating himself on getting a good price (twenty dollars for a five-hour excursion) when a short, dark, pudgy man tapped him on the shoulder. "Excuse me," said the Devil in all-too-understandable English. "I heard you bargaining. You must know you're crazy to take a cab. Just go to the bus station." Then he vanished in an evil-smelling puff of diesel smoke, leaving my husband pale and shaken.

"The book said there was a bus," Duke said, looking on the map for the station. Yes, but the book also said it was a two-hour ride to the closest town, from where we had to hitch fifteen kilometers to the ruins and pray we could get a ride back. "The book said the bus is only forty-five cents," he said.

I pointedly reminded him of our last guidebook-inspired economy. We'd just arrived in Albufeira, on the Algarve in Portugal, after a hellish drive from Lisbon. I wanted to check into a motel that had earned a small house, the "quite comfortable" rating from my red friend, the Michelin Guide, the one book I totally trust. But Duke was loyal to another volume, which stated if we walked down a certain street and knocked on doors, we'd find a charming room for a pittance. In fact, a harried mother with three screaming toddlers offered us a curtained-off alcove filled with laundry.

"You don't know what's there until you look at it," Duke rationalized later. But back in Ecuador, we took a cab to Ingapirca.

On the plus side, guidebooks lessen my fear of the unknown, even though they force me to deal with two unknown quantities—the country and the author. I wish there was a psychological profile at the back of the book so I could determine if we had anything in common: a limited enthusiasm for churches, for example, or a passion for folk art. Lacking such information, I have my own interpretations of key words: "peaceful," for instance, usually means in the middle of nowhere, "refugio," not on my life, and "overpriced," in my experience, is not bad at all.

Which is why I was looking forward to the few days we'd planned to stay in Salinas, reputed to be the "best" resort in the country, and malaria-free. But at the last minute Duke rerouted us to Bahía de Caraquez, an unspoiled (translation: primitive) port on the north coast. I was nervous because the major travel agencies in Quito had never heard of Aerotransportes Bahía, the small airline our guidebook claimed flew light planes to nearby San Vincente, and it was six hours by bus. But my husband was undaunted. He dismissed my concerns about malaria as "phobic."

Confident the book would be wrong again, I agreed to go. My blood froze when we returned to Guayaquil and Duke triumphantly led me to a teeny terminal with a nine-seater Cessna parked outside, where he bought two sixteen-dollar tickets. I made him take the seat without the seat belt and gnawed my fingernails as the plane took off and landed three times before finally touching down at what I believed was our final destination—a narrow stretch of coast with a huge runway long enough for a 747.

I sighed with relief and followed Duke down the airstrip, past a couple of pigs. Twenty minutes later I was still behind him as we trudged along the shore in the equatorial heat toward a rickety ferry dock. The next thing I knew, we were crossing the choppy half-mile-wide Rio Chone in a motorized rowboat equipped with wood slabs for life preservers. Naturally, the guidebook failed to mention this part of the experience.

The rowboat landed us in Bahía de Caraquez, a shrimp-farming center that appeared to have suffered touristus interruptus before developers' plans to turn it into a major resort were realized, leaving a group of unfinished high-rises. I was delighted to discover an "overpriced" hotel right on the beach. The shore was less than paradisiacal—Duke incautiously swam with the ebbing tide in the estuary and was nearly carried out to sea—but it could have been much worse.

So I was surprised when I awoke the next morning and found my husband looking distressed. He'd been bitten by a mosquito in the night, having turned down my offer of insecticide, and he was worried it might be malarial.

When I stopped laughing, I told him I had pills for malaria and he seemed impressed. Later, the manager assured him there was no malaria in town. "Cholera, yes," he said. "We have lots of cases." Duke had just wolfed down a shrimp omelette at a dubious-seeming café perched on stilts over the harbor, with no apparent source of running water, but I assured him I had pills for that too. Thanks to the book, I was prepared for everything.

Maybe too prepared, because soon after we returned home, Duke immersed himself in a new guidebook for Zimbabwe, Botswana, and Namibia. Thumbing through it, I note that in addition to all the health risks we encountered in South America, there are warnings about meningitis, diphtheria, sleeping sickness, crocodiles, and lions.

I think I'll go buy a Michelin Guide for France.

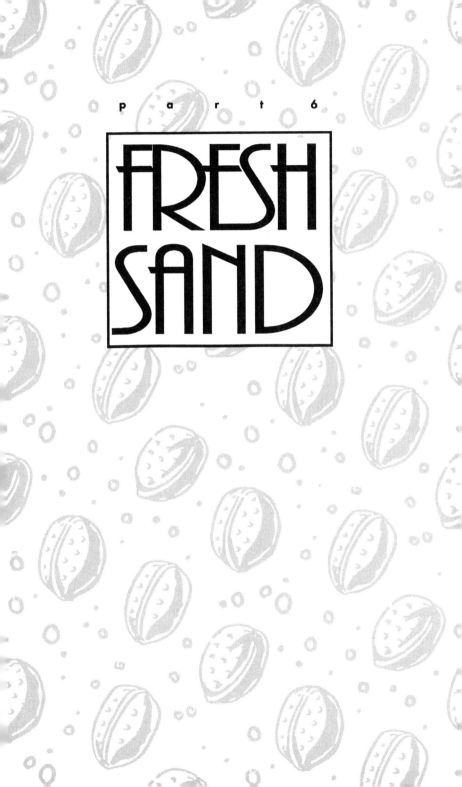

THE R.H. FACTOR

My sister called with what she thought was good news. "I dyed my hair red," she said. I gritted my teeth and resisted the urge to ask, "How dare you?" Ever since supermodel and hairdo harbinger Linda Evangelista went auburn, there's been a rash of women sporting faux Titian tresses. And as a born redhead (R.H.), I'm not amused.

"I wanted to do something funky," said Laurie, a born brunette, "and this looks as natural as fake hair can get."

I love my sister dearly, but I was ready to kill. Red hair is more than a fashion statement. It's a state of mind, a cornerstone of identity, a sign of instant recognition. If asked to describe myself, the first thing I'd say is that I'm an R.H.—and that's saying a lot. Being part of this minority (only 2 percent of the population) is like being in an exclusive club, whose members include Woody Allen, Mark Twain, Katharine Hepburn, Thomas Jefferson, and the Little Mermaid. And I resent a bunch of former mouse-heads trying to get in on the act.

My sister assured me it was just a temporary social experiment; she wanted to see if a dye job would make her more powerful. "I've been bullied my whole life by redheads," she said, alluding to me and our R.H. mother (who also greeted the news with a notable lack of enthusiasm: "You can't do that," Mother declared. "It's not your color.")

Laurie thinks "redheads get away with murder." But, actually, that's a myth, about as accurate as the Irish proverb "If a redheaded girl is born, there was a pig under the bed." Lizzie Borden not withstanding, an R.H. is far too noticeable to court trouble. Remember Thelma and Louise? Granted both actresses' red curls came out of a bottle, but still, the police were on their tails five minutes after they started shooting. With red hair comes responsibility. You have to be good at remembering names and faces, because, rest assured, everyone remembers yours.

"I've never been hit on so much in my life," Laurie said happily. "I work out at the gym every day. Guys I talked to all the time never gave me a response. Now they talk to me all the time." In fact, my sister had to get off the phone because she had lined up back-to-back dates.

I wasn't surprised. Men who like redheads *really* like redheads—even tawdry imitations with furniture-stained (mahogany? cherrywood?) manes. Typically, there's an R.H. in their immediate family and they've been involved with more than one. When I was single, I found it was a dependable litmus test; I knew Duke was serious about me when he mentioned that his sister's hair was the same color as mine. "She's bossy too," he noted.

My brother, Bobby, whose wife and two daughters all turn around when someone yells, "Hey Red!" concurred. "Redheads have very, very strong personalities," he said. "They all think they're special."

It's not our fault. Since childhood, strangers have been commenting on our heads. Red hair provides an instant topic of conversation, an easy way to approach me whether I like it or not. "People always say stuff," said my R.H. sister-in-law, Robbie. "They come up to the baby and say, 'Your hair's so pretty.' And at one and a half, she says, 'Thank you very much.' "

There's something indigenous to a true R.H.'s character that can't be faked any more than you can fake freckles. We have an inherent aplomb that comes from being the oddball in a world of blondes and brunettes. And we're about as subtle as the color red. Once, when I was in the throes of a post-divorce depression, Robbie said, "Cut it out. You're boring." I appreciated her frankness, though I admit sometimes this characteristic lack of tact can cause problems. Recently, a raven-haired friend complained about an R.H. doctor who greeted a patient with, "Hi, you're dying."

Even my sister, Laurie, admitted she wasn't sure she could handle the pressures of her new color. "It's a little weird," she said. "I went to a wedding and the guy I was with referred to me as the redhead. I looked around and I was the only one in the room with red hair. It was an instant mark of distinction. As a brunette, that was amazing to me. Brunettes have normal lives. Redheads don't."

Yes, but unlike the copycats who cop an attitude, a real R.H. has been tempered by reality. We have to endure endless childhood taunts of "carrot top," "Reds," "freckle-face," and "Bozo." We look best in dumb colors like khaki, peanut, eggplant, and rust, which come in fashion once in a blue (not a good color) moon. Back when tanning was still acceptable, while our brunette sisters lay basking in the sun, marinating in baby oil, we were forced to swim in T-shirts, our noses painted clown-white with zinc oxide. And every day of our lives we answer the same stupid questions: "Is that your real color?" and, "Where did you get your red hair from?" (Mother instructed me to answer, "I slept next door to the fire department.")

God forbid we should lose our temper, any emotional outburst is instantly blamed on our temperamental follicles— red hair being kind of a permanent PMS. And foreign travel, particularly to the Third World, is risky. Last year, in Ecuador, I asked a local señora if I could take a picture of her pig. "Sí," she said, but while I was focusing the camera, she came over and gave my hair a painful tug. "Maybe she was trying to see if you were wearing a wig," my husband said.

Still, I wouldn't trade being an R.H. for anything in the world so I really can't blame my sister for wanting to be one too. Of course, I can afford to be magnanimous because she called the other night and told me she had dyed her hair back to brown. "There's a redhead bond I'll never be part of," Laurie said wistfully, "but I don't think a brunette can pull it off if she grew up with the real things. They all flaunt their redheadedness, like, how dare I impinge on their uniqueness?"

I wanted to feel small and petty, but I didn't.

"Besides," Laurie continued, "having red hair is like having a spotlight on you all the time. And I don't have the energy for that."

"Good," I replied.

DIARY OF A MAD PUPPY OWNER

Dear Diary,

The new puppy is so cute! She's a little black pug, four months old, named Sophie—with huge bug eyes, a corkscrew tail, and a will of steel.

I got her from the actor Paul Winfield, who shares a spectacular house in the Hollywood Hills with a gang of wrinkled gremlins. Sophie was romping on an Oriental rug when first we met. She yanked off my sunglasses and pranced around the room. Immediately, I lost control.

I wish I could get it back. The puppy is now ensconced in her "nursery," which used to be our master bathroom. The floor is carpeted with newspapers, chew sticks, squeak toys, a water dish, and a wicker bed. My husband and I are sharing a tiny guest bathroom until she's housebroken.

Excuse me, Her Highness has just awakened from her nap.

Dear Diary,

I went to the Pet Department Store and wrote a sizable check for a twenty-pound sack of all-natural gourmet kibble, a state-of-the-art vitamin supplement, and brewer's yeast and garlic tablets for organic flea prevention. The puppy is better nourished than I am, or rather she would be if she would deign to eat. But the pug is on a hunger strike; all she'll chew is her wicker bed.

I called Paul Winfield. I learned that Her Highness is accustomed to dining on chicken livers and ground turkey, which he fried up nightly in Crisco oil and garlic. The actor also recommended goats' milk, eggs, sea kelp, and a weekly can of tuna in oil. I'm a vegetarian who rarely—if ever—cooks anything, let alone animal parts. But I made her a turkey burger.

Like most people who have sampled my cooking, she wouldn't eat more than two bites.

Dear Diary,

My husband, Duke, doesn't think pugs are real dogs. Whereas I believe the breed is living proof that God has a sense of humor, Duke prefers manly working dogs like border collies or wolflike creatures with immense teeth. Luckily, he doesn't have time to give a wolf the attention it deserves.

I was concerned that he wouldn't bond with Sophie. But as soon as he saw her, he exclaimed, "She's the cutest thing in the world." I expressed the obvious objection.

"You're not in her league," he replied.

Dear Diary,

I feel like I've been kidnapped and my captors won't let me sleep. I played with the puppy for hours. But as soon as I put her to bed, she whimpered pathetically.

Duke pointedly told me about his last dog, a shepherd so smart and skillfully trained I got the feeling it could play chess blindfolded, read Latin, and drive. My husband fancies that he is Gunther Gebel-Williams—the celebrated wild-animal tamer. He instructed me to ignore the pug's entreaties and turn out the light. I tried. She cried.

I sat on the bathroom floor and stroked her until she fell asleep.

Dear Diary,

The hunger strike continues. The vet suggested that I mix cottage cheese with her kibble. Her Highness condescended to eat a few mouthfuls out of my hand. But it was clear she was not amused.

Gunther Gebel-Williams contends I must show the dog who's boss. I suspect she already knows who's boss. "Give her the 'When She's Hungry Enough She'll Eat It brand dog food,'" he advised.

Dear Diary,

We went to the park. Children of all ages, jogging triathletes, and muttering derelicts flung themselves at the puppy and gushed, "Oh, isn't she cute!" I patiently answered the same questions ("No, she's not a pit bull") and tried not to grimace at the endless variations of "Someone hit it in the head with a shovel?" No matter what kind of dog you own, there's some inane remark you hear repeatedly (naturally, the speaker thinks he/she's the first person to think it up).

Her Highness accepted all the attention as her due.

I envy her sense of entitlement.

Dear Diary,

Puppies are like Barbie dolls. The doll is comparatively cheap; it's the accessories that kill you. I've had pugs for most of my adult life, and still, I'm in sticker shock. The dog should come with a label: WARNING: THIS ANIMAL WILL END UP COSTING MORE THAN A HYUNDAI.

So far I've made five urgent trips to my local pet emporiums (there are six within a two-mile radius). Foodstuffs notwithstanding, my purchases include: a canvas leash, a nylon training collar, three cans of fancy vegetarian dog food recommended by a friend with twelve poodles (my pug hated the stuff), a rubber flea brush imported from England, and "poison-free" flea shampoo that cost more than any hair product I have ever owned, which is saying a lot. A nylon bone, forty-eight "deli" sticks of colored rawhide, a king-sized box of Dispoz-A-Scoops, a Sky Kennel (for transport), and a vat of Nature's Miracle, a combination odor neutralizer/ stain remover that may or may not save my carpets.

And this doesn't include the vet bills.

Lest you think I lack self-control, I passed on the marble feeding bowl, electronic flea collar, plastic Frisbee (though my sister sent one), automatic feeder, sun visor, bandanna, and plaid trench coat.

Dear Diary,

Here's the division of puppy-related labor around my house. Pay close attention to the tasks performed by me and those performed by my mate.

MORNING SCHEDULE

5:30 A.M. Her Highness wakes up feeling manic. She stands on her hind legs and paws the puppy gate, yipping frantically for me to get up and play.

5:32 A.M. Drugged with sleep, I trudge warily into my former bathroom. I gather the soiled newspapers, carry them out to the trash, mop the floor, and put down more paper.

6:00 A.M. The puppy runs full speed around the house.

6:15 A.M. She drops a balled-up sock at my feet. She wants to play fetch. Obediently, I throw the sock. Again and again and again.

7:00 A.M. I scramble an egg and mix it with her kibble. She sniffs it suspiciously, takes four bites, and resumes her laps.

7:30 A.M. I fetch her leash and training collar. She darts away.

7:40 A.M. I wrestle her to the ground and put on her collar and leash. The pug assumes the paws-locked position. I drag her down the street. Passersby remark upon how cruel I'm being to the adorable little puppy.

8:00 A.M. I try to read the morning paper. It's wet.

8:30 A.M. My husband wakes up. He pats the dog. She joyfully hops into his lap and licks his ears, which he informs me is a sign of respect. After thirty seconds of adoration, Gunther Gebel-Williams orders her to stop. She obeys instantly and starts chewing my hair. I order her to stop. She continues chewing. He smiles and in a voice he has never used with me croons, "She's as cute as they come." He asks me, "Is there any coffee?"

Now, guess which one of us Her Highness views as the all-powerful giant and which one she views as her French maid.

Signed,
Fifi

Dear Diary,

The mother of Charlie, a fluffy white Japanese chen who lives up the street, knocked on my front gate at seven-thirty this morning and asked if our puppies could have a play date. This way lies madness, I thought. She hastily assured me that Charlie was fixed.

I wonder if I'm supposed to serve cookies and Milk-Bones.

Dear Diary,

I've got to get a grip. I spent half the day standing on the lawn waiting for the puppy to relieve herself. I'm trying to housebreak her. But Her Highness thinks that grass is "peasant." She waited until I brought her in. Then, when I wasn't looking, she went on the dining room rug.

After a pointed comment on how his last dog never messed the house unless she was grievously ill (and then, I got the sense he just handed her some paper towels and she'd clean it up), Gunther Gebel-Williams instructed me to rub the puppy's nose in it, shake her, and shout "Bad dog."

I couldn't. In the hopes of having a peak pet experience, I'd purchased the canine equivalent to the Dr. Spock baby bible—*Good Dog, Bad Dog* by Matthew Margolis and Mordecai Siegal. Margolis runs the largest dog-training facility in the world, and Siegal is a respected pet-care columnist. They maintain that it's wrong to punish a dog for going in the house because the dog is ignorant. Instead, they recommend correcting the dog with a firm "No!" and taking her outside. Unfortunately, I'm only allowed to do this if I catch her in the act.

"A few minutes after the deed has been done, the dog has no mental capacity to connect your wrath with what he did wrong," the experts state.

It could be days. It could be weeks.

Dear Diary,

My sister, Laurie, reminds me it could be worse. The pug isn't destructive, unlike her basset hound. "Elvis ate a couch," Laurie recalled. "I came home one night when I had left her a little longer than I should have. My apartment looked like the Arctic Circle. Everywhere you looked, there was foam and feathers. She ate everything but the springs."

Luckily, I work at home, so I can reprimand the puppy when she gambols around the house swinging my black beaded cardigan between her teeth. My sister works in an office and describes Elvis's puppyhood as living hell. "Once, I didn't completely bolt the closet. Elvis tore the innersoles out of my shoes. And then she went through a music-appreciation phase, where she ate cassette tapes."

Dear Diary,

I monitored the puppy's bodily functions all morning. She did nothing but bark. Then I got a long-distance call from an editor whom it had taken me weeks to reach. Her Highness began trotting in nervous circles under my desk. "No!" I shouted, loud enough to wake the dead.

"I'll call you back," I said to the editor. "I've got to take the puppy outside."

.   .   .

Dear Diary,

It's impossible to stay mad at a pug puppy. It's too cute. It must be Nature's way of making sure you don't wonder why you're keeping them. Otherwise you would—constantly.

Dear Diary,

I called Matthew Margolis. He has trained over twenty-five thousand dogs, including those of Elizabeth Taylor, Victoria Principal, Sally Struthers, Rich Little, Robert Wagner, and Kenny Rogers. He answered the phone, "Woof!"

I explained that in spite of all the housebreaking instructions in his book (a strict feeding and walking schedule, neutralizing odors, keeping her confined) all my puppy does outside is root in the garden.

Margolis told me to buy a puppy pen—a bottomless enclosure—and put it on the lawn with a piece of soiled newspaper. "Leave her there all day if you have to," Margolis said. "She'll cry and moan. But you can't run your life around her. You can't be a baby-sitter."

Yeah, right.

Dear Diary,

The Great Pugini escaped from the makeshift puppy pen I devised (I could fly to Albuquerque and back for what the real ones cost). I put her in the corral and went into my office. Not that I could work amidst the hellish squeals and frenzied scratching. Suddenly, there was an ominous silence. The puppy was missing. A panicked search located her burrowing under the house. And needless to say, she hadn't gone to the ladies' room.

This escape act was repeated all day, despite an impressive assortment of barricades. The sun was setting when I found two large pieces of plywood in the trash. The dog flung herself against the barrier for an hour. Then, eventually accepting the inevitable, she anointed the grass.

She got more praise for doing that than I've gotten for writing in the last ten years.

Dear Diary,

We had company for dinner. My husband, Mr. Let-the-Dog-Starve, roasted a turkey. There were plenty of leftovers.

Her Highness's appetite was miraculously restored.

Dear Diary,

She doesn't respect me. When my husband says "No!" the puppy looks remorseful. She slinks away with her tail between her legs.

But no matter how strict I am, she regards me as a sucker. (Maybe she figures anyone foolish enough to follow her around with a pooper scooper doesn't deserve consideration.) Today I was at my desk. The puppy trotted up and clawed my leg, her signal for me to put her in my lap. "No," I said firmly. She raked my leg vigorously and added a plaintive moan. I ignored her for a while, but at last, in the interest of getting some work done, I succumbed.

How did she thank me?

She bit my ass.

Dear Diary,

Gunther Gebel-Williams and I went to the beach. A ripe young nymphet wearing nothing but a black lace G-string was sprawled on her stomach sunbathing. She'd attracted more male onlookers than a dog in heat.

"I think she needs some help with her suntan lotion," my husband said.

"Down!" I snapped automatically. "Stay!"

"Now you've got the tone to use with the dog," he said.

That evening, Her Highness started chewing my shoelaces. "Remember the girl in the lingerie," Gunther prompted.

"No!" I snapped. "Sit!" The puppy obeyed instantly.

I think this could be the beginning of a beautiful friendship.

TALK OF THE CLOWN

It used to be the conventional wisdom in Los Angeles that nothing was too weird for Venice, the beachfront community whose boardwalk has become a nationwide synonym for freak show. But that was before Jonathan Borofsky's thirty-foot fiberglass *Ballerina Clown* began pushing the tolerance envelope.

Take me, for example. The first time I saw the clown, I nearly crashed the car. I was three blocks away from my house when a Brobdingagian toe shoe loomed into view. I didn't mean to slam on the brakes. But there was a ballerina the size of the Lakers entire front line standing one on top of the other. It was wearing a tutu and a leering clown mask with a five-o'clock shadow. Huge white gloved hands outstretched, he or she appeared to be blessing the intersection, like the pope of mutant fast-food icons. More startling, it was standing on half pointe doing a mechanical battement atop the North Beach Bar and Grill.

Don't get me wrong. I like art. And I live near the boardwalk. Chain-saw jugglers, limbless dancers—no problem.

But, well . . . I've got to keep my car insurance, for one thing. "What the hell is that?" cried the gawker who almost rear-ended me. He craned his neck out the window, shook his head, then gave the Joan Rivers open-mouth, finger-down-throat salute.

Art consultant Elaine Gans, the woman responsible for the installation, is thrilled with this public response. "It's the most provocative piece of public art in the country," she said proudly, after I managed to get my car into the driveway intact and make a few calls to find out what was going on. "Public art needs to be something that touches people, whether they like it or not," said Gans. "If they start driving by and they don't care, then we haven't accomplished anything."

"We" includes real estate developer Harlan Lee, creator of the "Venice Renaissance" complex that the sculpture adorns, who hired Gans and laid out the estimated $150,000 to "make a significant cultural contribution to Venice," as his spokesman, Michael Diedon, put it. (Lee was safe in Europe and couldn't be reached when I called.) Artist Jonathan Borofsky, a certified American master whose work has appeared everywhere that's anywhere, did acknowledge that this particular piece "is not a piece that fits in everywhere."

Borofsky continued, "We all knew that it would have an impact and create discussion. And as an artist you look for new possibilities. Sometimes you create a little dissonance. We could have put a clock up there that would have confronted nobody."

"What's wrong with a clock?" exclaimed a Disney executive who almost hit a parked car. "That atrocious piece of kitsch looks like something they sell at the Tinder Box." (Or one of Batman's enemies.)

"It's about taking opposites and throwing them together," said Borofsky, who previously threw together an eleven-foot ballerina clown, which tours with his exhibition. "It's not an image in our psyche that we recognize right away, like a man picking apples. This is more radical. More psychologically disturbing. You have to think. What is that? It seems to be a clown and a dancer. Right away you're confronted with a combination not in the known dictionary of the brain."

At least, brains that don't belong to art critics. "Like lightning that suddenly explodes from the quiet gathering of invisible, charged particles in the atmosphere, Jonathan Borofsky's best work manages to pull you up short by igniting a sudden crack! of recognition," raved Christopher Knight of the *L.A. Times*. "In my experience, however, nothing, anywhere is quite like Borofsky's sleeping giant."

"It would be nice if it were six inches tall and in the corner of a living room in Silverlake," said public relations maven Josh Baran, a self-described "liberal kind of guy" who lives on Ocean Front Walk. "That thing makes me pray for an earthquake. (Sorry, it's earthquake-proof.) At first I thought it was only temporary. Then I realized that it was going to be here forever."

"I wouldn't say that it doesn't have a right to be here," said Shana Weiss, a political organizer for the Hollywood Women's Political Committee. "But every time I walk by it, I cringe. It feels pretty smug. Anytime you have a clown doing something unclownlike, it feels sinister."

Still, some residents are slowly beginning to accept, and even appreciate, their flamboyant neighbor. "How many other places could you live and have a major work of controversial and critical importance in your own backyard?" said screenwriter Howard Cushnir, whose apartment overlooks the *Ballerina Clown*. "I wouldn't want the Statue of Liberty on that corner. But the *Ballerina Clown* is a perfect reflection of the world in which it sits. And by fall you can probably go trick-or-treating anywhere on the West Side and everyone would understand your costume."

It has certainly made it easier to give directions. All you have to say is turn left at the clown.

Besides, it could be much worse. The smaller version of the

Ballerina Clown has a tape of the artist singing "My Way" playing constantly. While the larger version is wired for sound, and it did sing at the opening, the tape wasn't included in the package. "It's a lot to ask for people to have to listen to that on a daily basis," Borofsky said.

It's good to know that something is still too weird for Venice.

UNEMPLOYMENT AND THE NEW AGE

Settling into my role as an unemployed columnist, I did what thousands of laid-off, pink-slipped, or put-on-ice women do—I turned to superstition and the occult. It's amazing how much metaphysical guidance is available to a person in doubt. No matter how depressing the recession or how many résumés fail to produce a bite, there's always some New Age magus or oracular instrument to predict that it will all be all right.

Perhaps this is a predominantly female coping mechanism. Men, with a few notable exceptions (Hitler, Reagan) usually eschew the supernatural and opt for something more direct. "Guys go to bookies or bartenders," my husband says. "Women turn to fortune-tellers."

For years, my first line of psychic defense has been the *I Ching,* the book of ancient Chinese divinations. While I waited for my initial volley of cold calls to prospective employers to be returned, I tossed my three old bronze coins. It was disconcerting when I drew the hexagram Abysmal, with the cheery notation from the Oracle, "In the abyss one falls into a pit. Misfortune." But I tried to look on the bright side. At least the Oracle was right.

I decided it couldn't hurt to take a teeny peek into the future for some career direction. After a wrenching debate over which medium—channeler? numerologist? palmist? stargazer?—could best deliver the message, I opted for a "metaphysical counselor" who read playing cards. In these uncertain times, Louise was booked solid, but she managed to squeeze me in.

I watched nervously as she contemplated a deck mono-grammed with her phone number and logo. "Prosperity is there for you," she said, hastily adding that for the moment I should be conservative with money "for peace of mind." I immediately felt guilty for crossing her palm instead of the gas company's.

The seer foresaw three writing projects in my future, all of which looked good (this is the recession version of the tall, dark, handsome stranger coming to you from across the ocean. In a leading economic indicator, mystics now assume women want to talk business instead of romance.) She offered to channel one of her spirit guides to see what was holding me back. I passed, but I did spring for her how-to book, *Reading Your Future in the Cards,* which I figured would not only give me a leg up in a growth industry but also provide a snappy answer to the job hunter's most dreaded question: "So what are you doing now?"

"Don't start anything until Mercury goes direct," Louise cautioned.

Los Angeles may be the only place on the planet where a seer can give you advice like that and your friends will whole-heartedly agree.

"You'll have a new burst of energy when Mars is in Leo again," Sally concurred, citing her guru of the moment—MacAstrologer. Despite its input, my friend, a well-published author, had also fallen victim to the economic slump.

But she was still in control. "There's hardly a thing I don't have going," Sally said on the phone the other day. "I've been doing the tarot excessively. And Runes. Of course I have a green candle, which is good for money. And I affirm, 'I love money, and money loves me.' As we speak I am lighting the candle."

Maybe it's foolish to do all of this. Then again, maybe it's foolish not to. At least it gives you the sense you're being productive. And it's easier than finding work.

"Maybe it's because women are more likely to be in therapy," says Charlene, who is seeing a swami who does past lives. Well, swamis are a lot cheaper. "Besides, a psychic is much more optimistic. You don't have to say much. You just sit there and dream and hope."

"Do you know about your money corner?" Sally asked. Blessedly, I did not, but she explained that according to the Chinese philosophy of feng shui, my house is a metaphor for my life. The far left corner represents wealth, and if it's somehow stopped up—cluttered with old newspapers, for example—it's helpful to do something to enliven it. "Fish tanks are good," Sally said. "Or plants, or wind chimes to stir the chi around."

I thought about trying it, but even I have limits.

I consulted the *I Ching*—Abysmal again. "The abyss is dangerous," the Oracle warned. "One should strive to attain small things only."

Not a bad idea. I decided to get a grip on something simple—my mind. The enlightened sages at the Dawn Horse bookstore recommended *Reflections in the Light,* an affirmation-of-the-day handbook. The most memorable exercise directed me to imagine what I want, surround it with a pink bubble, and release it into the universe, all the while chanting, "My heart's desire is coming true."

So far, neither a lucrative book contract nor a three-picture deal has appeared at my door. But I did manifest a parking space in Westwood on Friday night.

Meanwhile, back at the coins, after six consecutive Abysmals, I moved to a new hexagram—Oppression. "It furthers one to offer sacrifice," the Oracle said.

I decided to sacrifice the Oracle. Instead I turned to the Queen of Cups, a picturesque tearoom in Venice Beach that is attempting to do what the Federal Reserve so far has been unable to accomplish—restore faith in the economy. There are in-house mystics on duty around the clock.

One offered me a basket of M&M's. "Take a green one, your wish will come true," the mystic said. Then she divined four things about me ranging from wrong to grossly, ludicrously wrong. "I see you coming and going in an office," she announced. I perked up. Could this be the job of my dreams?

"No, this is definitely past, not future," the mystic said. "Do you work in an office?" I shook my head. "Did you ever work in an office?" Actually, I've always worked at home. "Does your husband work in an office?"

"Yes," I conceded. (Fortunately one of us is employed).

"Ah," she said brightly. "Well, maybe it's him."

That's when I decided to focus on the present and let the future take care of itself. Accepting my role as an unemployed person, I considered doing what millions of made-redundant, canned, or dehired women have done. Write a screenplay, buy a lottery ticket, sue someone. Then I had a better idea. I called my broker.

"Is there such a thing as green candle and *I Ching* futures?" I wondered.

ANOTHER DAY IN PARADISE

I t looks like we won't get off the island today. The mouse-like representative of Indoavia Airlines has just informed us that our flight from Bandanaira (the teeny capital of the Banda Islands) to Ambon (the gateway to civilization as we know it) has been canceled—again! So, it's at least another day on this legendary spice archipelago in Eastern Indonesia.

Oh well . . . we've got sunlight on the sand. We've got moonlight on the sea. . . . We've got a location scout's vision of a South Pacific paradise complete with crystalline waters, cinnamon groves, luminous coral gardens, ruined Dutch forts, colonnaded plantation big houses—even a central-casting volcano venting smoke.

What ain't we got? We ain't got planes.

The Bandas are served by a single airline, Indoavia (or Indoalibi, as it should be called), which runs a seventeen-seat Twin Otter from Ambon two or three times a week. Since we arrived, our return flight has been off and on more often than the generator. We could charter a plane for a thousand dollars—but who's in that big a hurry?

"What do you want to do today?" asks my husband, Duke, who has gone completely native. "Maybe I'll go hang out with those guys building the war canoe." They're carving the kora-kora out of a single kaputi tree log, the only concession to modernization being they're using a chain saw.

"Who wants to hike through my nutmeg plantation?" cries our host, Des Alwi, the exuberant Orang Lima Besar (chief) of the Bandas. He owns the hotel—the Maulana Inn, a tatty semirenovated former Dutch nutmeg planter's mansion on the banks of the lagoon—and virtually everything else on the island. Every morning and afternoon, the plump middle-aged rajah proposes (and usually leads) a "Club Des" expedition.

"It's not like climbing Gunung Api?" I ask anxiously. Yesterday, the morning excursion was a daunting ascent of the active volcano, a near-death experience that I don't care to repeat.

Mr. Alwi, or, as they say on Banda, Tuan Alwi, promises that we'll enjoy this outing even more than we enjoyed snorkeling in the oceanic hot springs (actually, Duke was the one who appreciated swimming with a profusion of astonishingly colored tropical fish. I was simply grateful to be in the only place on the island with hot water).

"I'll check out the war canoe when I get back," Duke decides. So we slather on yet another layer of sunscreen and industrial-strength Bugs-B-Gone spray and jump into one of Tuan Alwi's boats—a flat-bottom thirty-foot centerboard sloop—along with eight of our fellow guests.

Three hundred and twenty-three years ago, in the Treaty of Breda, the English reluctantly gave up their claim to the Bandas, at the time the world's prime source of then precious nutmeg and mace. In exchange, the Dutch gave up a minor possession in North America called New Amsterdam. "You think they'd trade it back?" asks Tuan Alwi.

As we sail around our base island of Neira, he points out Fort Belgica and Fort Nassau, two seventeenth-century Dutch strongholds. There's another decrepit fort—Hollandia—on the island of Bandar Besar, to which we are headed, and an English bastion on the outer island of Run. We've already visited a small museum filled with rusting war toys— souvenirs of the ferocious centuries-long European struggle to control the precious prerefrigeration Bandanese nutmeg trade, which fetched profits of 1,000 percent in the spice-starved 1700s. "Someday, I'll show you the cannon that Magellan brought here," Tuan Alwi promises.

Someday, I'll get off this island, I suppose.

"You can always go back on my big boat," he says grandly, like Oz offering Dorothy his balloon. I'm not eager to take an all-night cruise aboard this vessel—a none too clean three-hundred-ton Taiwanese fishing junk with a deep, suspicious gash in the stern and rumors of a temperamental engine—that he acquired at auction after it was seized by the Indonesian navy.

Of course, it beats the Perintis Ferry, which is what the rodentine Indoavia agent suggested we take the day before yesterday when our plane was—surprise!—canceled. I saw no reason to embark on a fourteen-hour boat ride that even the most bohemian of our guidebooks described as an "endurance test." And that was before we even saw the ferry, which listed precariously as it left the shore without us. Perhaps a thousand people and their livestock were crammed on board, along with four lifeboats and a sound system that could have been heard on the island of Ceram, 120 miles away.

"They time it so they get to Ambon late at night, when the harbor people won't see the violations," Tuan Alwi explained.

We approach the shores of Bandar Besar. Duke is cheerfully eating fresh nutmeg fruits, discussing with Rudolph, a Dutch aerospace engineer who is fresh from a trek through the highlands of Irian Jaya, the best place to take a dive. Rudolph shakes his head and points to a dive regulator completely filled with water. "The equipment is not so good," he says in his slow, meticulous English.

"So what?" my husband says blithely. "Nothing's perfect."

"When is your boat sailing?" I ask. But Tuan Alwi doesn't hear me. He has jumped overboard and is merrily splashing up the beach of the largest island in the chain.

It looks like an enchanted forest. I have never seen a place so green. The air is cool and clean and all the houseplants I've ever killed (especially the species the florist insisted would thrive in low light) are nine feet tall and flowering. There are mangoes and bananas we can pick right off the trees—and coconuts, papayas, durians, and jackfruits. A tiny deer walks out, stares at us, and walks back in the glade.

Tuan Alwi leads us along a winding trail shaded by gigantic kaputi trees and tamarinds, banyans, and cinnamon groves. He stops in front of the pride of the archipelago—the stately nutmeg tree. "No single canned food can last six months without nutmeg," he says proudly. "And Bandanese nutmeg is the best."

In the distance, we can see native farmers hacking at the jungle with machetes. "Oh look," exclaims Rex, the extremely pale Australian ballet master usually dressed in diaphanous white. "They're working!"

Actually, by the time we reach the end of the trail, almost everyone on the island has stopped working to pay homage to the Orang Lima Besar and gape at his guests. Only five hundred outlanders a year—mostly divers and mostly Japanese—come to these tiny islands. Wherever I go I'm surrounded by gawking children who have never seen red hair. I imagine it's the closest I'll ever come to feeling like Princess Diana on tour.

The sun is setting over the volcano when we arrive back on Neira. We are greeted by the only shop on Banda—a wizened man in a dugout canoe who floats by every evening to peddle his wares: nineteenth-century Dutch gin bottles, nautilus shells, tarnished two-hundred-year-old V.O.C. coins, and antique Chinese porcelain, brought here as trade goods centuries ago. He holds up a bowl and flicks it with his forefinger. It rings like a bell. "Thirty thousand rupiahs," he says. (About seventeen dollars.)

Margaret, the tough Australian importer, examines it hopefully, then sighs. "Qing," she says. "Not Ming. Still you'd pay a hundred dollars for it in Melbourne."

The mouselike representative of Indoavia scuttles to the dock and squeaks out that the plane is leaving tomorrow. He skitters away with a thick wad of our rupiahs in his paws. I have to admit that my tolerance for the *mandi*—the cistern of more or less cold, more or less clean water meant to be dippered over your head as a substitute for a shower—is waning. And I would give anything to spend the night between clean sheets. But we still haven't seen the island of Ai, with its antique church, and Fort Revenge.

"It looks like we may get off the island tomorrow," I tell Duke.

"I'll see if I can rent a motorboat," he replies.

REQUIEM

Please don't hate me for killing Stella. I really didn't have a choice.

Fourteen years ago, I bought two pug dogs. From the start, Bess, an energetic black puppy, adored me. And Stella, a sluggish fawn one, adored her dish. Loyal little Bess followed me everywhere; she was never happier than when she was in my lap. Stella only followed me if I was going to the kitchen; her joy was a plate of dinner scraps.

In a way, I had myself to blame. I bought Stella sight unseen from a Breeder-of-Champions (B.O.C.) in Chicago. I was there on business and I stopped by the renowned pug farm, hoping to find two little girls who would keep each other company. Bess and I bonded at first sight. As for Stella . . . well, Mrs. B.O.C. explained that she didn't have a fawn puppy on the premises, but one of her dogs had fathered a litter in Iowa. She promised that she'd send me the cream of the crop.

Either Mrs. B.O.C. was less than frank or the kennel was in the middle of a toxic waste dump. The pug equivalent to

Rosemary's Baby arrived apple-headed and bunny-footed. Whereas Bess bounded out of her Sky Kennel, flung herself in my lap, and smothered me with kisses, Stella was totally indifferent. Within thirty-six hours, I suspected she was borderline autistic, but Mrs. B.O.C. insisted that she was merely "shy." I didn't have the heart to ship her back.

For the next decade, I supported a pet that wouldn't look up when I came home unless I was holding a doughnut. Twice a day, I walked her—make that dragged her; she didn't like to move much—around the block. I took her on vacation. I kept her in kibble and chew sticks. But not once did Stella crawl into my lap. "She's not a dog, she's a goldfish with fur," said my husband, Duke, who actually came to admire her total fixation on her own comfort. The nicest thing I can say is that she wasn't a lot of trouble.

Then she turned twelve, and began to develop a series of costly but never life-threatening ailments. Unlike Bess, who had the decency to provide me with genuine medical catastrophes—a stroke, for example—that I could rescue her from by writing a sizable check, Stella's difficulties offered no such emotional satisfaction.

First, she succumbed to a chronic eye infection that could only be cured by a mysterious forty-dollar-a-gram solution, which, according to my longtime vet, Dr. Weiner, was accidentally discovered in the course of cancer research. Why the scientist was inspired to test his breakthrough on pug eyes was beyond me, but what I did grasp immediately was the financial impact. "How long will she need these?" I asked, as my vet instructed me to put them in three times a day.

"Forever," he replied.

I remained sanguine even after Stella acquired a matching ear infection that required another pricey miracle elixir and meant that I was always washing mucus out of one pug orifice or another. But I began to lose it when Dr. Weiner found a small $350 tumor on her leg. He was positive it was nonmalignant (naturally) but "just to be safe" he insisted on remov-

ing it. "Don't worry," he said. "She won't die on the table."
Maybe I'll get lucky, I thought. But no such luck.

Before I could pay off my Visa bill, Stella's legs went out.
She woke one morning so crippled by arthritis she couldn't
even waddle to her dish. I braced for what I presumed—dare
I say hoped?—was the inevitable. "I think it's time," I told
Dr. Weiner.

"Oh no," he said. "There's something we can try."

"Something" turned out to be a sequence of wonder shots
that had proved effective in racehorses.

"Will she get well enough to walk around the block?" I
asked.

"I don't know," Dr. Weiner said. "But I won't put her
down. She's still eating."

Stella will probably be eating three months after she's dead,
I thought helplessly. My friends suggested that I find another
vet, but what was I supposed to do? Get out a Yellow Pages,
call around, and say, "Hi, will you kill my dog?"

Four hundred and thirty-two dollars later, Stella could
waddle to the corner if I carried her up and down the front
stairs. I didn't see what she would miss if she was put to sleep,
since she already spent twenty-three and a half hours in slum-
berland. But she still came magically alive—eyes glistening,
dancing like Pavlova, uttering joyous yips—at mealtimes.
Around this time my husband and I saw the movie *Awaken-
ings,* in which a group of lifelong catatonics undergo similar
transformations after being given L-dopa. We turned to each
other. "Stella," we said.

I knew I was over the edge when my friend Marcella
called, despondent. A coyote had snuck into her yard and
eaten her cat. "Would you keep Stella for a few days?" I asked
hopefully.

On her fourteenth birthday, I calculated I had spent close
to two thousand dollars keeping her in a wheezing-sofa-
cushion-with-fur state. Duke suggested that I practice triage.
"No-code her," he said. "Make her comfortable but don't

spend any more money." This was easy for him to say; he didn't have to endure the look of disapproval on Dr. Weiner's face when I announced my decision to forgo the mysterious eyedrops for Visine.

Finally, not long ago I needed major surgery. I was lying in a special hospital unit, doped to the gills, when Duke approached my bedside, waited for my eyes to flutter open, and gave me the bad news. "Honey," he said. "Stella's got a cough."

"Put her to sleep," I moaned, and fell back into a morphine haze.

When I came to again, my husband was at my side. "I took Stella to Dr. Weiner," he said. "He gave her an eighty-five-dollar cough medicine and said she needed to go on a diet. I got her a sack of diet kibble."

"Get her a gun," I said.

The nurse had just finished drawing my blood when my neighbor Barbara called. She was watching the pugs while I was in the hospital. "Listen," she said, holding out the phone so I could hear a hacking cough. "Stella's not doing so well."

"Neither am I," I said.

Stella was rasping like Camille when I arrived home from the hospital. What's more, she was incontinent (but Dr. Weiner had already assured me he had pills for that). "I guess I should have taken her to the Humane Society," Duke said. "But I wasn't emotionally up to it." With that, he left for work.

Blame it on the painkillers. There was no way I was spending another day with Stella, and I couldn't afford another trip to my right-to-life vet. I called the Humane Society and explained the situation. A volunteer assured me they would be glad to put her to sleep, painlessly by lethal injection—for free (a first!). "We do have to make sure she's not adoptable," he added.

"Trust me," I said. "If someone will adopt her, I've got swampland in Florida they can buy."

The volunteer told me to bring Stella in right away. I would have been glad to, but I wasn't allowed to drive. I called my neighbor Barbara. Her car had just been stolen. In desperation, I called a cab. The dispatcher said it would cost forty dollars round trip. I didn't have that much cash in the house, and I was too weak to run around town. Luckily, I had an inspiration. I called One-Two-Three, my trusty messenger service. "Could you take my dog to the Humane Society?" I asked.

"Sure," the dispatcher said. "We do it all the time." She promised to send a compassionate driver who would wait and make sure the deed was done. She told me it would cost ten dollars. "Unless you want to send her express."

Stella never rushed for anything in her life. It seemed like a bad time to start. A short while later, I kissed her good-bye, handed her to the courier, and heaved a sigh of relief. I didn't have a twinge of guilt until I got the receipt that said "Stella." And then it passed in a flash.

Rest in peace, Stella. Wherever you are, may your dish be full.

ABOUT THE AUTHOR

MARGO KAUFMAN lives in Venice, California, with her husband and pugs. Her work has appeared in *The New York Times*, the *Los Angeles Times Magazine, Cosmopolitan, USA Today,* and *The Village Voice* and she is the Hollywood correspondent for *Pug Talk* magazine. At the time of this writing, she was not nuts.

ABOUT THE TYPE

This book was set in Bembo, a typeface based on an old-style Roman face that was used for Cardinal Bembo's tract *De Aetna* in 1495. Bembo was cut by Francisco Griffo in the early sixteenth century. The Lanston Monotype Machine Company of Philadelphia brought the well-proportioned letter forms of Bembo to the United States in the 1930s.